THE PRINCIPLES OF CHRISTIAN APOLOGETICS

AN EXPOSITION OF THE INTELLECTUAL
BASIS OF THE CHRISTIAN RELIGION

SPECIALLY WRITTEN FOR SENIOR STUDENTS

BY

REV T. J. WALSHE

"Le siècle porte au besoin d'examiner : vous le combattriez
en vain ; c'est du besoin d'examiner que vous devez faire
sortir le besoin de croire."—MADAME DE RÉMUSAT

WIPF & STOCK · Eugene, Oregon

Wipf and Stock Publishers
199 W 8th Ave, Suite 3
Eugene, OR 97401

The Principles of Christian Apolgetics
An Exposition of the Intellectual Basis of the Christian Religion
By Walshe, T. J.
ISBN 13: 978-1-5326-5641-5
Publication date 4/27/2018
Previously published by Longman's Green and Co, 1919

NIHIL OBSTAT

C. SCHUT, D.D.,

Censor Deputatus.

IMPRIMATUR

EDM. CAN. SURMONT,

Vic. Gen.

Westmonasterii, die 30 Decembris, 1918.

THIS BOOK IS DEDICATED

TO

RELATIVES AND FRIENDS

LIVING AND DEAD

WHO ARE TO ME A SYMBOL OF

GOD'S FIDELITY AND LOVE

PREFACE

THE study of the science of Apologetics is very necessary in these days of doubt and agnosticism. The fundamental principles which underlie all religious belief are daily called in question. And even if the urgent need of a reasoned grasp of the foundations of Faith did not exist, the interest of the subject of Apologetics, the large outlook upon life which it involves, the coherence of its parts and the cogency of its conclusions make it desirable that an examination into the principles of Theism should be an indispensable adjunct of Christian teaching.

The first step to take in the investigation of the claims of Natural Religion is to prove that an objective world exists, a world external to consciousness. The ground for this belief must be examined so as to justify the transit from consciousness to reality. In the process, one begins to realise, perhaps for the first time, the truth that there are many characteristics of the external world which our perceptive faculties are not keen enough to observe. At the same time, it can be shown that our perceptions, though not adequate, are true as far as they go, and this conclusion is sufficient for the validity of the well-known argument that contingent beings postulate the existence of a First Cause upon whom all contingent existences depend, the necessary personal Being, to whom we give the name of God. God exists. Man has been created by God. Man has been endowed with a spiritual soul—spiritual because for its existence and action it is independent of matter, and therefore persists after the death of the body. Man owes to God the debt of private and public acknowledgment and worship. Here in brief are the main theses of Natural Religion. Supported by this basis of Natural Religion, and aided by the application of the criteria of miracles and prophecy, the enquirer is led to the further conclusion that there is one and only one true form of Supernatural Revelation, namely Christianity. In the following chapters an attempt has been made to reproduce in English form the classical arguments which are set forth in text-books of Apologetics written chiefly in Latin, French and German. The aim has been to avoid as far as possible technical nomenclature, so that Senior Students of Secondary Schools may follow the trend of the discussion. If such students are called upon to unravel the intricacies of the Differential and Integral Calculus set for B.A. and B.Sc. degrees, it is surely not too much to expect that the metaphysical principles which are the support of Natural and Supernatural Religion should have some share of their attention.

In the development of the Apologetic argument, I desire to acknowledge my indebtedness to the Dominican work—Père Garrigou-Lagrange's " Dieu, son existence et sa Nature,"[1] and to another work of great merit, " Foi et Raison," written by M. le Chanoine Valvekens.[2] Whilst following these authors in the more formal and " scholastic " portions of their works, I have not hesitated to adopt another treatment if such appeared preferable. I desire to thank the Editor of the " Irish Theological Quarterly " for permission to republish some articles on Apologetic subjects contributed by me from

---

[1] " Dieu, son existence et sa Nature," par P. Fr. R. Garrigou-Lagrange. Paris, Gabriel Beauchesne, 1915.
[2] " Foi et Raison " (Cours d'Apologétique), par M. le Chanoine Valvekens.

time to time. I desire also to thank Dr. Keith,[1] and his publishers, Messrs. Williams and Norgate, for the use of two illustrations which appear in Chapter IX, and the Rev. H. Thurston, S.J., for valuable suggestions and for the time and trouble involved in the correction of the proof sheets.

Regret has often been expressed that more use has not been made by writers on Apologetic subjects of the various branches of Natural Science—Physics, Astronomy, Biology, Geology, Anthropology—sciences which point to conclusions relevant to the theistic argument. Surely it is by endeavouring to comprehend the Natural as well as the Supernatural Revelation that foundations are more securely laid, and a better opportunity given of appreciating the harmony, beauty, and stability of the Divine edifice of Faith. Should any measure of success attend the present effort, should reflection be aided, doubt removed, reverence increased, I shall indeed be amply rewarded for my labour. But in the investigation of Divine Truth, we must not forget our limitations, so admirably expressed by the earliest of Christian Apologists: "O the depth of the riches of the wisdom, and the knowledge of God! how incomprehensible are His judgments, and how unsearchable His ways!" The "windows into the Absolute" permit us to see but "through a glass darkly." It is the trial of Faith. Presently we shall see "face to face."

T. J. W

[1] "The Antiquity of Man," by Dr. Keith.

CONTENTS

PREFACE *Page*

CHAPTER I
THE EXTERNAL WORLD

Objective value of sense impressions—Scepticism—Idealism—Critical Realism—Natural Realism—Primary and secondary qualities of bodies—Qualities of Sound—Qualities of Colour—Neo-Scholastic theses in regard to secondary qualities—Arguments in support of Neo-Scholastic view—The old scholastic teaching—Arguments in support of the same—Conclusion 1

CHAPTER II
THE APOLOGETIC AIM

I. Logical divisions of "Natural Religion"—Definition of Vatican Council—Terms of oath against Modernism—Encyclical "Pascendi" 16

II. Proofs which are "Scientific"—St. Anselm's à priori argument—Arguments à posteriori—Empirical Agnosticism—Hume—Mill—James—Comte and Littré—Idealistic Agnosticism—Kant, his categories and antinomies 20

III. How knowledge is acquired—First principles are intuitive—Rule and motive of certitude—In what sense there exists a subjective element in Knowledge—Bergson's philosophy of action 24

IV. Transcendent value of primary notions and principles—How legitimately applied to the Infinite—Kant's and Spencer's erroneous application of primary notions in their univocal sense 28

CHAPTER III
PROOFS OF GOD'S EXISTENCE

The five aspects of the metaphysical proof—General proof—Proof based on moving bodies—Efficient cause—Contingent Being—Degrees of Being—Manifestation of Order—Résumé—Human opinion—"Les fanfarons petits-maîtres de la Science"—The testimony of distinguished men in Science and Literature—Bacon, Pasteur, Brunetière, Huysmans, Bourget, Coppée, Kelvin—Dr. Dennert's chart 32

CHAPTER IV
ERRORS OPPOSED TO THEISM

The connotation of the word " Atheist "—Positivism and Agnosticism — Materialistic Monism — Materialistic Evolution — Spiritualistic Evolution—Lamarck—Darwin—Natural Selection—Mendel—De Vries – Phylogenetic tree of plants—Conclusion *Page* 51

CHAPTER V
A GENERAL VIEW OF THE NATURE AND ATTRIBUTES OF GOD

I. Preliminary distinctions—Fundamental perfection of the Divine Nature   68

II. Attributes bearing directly upon the " being " of God—Unity and Simplicity – Truth—Perfection and Goodness—Infinity—Immensity—Immutability—Eternity—God is from the human standpoint invisible, incomprehensible, and withal cognoscible   70

III. Attributes which bear upon Divine Work—Wisdom—Love with its characteristics of Mercy and Justice   72

IV. Attribute of Infinite Power—Creation and Conservation—Divine Concursus—Miracles—Intimate Life of God   77

CHAPTER VI
SOME SUPPOSED ANTINOMIES

I. Difficulties arising from the attributes of Simplicity and Immutability—Maimonides—Duns Scotus—Approved teaching—Perfections not virtually distinct one from another—Perfections between which there is a virtual distinction by reason of the different relations of creatures to God—Perfections virtually distinct independently of creatures   88

II. Difficulties arising from the existence of evil, physical and moral—Natural standpoint—Supernatural standpoint   95

III. Difficulties arising from the consideration of the Divine Nature as seen from the standpoints of Reason and Revelation   105

CHAPTER VII
POLYTHEISM AND PANTHEISM

I. Infinite Perfection of God involves His unity—Unity of purpose in Nature witnesses to Unity of Creator—Unity of development manifested in our Solar System—Mosaic cosmogony and the geological record—Polytheism a decadent belief   108

II. Immanence and Transcendence—Personality—Illustration from the Human Nature of Christ—Pantheism the negation of Personality—God of Theism and the " Eternal Axiom " of Taine   113

CONTENTS

CHAPTER VIII

THE NATURE OF MAN

I. Spirituality of the Soul—Proofs—Materialistic objections—Size of brain and mental ability *Page* 116

II. Freedom of the Will—Liberty from constraint—Liberty of indifference — Proofs — Corollaries — Power of sinning an imperfection of free-will—Psychological power of habit—Determinism in its different forms 119

III. The Natural Law—Proofs of its existence—Primary, secondary and remote principles of the Moral or Natural Law—Promulgation and Sanction—Independent Morality 124

CHAPTER IX

ORIGIN AND DESTINY OF MAN

I. Substantial union of Soul and body—The Oldest Human Relics—Chart of Post-Tertiary times—Neolithic Age—The Tilbury man—The first glimpse of Palæolithic times—Father McEnery of Torquay—Deluge at end of 4th glacial period—Azilian culture and script—Magdalenian—Solutrean—Aurignacian cultures—Summary of discoveries of Later Pleistocene period — Mid-Pleistocene period — Mousterian Man — Abbés A. and J. Bouyssonie and Bardon—Abbé Breuil—Early Pleistocene period—Pre-Chellean man—Large cranial capacity—Dr. Gladstone on size of skull and mental power—Piltdown Skull—Antiquity of Man—Theological aspect—Unlikely assumption—Conclusion 127

II. Origin of the Soul—Creative act of God—Unity of the human species—Unity of origin 141

III. Destiny of man—Immortality a consequence of spirituality—Need of adequate sanction for the Moral Law—Specific punishment a truth of Revelation 142

CHAPTER X

RELATIONS BETWEEN GOD AND MAN

I. Necessity of Religion for the Individual—Utility of Religion for the Individual—Necessity of Religion for Society—Catholic and non-Catholic countries compared 144

II. Necessity and Utility of Worship—Interior—Exterior—Social Worship 150

CHAPTER XI
RELIGION FROM THE STANDPOINT OF HISTORY

I. China and Japan—Brahmanism and Buddhism—Persia, Babylonia, Assyria, Syria—Arabia—Egypt—Greece and Rome—Primitive Races—Australian—African—American tribes . . *Page* 153

II. The comparative method—Belief in a Supreme Being and Immortality of the Soul universal—Polytheism a declension from primitive Monotheism—Probable process of degeneration—St. Paul's anthropological doctrine—Census of the different forms of Religious belief 163

CHAPTER XII
REVELATION AND ITS CRITERIA

I. Divine Revelation—Natural and Supernatural Orders—Possibility and congruity of the Supernatural Order—Mysteries—Absolute necessity of Revelation in regard to certain truths—Moral necessity of Revelation for the prompt, universal, certain and complete knowledge of the truths of Natural Religion—Criteria of Revelation 167

II. Miracles—Nature of a miracle—Possibility—Possibility of proving a miracle—The suggested commission of scientists—Miracles and Science—Suggestion, faith-healing and hypnotism—The Divine causality can be established—Probative force of a miracle 173

III. Prophecy—Nature of prophecy—Possibility—True prophecies have taken place—Probative force of prophecy 178

CHAPTER XIII
FAITH AND REASON

I. Rationalism—Is Reason autonomous?—Does Reason follow an upward course?—Rationalistic claim regarded from the standpoint of History and Philosophy 181

II. Faith and Science—Apparent contradictions arise either from misapprehension of dogma or from confounding hypothesis with truth—How Reason helps Faith—How Faith helps Reason—Relation between Faith and Science 183

CHAPTER XIV
THE FACT OF REVELATION

I. Three historical phases, Primitive, Mosaic, and Christian 186

II. Historical Authority of the Gospels—Their integrity—Authenticity—Veracity 187

III. Divine authority of the Gospels—Nature of Inspiration—Aim and extent of Inspiration 191

CONTENTS

CHAPTER XV

THE DIVINITY OF THE CHRISTIAN FAITH

I. Attestation of Prophecy—Claim of Christ to be the Messias—Confirmed by prophecies . *Page* 194

II. Attestation of Miracles—Miracles wrought on irrational beings—Wrought on human beings—Characteristics of their performance 198

III. Attestation of the Resurrection of Christ—Christ predicted His Resurrection in confirmation of His Mission—Witnesses to His Resurrection 200

CHAPTER XVI

"THOU ART CHRIST, THE SON OF THE LIVING GOD"

I. "Thou art Christ"—Realisation of Messianic Prophecy—Detailed exposition of Messianic prophecies—Fulfilment 204

II. "Thou art the Son of the living God"—Divinity of Christ proved from the Gospels—First group of texts—Criticism of the same—Second group of texts 209

III. Cumulative force of testimony—Résumé 213

CHAPTER XVII

ESCHATOLOGICAL APOLOGETICS

Schweitzer's book—Modernism described as Pantheism in philosophy and Unitarianism in Divinity—The Kingdom of God—"The advent of Messianic consciousness"—The eschatological theme—Père Lagrange's critical analysis—Concluding remarks 215

CHAPTER XVIII

THE DIVINITY OF THE CHRISTIAN FAITH DIRECTLY PROVED

I. Propagation—Quantitative—Qualitative—Supernatural Character—Objections . 226

II. Conservation — The fact — Supernatural character — Objections 230

III. Transformation of the World—Fact—World before Christ and after Christ as regards the Individual, the Family and Society—Objections . . 232

IV. Heroism of the Christian Martyrs—Their number—Circumstances of duration, universality of the persecution, and the ferocity of the persecutors—The martyrs suffered for Religion—The true force of this argument—Objections—Résumé in the words of Lamy 235

BIBLIOGRAPHY 241

INDEX 245

THE PRINCIPLES OF CHRISTIAN APOLOGETICS

CHAPTER I

THE EXTERNAL WORLD

THE student, who is accustomed to accept implicitly the testimony of the senses, finds at first the suggestion bewildering that sense-impressions do not represent accurately external qualities and objects. But once raised, the question, how far subjective states correspond to objective reality—how far our faculties may be trusted in the search after truth—is obviously of primary importance. Doubtless the student has many times watched a sunset with its gorgeous manifestation and changing panorama of colour; many times too perhaps has he admired a landscape in which "meadow, grove and stream" seemed "apparelled in celestial light," or listened in time of storm to the roar of the angry waves as they lashed a rock-bound coast. Should science analyse the feast of colour into mere undulations of ether, resolve the roar of the angry ocean and the song of the lark into wavelengths of air; should the redness of the rose, the whiteness of the lily, the verdure of the fields be merely a subjective vision, the objective world becomes indeed drab and uninspiring, and the gain in knowledge will never compensate for the loss of the "vision splendid," and the loss of Nature's orchestration with its sacramental suggestion of invisible power and beauty.

The attitude of students of philosophy in regard to the

objective value of sense-impressions may be classified as threefold—the attitude of the Sceptic, of the Idealist, and of the Realist.

First, the contention of the sceptic confronts us—the contention, namely, that objective knowledge is impossible, that between states of consciousness and their external causes there may not be the remotest resemblance, that it is impossible to bridge over the gulf which separates the subjective from the objective (if in truth the latter has any existence), that under the circumstances doubt is the truest wisdom :

> There lives more faith in honest doubt,
> Believe me, than in half the creeds.

An examination, however, of this position shows inconsistency and indeed contradiction. The assertion " doubt is the truest wisdom " is put forward either as (*a*) a sure principle, or (*b*) as a doubtful one, or (*c*) as neither certain nor doubtful. If the first supposition be taken, it is clear that a positive and certain principle is laid down in direct contradiction to the fundamental tenet that " nothing is certain," and in the second and third hypotheses the element of doubt is fatal to the value of the statements. Nay, the expression of an opinion on the part of the sceptic involves at least three contradictions : (1) he assumes as certain his own existence ; (2) he accepts the truth of the principle of contradiction inasmuch as this principle underlies every statement ; and (3) he draws a distinction between knowledge and ignorance, between certainty and doubt. Scepticism stands self-condemned.

Idealism is a modified form of scepticism. Idealists admit the certainty of states of consciousness. The " monistic idealists " recognise the unity of the subject which experiences the states of consciousness in contradistinction to the " pluristic idealism " of Hume and others who held that the succession of conscious states are so many separate experiences without an underlying unity of subject. Monistic idealism is subdivided according as the percipient subject is believed to be the individual "ego" (subjective monistic idealism); whereas if the percipient subject be a world mind (universal consciousness, of which the individual mind forms but a manifestation) another form of idealism emerges, objective monistic idealism, of which Fichte, Hegel and Schelling were the chief supporters. Berkeley, bishop of the Irish diocese of Cloyne, taught that God acts upon our sensitive powers so as to produce the appearance of an external world, whereas the only real objective beings are spirits. This form of idealism is no longer held, nor did Berkeley ever succeed in reconciling the deceitful appearance of phenomena with the truthfulness of God. Perhaps the most striking example of an idealistic system logically developed is that of Kant. He attributes to the human mind three main cognitive faculties—perception, understanding and reason. Each of these faculties contains forms of thought by the application of which to the materials given in the senses knowledge in the scientific sense is produced. Perception has two forms—time and space. Understanding has twelve categories under four general heads—quantity, quality, relation, modality; and reason seeking after unity places before itself ideals in which the phenomena of consciousness, of the outer world and of possible existence are summed up. Hence the ideals of the soul, of the universe, and of God. And these ideals are not objects of actual and positive knowledge, but regulative principles which guide reason in its search after highest truth.

It will be sufficient in this chapter to point out two objections fatal to Idealism. First it misapprehends the true meaning of Knowledge. The mere succession of mental phenomena can never furnish materials for scientific knowledge, unless the mind can grasp the causal relations which bind them together. The discovery of the planet Neptune is a case in point. Leverrier and Adams both noted irregularities in the orbit described by Uranus which led them finally to postulate the existence of another planet. Here surely was a suggestion, the truth of which depended upon the reality of the force of attraction, the respective positions of the planets and other objective considerations. And though

Neptune had never been recognised as belonging to our solar system and was invisible to the naked eye, the astronomer relying upon the objective truth of physical principles was able to indicate the portion of the heavens where the new planet would be seen, if suitable optical means were employed. Physical science and Idealism are not compatible. The second objection is equally strong: every form of Idealism questions the truth of the information derived from the perceptive faculties, and thus logically leads to Scepticism.

Some students of philosophy take up a position midway between Idealism and Natural Realism. They are known as Critical Realists. Their system rests upon a fundamental principle which may be stated thus: states of consciousness are primarily known and from them by aid of the principle of causality, the inference to the objectivity of the external world is made. But the question arises how can the truth of the law of causality be known unless we are assured of the real existence of cause and effect which our sensitive faculties perceive? The intuitive principle of causality is recognised by the intellect from the materials furnished by sense-perceptions; so that to invoke the aid of causality in order to establish the objectivity of sense-perceptions is a flagrant instance of the logical fallacy known technically as "petitio principii," or in more familiar language the fallacy of the "vicious circle." But even if the truth of the principle of causality be granted, the only inference which can be made is that there is an external cause of sensitive cognition, but of the nature of the cause nothing is known. Critical Realism is thus seen to be practically identical with the phenomenalism of Kant alluded to above.

Special attention must now be given to an examination of the chief principles of Natural Realism, the most fundamental and important of which asserts that we have an *immediate* perception of the outward world, that sense-impressions are not directly perceived but determine the sense to the *immediate* perception of the outward object. This is the complementary truth which, overlooked by Idealists, vitiates their conclusions. No matter how logical their reasoning may be, if it sets out from faulty premises, the harvest of error will be more abundant in accordance with the efficiency of the logical process.

Scholastic writers distinguish between the primary and secondary qualities of bodies : the primary qualities, extension, movement, etc., capable of being tested by more than one sense are called " sensibilia communia," whereas each of the secondary qualities appeals to one particular sense, colour to the eye, sound to the ear, odour to the nose, taste to the palate, sense of resistance, of heat and cold, to the touch. Hence a secondary quality is appropriately named " sensibile proprium." Students of Natural Science have succeeded in making interesting discoveries regarding the nature and causes of secondary qualities of bodies. Sound, for instance, has been analysed as the energy of a body propagated by air—an energy which is perceived when the air-waves reach the ear. There are three qualities of sound well known to students of the subject : (1) intensity (loudness), which is due to the amplitude of the vibration ; (2) pitch, due to the length of the vibrating body, and consequently to the number of vibrations per second ; and (3) timbre or quality of tone. " Doh," for instance, sounded on a piano may have the same intensity and the same pitch as " Doh " sounded on a violin, but the two notes will differ markedly in timbre. The strings both of the piano and violin vibrate as whole strings, but there are minute vibrations of portions of the strings forming " overtones," which, coalescing with the principal tones, give to each note its peculiar quality. The number of vibrations per second of a note compared with those of an octave higher gives the proportion $1:2$. The vibrations per second of C and G are as $2:3$. Those of C and F are as $3:4$. The number of vibrations of F, A, and C' are as $4:5:6$.

Interesting discoveries and speculations have been made also in regard to Colour. The energy of the molecules of a body (e.g. the Sun) propagated by transverse vibrations of ether are said to be the fundamental cause of colour, and the perception by the eye of this undulatory energy constitutes the sensation of colour. It is well known that the light of the Sun may by means of the spectrum be split up into seven different colours—red, orange, yellow, green, blue, indigo, violet. The analogy between the seven notes of the musical scale, doh, ray, me, fah, soh, lah, te, and the seven spectral colours is striking and suggestive. It has been estimated that the vibrations per second of the red rays of the spectrum are about 460 billions, and those of the violet rays 670 billions. Whence it appears that colour is the "pitch" of light. Again we are assured that when sunlight falls upon a body— say upon the red petals of a rose—owing to their molecular constitution the petals absorb all the rays except the red which are reflected to the eye. In case of black objects all the rays are absorbed, whilst all the rays are reflected from white surfaces. And the conclusion is formed generally by scientists that colour exists in bodies in the sense that they possess a certain selective or absorptive power. Colour exists fundamentally or causally in the external object, and exists in its formal character of colour only in the eye.

Many writers of the Neo-scholastic school accept the general teaching of scientists in regard to the subjectivity of secondary qualities of bodies and justify their acceptance by the following arguments to which we shall endeavour to do the fullest justice. Our criticism of this aspect of Natural Realism will follow in due course.

A. Thesis in Regard to Sound

If the truth of perception requires that in the vibrating body or air, sound should exist objectively as it is perceived, then it must exist objectively with the same intensity, pitch and timbre wherewith it is perceived.

But that is impossible.

Therefore the truth of the perception does not require, etc.

The minor is proved as follows :

(*a*) Intensity. Loudness or intensity decreases as the square of the distance. Two men placed at different distances from the sounding body perceive different intensities. But if they both hear the sound as it exists in the body, there must be different intensities there at the same time.

(*b*) Pitch. A simple diagram will illustrate the argument in this case.

$$A \text{————————} S \text{————————} A^1$$

Let S represent a railway station. A indicates an approaching train. The pitch of the engine's whistle when first heard as it approaches the station is recognised to be soh (G), but when the whistle is sounded in the station preparatory to departure, the pitch is fah (F), and as the train recedes in the direction A^1, the pitch sinks to me (E). From the scientific standpoint there is a satisfactory explanation. The air-waves created by the whistle of the approaching train, falling with accelerated frequency upon the ear, raise the pitch, whilst falling with less frequency as the train recedes, the pitch is lowered. And many writers of the Neo-scholastic school appeal to this experiment as showing that sound does not exist formally outside the sense. "The engine-driver," they say, "hears the note fah (F) all the time. The listener at the station hears soh, then fah and finally me. If sound exists objectively as heard, we have contradictory and confusing results."

(*c*) Timbre. The quality of a tone can be artificially produced by the vibrations of a number of distinct bodies (tuning forks). In this case of artificial production no individual body can lay claim to the formal sound. But the quality of a note is due, as explained above, to the overtones which come from segments of the string and which correspond to the tuning forks. In no case then can the particular formal sound (timbre) exist objectively.

B. Thesis in Regard to Colour

The Neo-scholastics for the most part accept also the subjectivity of colour. "Colour exists fundamentally in the object and formally in the sense." And the following arguments are advanced in support of this thesis.

(a) Argument based on the "interference" of light. In the case of a soap-bubble if observers be differently stationed, one notes that a certain part of the bubble is red, another judges that same part to be green, whilst a third concludes that it is violet. It is contended that if formal colour existed objectively, each observer would see the same colour in the same place.

(b) Argument based on mixture of colours. Blue and yellow pigments produce greenish colour. Now the green (if formally present) must inhere either in the aggregate of the particles or in the particles themselves. Not in the aggregate of the particles, which is a mixture of blue and yellow; and not in the particles themselves, which have their own respective colours. The colour of the aggregate, therefore, cannot be explained on the hypothesis of "formal" colour in the object.

(c) Newton's disc. The experiment with Newton's disc is well known. It depends on the fact that the eye requires $\frac{1}{8}$ of a second to discriminate colours. The spectral colours on the disc rotated rapidly produce the sensation of white colour. Formal colour is therefore claimed to be subjective.

(d) Change of Light. Finally the change of colour produced by change of light points also to subjectivity. Blue and green, distinguishable in daylight, appear in both cases to be green in candle light.

An endeavour has been made to state the arguments for the subjectivity of formal sound and formal colour in the fairest way, but this teaching is open to the serious objection that it favours Idealism. If in truth secondary qualities of bodies are not objective, the inference follows that even primary qualities lose their claim to objectivity, since they are revealed to us by secondary qualities. The extension of a body is known through its colour, and if there is deception in regard to colour, the deception affects the extension. Indeed both Berkeley and Kant deduced their idealistic views from the supposed subjectivity of secondary qualities.

It will be well to indicate first of all the answer to a few general difficulties before treating specifically those which arise from sound and colour.

1. It is asserted that sound, light and heat are " modes of motion." Granted. But motion is not the *total phenomenon*. Scholastic writers of the greatest weight from Albert the Great and Thomas Aquinas down to exponents of philosophical science at the present day (Gredt, Pesch, Farges, Mivart, etc.) claim that sound and colour and the other sensibilia propria exist objectively as sensible qualities. The total phenomenon is sometimes very different from its constituent parts. Water has no resemblance to either hydrogen or oxygen. Both sound and colour are far more than wave-motion of air or ether.

2. The objection is urged that electrical action conveyed to the retina produces light, applied to the ear produces sound, the phenomena in both cases being subjective.

We do not contend for a moment that there may not be purely subjective phenomena due to artificial stimuli or to some abnormal condition. Our contention is that when the senses in their normal condition perceive sound or colour, these sensible qualities have an objective existence as sound and colour apart from the sense.

3. The Weber-Fechner law is sometimes quoted in favour of subjective sensation. The law claims that increase of sensation (intensity) in arithmetical progression 1, 2, 3, 4, etc., requires increase of the stimulus in geometrical progression 1, 2, 4, 8, etc. The application of mathematical measurement to psychological phenomena must be received with caution. Many question the truth of this law, but granting its truth, it does not in the least tell against the objectivity of sensation. Scholastics have always contended that what the sense perceives is true *as far as it goes, but is not the whole truth*.

We proceed now to criticise the specific arguments adduced by many Neo-scholastics to prove the subjectivity of formal sound and colour.

I. Intensity, pitch and timbre of sound.

(*a*) Intensity. Experiments show that the same sound is

heard with different intensities in accordance with variation of distance. This fact is in perfect accord with the objectivity of sensation which Realists claim. The physical law is well known which states that if an observer doubles his distance from a sounding body the intensity perceived at the new position will be only ¼ of what it was at the former position. But the lessening of intensity in accordance with distance is not a positive error. The sense-perception is true as far as it goes. The sound has *in the ear* the exact intensity which is perceived.

(*b*) Pitch. The argument based upon the change of pitch of the locomotive whistle as it approaches or recedes is not convincing. The supposition is that though the whistle sounds fah (F), the ether vibrations of the rapidly approaching train, when wave overtaking wave they reach the ear are interpreted as sounding soh (G). Realists readily assent. The ear perceives the note soh (G), because the note soh (G) is actually produced *in the ear* by the increase of undulations per second. And if the objection be raised that there is in this case a positive error—inasmuch as the note perceived differs from the actual note—the answer is at hand. The ear perceives not only the pitch of the whistle but witnesses to the fact of the whistle's rapid approach, so that the correspondence between the perception and reality is maintained. Should the ear have perceived fah (F) in this case, the fact would favour the subjectivity of sensation rather than support its objectivity. The note soh (G) is produced in the ear and perceived as such, and if the judgment be made that soh is the actual note sounded by the whistle, the error obviously belongs to the judgment.

(*c*) Timbre. Let it be granted that the ear does not as a rule catch the overtones which, added to the principal tone, cause the quality of a note. But from this fact nothing more can be inferred than that the sense fails to perceive the whole objective phenomenon. As laid down before, the perception of the sense is true as far as it goes, but is not the whole truth.

II. Colour and its manifestations.

(a) Example based on "interference" of light. It will be remembered that in the case of the soap-bubble, the same part viewed from different positions appeared red to one observer, green to another, and violet to a third.

It is curious that an experiment which is regarded as a crucial test of the subjectivity of formal colour should lend itself admirably to establish the opposite conclusion. Spectators differently placed viewing the same part of the soap-bubble receive (owing to "interference") some and not others of the spectral rays. The red rays forming red colour are received by one, green rays forming green colour by another, etc. The sense reports truly but the judgment erroneously refers the colour to the object. Indeed the Neo-scholastic argument in this case proves too much, for not only secondary qualities but the primary quality of extension is apparently affected by distance. A circle appears as such to one spectator, and to another differently placed seems to be an ellipse. And yet the Neo-scholastics contend strongly for the objectivity of the primary qualities.

(b) Mixture of colours. Blue and yellow powders give out when mixed a greenish tint. The perception is not false but insufficient. The eye cannot appreciate the inequalities which undoubtedly exist in what is regarded as a straight line, and similarly the eye sees but indistinctly the blue and yellow ingredients. The resultant impression produces objectively a sensible quality resembling green which is accordingly seen.

(c) Newton's disc. The experiment with Newton's disc depends upon the fact that the eye requires $\frac{1}{8}$ of a second for the discrimination of colours. When the disc is rapidly rotated, the rays from the spectral colours blend, and reaching the eye simultaneously they form for the eye the quality of whiteness. An authority of great weight records very briefly his judgment on the merits of the view favoured generally by Neo-scholastic writers: " The view you describe is the one which is, I suppose, commonly accepted. It certainly seems to me to imply that the mind, or else, as some think, the sense organ or sense apparatus, including nerve centres, creates colour, and so it is idealistic (Locke). I do not think that the white appearance of the rainbow disc can be explained by an act of judgment. It is rather purely physiological. Under the conditions the eye is stimulated in the same way as by a white surface and it sees white. There are different theories, as you know, of what the physiological process is. On the Hering theory all the other colour excitements except white cancel each other out and leave only white. There is no judgment involved in seeing white when the eye is excited in the white way. White is the corresponding object. You may say if you like it is hallucination, but in that case every sensation is a hallucination. In like manner when you stimulate a cold point on the skin with a hot tube you have the sensation of cold. The rainbow disc in revolution produces the excitement specific to white and white is seen. I vote for the old scholastic view."

But does not the example of the stimulation of cold points on the skin suggest a want of correspondence between the sensation and the non-mental object and thus favour a subjectivist view ? The writer continues : " I do not think that the paradox of the sensation of cold when a cold point is stimulated by a hot tube or metal point favours the view of subjectivism. Of course the solution involves the whole of the opposite or realistic view. The apparatus set going by excitement of the cold point is the machinery for mental response to the non-mental object cold. No matter how it is excited, the object is the same. The way I put it is that this mental response is compresent with cold in the external world. The metal point is not as it happens cold but hot. Consequently it is an illusion if you think that the metal point is cold. But the cold is still not mental but external. It does not happen to be in the metal point but somewhere else. The illusion consists in referring it to the metal point. I am accustomed to describe the process of apprehending the external cold under these conditions in this way. I compare it to turning round to see something which is not in front of you. When the cold machinery is set going you turn round to see the cold in the world. And so the illusion that the metal point is cold is like squinting. You see the metal point with one eye and the cold with the other. I wish I knew the scholastic writers, old or new. But is not my answer in the spirit of the older writers? You know better than I."

(*d*) Change of light. The colours blue and green cannot be distinguished in candle light. For this light, differing in composition from sunlight, is differently absorbed and reflected by the bodies upon which it falls. Falling upon a blue object, the green rays of the candle light are strongly reflected, thus partially or wholly masking the blue colour. And as green rays are reflected both from blue and green objects, the sensible quality of green is formed and perceived by the eye.

It is sometimes said that the subjectivity of the sensations perceived by the faculties of taste and smell is especially noticeable. The same food, for instance, is appraised differently in accordance with individual taste. "One man's meat is another man's poison." But it must be remembered that the "sensibile proprium" (i.e. the object) of taste is not the food alone, but the food mixed with saliva. Hence individual idiosyncrasies. In regard to odour, it is recognised as due to small particles which are given off by the odour-emitting body, which particles reach the nose and produce objectively the sensible quality. The "sensibile proprium" of touch—the sense of resistance, of the roughness and smoothness of bodies, of cold and heat, etc., have likewise objective existence. Heat, for instance, like light and sound is a mode of motion, but the motion is not the whole phenomenon.

Conclusion

What then do we see when we look at an orange?

1. We see *directly* the orange, the reflected rays from which constitute formal colour which is perceived by the eye.

2. The perception of the colour (or sound) is of course affected by distance. The intensity of the formal colour (or formal sound), which is in the eye (or ear), though distinct from the sense, is the sensible quality which is perceived. In other words, the sense perceives what is true but not the whole truth.

3. The coloured object (orange) is seen under a certain visual angle, and in a certain direction of space.

4. The real magnitude of the object and its form of three dimensions are estimated by association with past experience.

These conclusions are in perfect agreement with the teaching of Albert the Great and Thomas Aquinas. Their judgment was that colour and sound exist materially in the object and formally in the medium. " Hypostasis coloris est lux." To admit that sensitive perception represents objects with a positive element of error is to cast serious doubt upon the accuracy of our cognitive faculties and to encourage the adoption of idealistic principles which inevitably lead to scepticism. Belief in the trustworthiness of the senses enables the human mind to look with true insight and deep appreciation into the wonders of creation and to recognise therein the hall-mark of Supreme Power and Beauty. A striking passage in Goethe's " Faust " records the utterance of the Earth-spirit :

> 'Tis thus at the roaring loom of time I ply,
> And weave for God, the garment thou seest Him by.

The garment displayed before our eyes—stimulating our powers of thought so that they comprehend in some small measure the majestic power of God—this beautiful vesture of Nature is often misinterpreted because analysed in a too formal and pedantic way :

> Sweet is the lore which Nature brings ;
>   Our meddling intellect
> Mis-shapes the beauteous forms of things :
>   —We murder to dissect.

In conclusion, some words of Dr. Hans Driesch (" Science and Philosophy of the Organism," Vol. II, p. 362) are relevant. In the course of a discussion on what he calls " Three windows into the Absolute," he writes that " the last window into the Absolute is the contingency of *immediate* Givenness and the immanent coherence of the single phases of Givenness in spite of its contingency. Let the reason of immediate Givenness be what it may, 'I,' as the conscious Ego, *do certainly not create it consciously out of myself;* it is very often contrary, or at least indifferent, to my will."

From the theistic point of view, the phrase "window into the Absolute," as applied to the External World, is a happy one, inasmuch as the contingent enables us to extend our intellectual vision to Necessary Being.

CHAPTER II

THE APOLOGETIC AIM

1. A TREATISE on Natural Religion may be conveniently divided into three sections :
    I. The existence and nature of God.
    II. The origin, endowments and destiny of man.
    III. The relations between God and man.

I propose to follow this order. But as Human Reason is the only court of appeal in all questions of Natural Religion, it will be necessary first of all to establish the validity and cogency of those principles and methods which Reason uses in order to reach its conclusions. An introduction, therefore, is prefixed and therein answers are given to the following questions : what religious truths can be proved by the natural light of Reason, what is the objective value of those primary principles (e.g. the law of causality) upon which Reason bases its conclusions ? Having settled these preliminary difficulties, we shall be at liberty to demonstrate the existence and nature of God, to show that man possesses endowments of spirituality, freedom of will, immortality, etc., and that there is an obligation upon rational creatures to recognise the Source of their origin, and to give to God the tribute of their worship, obedience and love.

2. " The holy Catholic Apostolic Roman Church believes and professes that there is one only true and living God, Creator and Lord of heaven and earth, all-powerful, eternal, immense, incomprehensible, infinite in intelligence, in will and in all perfection ; who being by nature a unique spiritual substance absolutely simple and unchangeable, must be declared really and essentially distinct from the world, happy

in Himself and by Himself, and raised above all which is, or can be conceived, outside of Himself."

In this definition of the Vatican Council (constitution " Dei filius," Cap. I) the existence and nature of God are first set forth. Next comes the statement of the real and essential distinction between God and the universe with reasons assigned—a clause directed against all forms of pantheism. God is distinct from the world because He is (1) unique by nature; (2) absolutely simple; (3) unchangeable. The words of the Council proceed : " because of the goodness of God and His almighty power, and not with the object of increasing His happiness nor of accomplishing His perfection, but to manifest His goodness by the benefits accorded to His creatures, this one true God did with absolute freedom create from nothing at the beginning of time creatures spiritual and corporal, i.e. the angels and the world, and finally man whose nature is made up of matter and spirit. By His Providence God preserves and governs all that He has produced ' reaching mightily from end to end and disposing all things with sweetness ' (Wisdom viii. 1). For all things are ' naked and open to His eyes ' (Hebrews iv. 13), even those acts which belong to the future and proceed from the free choice of creatures."

The Vatican Council has also declared that human reason can by its own power attain to the knowledge of God.

" The same Catholic Church holds and teaches that, by the natural light of reason, God the beginning and end of all things can with certainty be known from created things, for from the creation of the world His invisible perfections are perceived by human reason, being understood by the things that are made (Romans i. 20). Nevertheless it has pleased the wisdom and goodness of God to reveal Himself and the eternal decrees of His will in another—a supernatural way."

These words of the Council are aimed against

(a) Fideists and Traditionalists who maintained that the existence of God can be known only by the aid of Revelation or of the positive teaching of Tradition.

(b) The Kantian doctrine that *speculative reason* cannot

furnish satisfactory proofs of God's existence. Kant allowed that from *practical reason* some sort of proof may be deduced —a proof "subjectively sufficient but objectively insufficient."

3. Further light is thrown upon the teaching of the Vatican Council by the terms of the oath against Modernism prescribed to the clergy by the Motu Proprio "Sacrorum Antistitum" of September, 1910 :

"I profess that God the beginning and end of all things can be known and proved to exist with certainty through the natural light of reason by means of the things which He has made, i.e. the visible works of creation, just as a cause is known from its effects."

Some points in this profession merit attention :

(*a*) The object to be known, "God the beginning and end of all things," i.e. "the one only true and living God, creator of Heaven and earth," the notion of whom contains virtually or implicitly the attributes characteristic of Him as well as the falsity of contrary opinions. In his "Philosophy of experience," W. James writes : "the only opinions (regarding the nature of the Deity) which truly merit our attention belong to the order of ideas which may be broadly termed the pantheistic vision, i.e. the vision of God regarded as immanent in the universe." The pantheistic idea of God immanent but not transcendent is, as we shall see, wholly inadmissible.

(*b*) "The natural light of reason," i.e. the natural faculty man possesses whereby he recognises the intrinsic truth of primary principles, e.g. the law of causality. Kant's "practical reason" does not lay claim to any such power, but it is supposed to beget a kind of moral belief "subjectively sufficient but objectively insufficient."

(*c*) The natural light of reason directed to the "visible works of creation" perceives the necessity of a cause. The mind sees *directly* the existence of contingent things and perceives *directly* also the force of the law of causality. The conclusion reached (often subconsciously) may in explicit form be stated as follows :

> All contingent things require a cause.

The " visible works of creation " are contingent.

They, therefore, require a cause.

(d) The existence of a First Cause can be " certainly " known and proved.

(e) Finally in declaring that the knowledge of God's existence can be thus attained, the Church speaks of the physical possibility of such acquisition. Most people first learn of God's existence from religious instruction based on Revelation. But the Church wishes to convey the truth that speculative atheism is not possible to a man who uses his reasoning powers normally and seeks the truth in good faith. Confirmatory evidence comes from the researches of men like Andrew Lang (" The Making of Religion ") and P. Schmidt (" Anthropos "), who hold that the origin of the idea of God is not due to any form of animism nor to the worship of ancestors or of nature, but is anterior to all such superstitions, beliefs and practices and originates from the deduction of a First Cause. Such conclusion is reached spontaneously by the savage mind, not—it is needless to say—through formal syllogistic reasoning.

There is no contradiction later when the words of the Council insist upon the moral necessity of Revelation. Revelation is morally necessary so that truths of religion, which are not inaccessible to human reason, may be known *by all, without difficulty, with certitude* and to the *exclusion of error*. Obviously everyone has neither ability nor opportunity to investigate these matters and for such Revelation is morally necessary.

4. The anti-modernist oath is supplemented by the teaching of the Encyclical " Pascendi " of Pius X, which condemns the agnostic doctrine that we know nothing but states of consciousness, and condemns also modernistic " Immanence." Immanence is another form of the idealistic contention that we cannot reach objective truth, that we know merely our own ideas and impressions, but that nevertheless there is an intuition of the heart whereby one becomes convinced of the reality of God's existence. " L'immanence c'est l'intériorité." Bergson—a subjectivist of this type—

upholds the old view that external things owe their supposed material existence to the mind, that in reality all is action. God is incessant life, action, liberty whence all action radiates. Immanence as a philosophical system or a philosophical method, so far from leading to objective truth, tends to Agnosticism and pseudo-mysticism. It involves the destruction of all knowledge, profane as well as religious.

Hence in answer to the question what religious truths can be demonstrated by Reason, we need but repeat the logical divisions of this treatise on Natural Religion

(1) the existence and transcendent nature of God ;
(2) the origin, endowments, and destiny of man ;
(3) the relations between God and man.

II

In answer to the question can the existence of God be established by a scientific proof, it is necessary first of all to determine what precisely is meant by the term "scientific." Students of the physical sciences claim and claim reasonably that in their department the word "scientific" connotes a proof which is based upon observation and experiment. But as the physical sciences do not constitute the sum total of knowledge, as there are other branches such as Metaphysics, Rational Psychology, Logic, Ethics, Pure Mathematics, etc., which do not treat of the properties of matter and cannot be subjected to the test of observation and experiment, there must be other bases of certitude besides those on which the physical sciences depend. The aim of the present chapter is to show that "philosophical certitude" is just as valid as the physical certitude named "scientific." In fact, Certitude may be threefold. Certitude based upon an intuitive first principle such as the law of causality is called "metaphysical" or "philosophical." Certitude depending upon the uniformity of Nature's laws is termed "physical," and Certitude resting upon adequate human testimony is named "moral." Catholic philosophical writers deny (1) that the human mind has an immediate intuition of God, i.e. that the existence of God is evident in the same way as the principles of identity and contradiction are evident ; (2) that there is any valid à priori proof of God's existence. St. Anselm indeed attempted to formulate such a proof. He argued thus : the idea of God connotes the most perfect Being conceivable. But if He does not exist, we can conceive a being more perfect (because existing) than the most perfect being conceivable, which is absurd. God, therefore, exists. An examination of this mode of reasoning reveals its inconclusiveness. We are justified in accepting from St. Anselm's argument, not that God exists, but that the idea of God, as the most perfect Being conceivable, implies His existence in idea. But the passage from the domain of thought to that of actual existence is inadmissible.

Catholic apologists do claim that there is a demonstration à posteriori—from effect to cause—which gives a true if limited knowledge of God and the assurance of His existence, showing that He is :

    1. Supreme Mover, Himself unmoved,
    2. Supreme Efficient Cause,
    3. Necessary Being,
    4. Most Perfect Being,
    5. Supreme Intelligence.

These five predicates belong, as we shall see, to God and furnish an analogical knowledge of His Divine Nature—an analogical knowledge, for between the human conception of infinite perfection and actual Infinite Perfection there can be only an analogical resemblance.

The validity, however, of the à posteriori argument is called in question by the representatives of both forms of Agnosticism—the empiricist and the idealist. The empiricist denies that the principle of causality is a necessary truth. " Necessary truths have no existence as we know nothing but appearances (phenomena) and states of consciousness."

The Kantian idealist explains the law of causality as a mental category, which, owing to its subjective character, affords no guarantee of objective reality.

A. Empiricist Agnosticism

David Hume. The sensist theory of knowledge (epistemology) which Locke popularised in his work on the Human Understanding has been happily summed up in a short sentence by scholastic critics. "Nihil in intellectu nisi prius in sensu." The critics in question emphatically disagree with this dictum and claim that the intellect penetrating beneath phenomena perceives being (noumena) and the primary principles which depend on being. Hume was a follower of the nominalism and phenomenist system of Locke. To Hume an idea or concept was merely an image to which a general name was attached. Hence the idea of cause was nothing more than a case of invariable and unconditional succession. The sense of effort (nisus) which is felt in moving a body is (according to Hume) illogically transferred to inanimate things. And even when one moves a body, it cannot be said that the voluntary effort exercised really produces the movement; there are other intermediate factors called into play, muscles, nerves, etc. The law of causality being succession of antecedent and consequent without a true causal relation, no valid argument can be based thereon to establish the existence of a First Cause. And yet he writes in his "Natural History of Religion": "the ordered arrangement of nature speaks to us of an intelligent Being."

John Stuart Mill was also of the school of Locke and Hume. "We know nothing but states of consciousness"; "causality is nothing more than invariable and unconditional succession"; "all knowledge comes from experience." The late Dr. Ward, however, convinced Mill that the infallibility (within limits) of Memory, upon which the fabric of human knowledge is necessarily erected, is a truth incapable of proof —a truth always and unavoidably presupposed in every statement, so that the contention that all knowledge comes from sense experience cannot be maintained.

Herbert Spencer admits the existence of a material world, but attributes the supposed necessary character of the law of causality to the fact that the association of antecedent and consequent has become intensified by heredity into a causal relation. Spencer recognises a difference only of degree between the senses of the lower animals and the intelligence of man. He finds contradictions (antinomies) between the ideas of infinite justice and infinite mercy, between the exercise of infinite wisdom and free will, between the conception of an infinitely powerful benevolent God and the existence of evil. The attributes which he ascribes to the Deity are, though magnified, still human. Spencer forgets that between the attributes of the Infinite and the finite, there cannot be univocal but only analogical resemblance.

William James judges the idea of cause to be too obscure for the basis of a theological conclusion.

Comte, Littré and the French positivists hold views practically identical with those of the English Empiricists.

B. IDEALISTIC AGNOSTICISM

Kant, as noted above, endows man with three main cognitive faculties—Perception, Understanding and Reason, each of which faculties contains principles or forms of thought by the application of which to the materials given in the senses Knowledge in the scientific sense is produced. Perception has the forms—time and space, under which external objects appear. Understanding has twelve of these inner categories under the general heads of quantity, quality, relation and modality, and Reason has three forms which seek after unity. States of consciousness are unified under the category "soul," outward phenomena are all included under the category "universe," and possible existence is summed up under the category "God." The law of causality is due to the category of "relation." But as these categories are mental and subjective—"principles synthetic à priori"—they have no objective validity.

Moreover, in the idea of an Infinite Being, Kant discovered antinomies which he regarded as incapable of satisfactory explanation. For example, a necessary being cannot exist in or beyond the universe because (1) if he exists in the universe he is either (a) an integral part of cosmos or (b) identical with the totality of phenomena. But a part of cosmos, necessary and uncaused, can have no relation with the rest, whereas if identical with cosmos, the absurd consequence follows that a number of contingent beings taken together make a necessary being. If (2) on the other hand, a necessary being exists outside the universe, when he begins to act he enters into time and into the world contrary to the hypothesis. Kant's difficulties in this connection arose from the same source as those of Spencer—the substitution of the univocal for the analogical conception of Divine perfection.

Agnostics therefore claim that the law of causality has neither an ontological nor a transcendental value, i.e. that it can prove neither the objective existence of being nor the existence of a transcendental First Cause.

III

How is knowledge acquired? To what extent is knowledge objective and accurate? These questions have been discussed for thousands of years, and the divergencies of view in the past and at the present time are due to fundamental differences regarding the origin and validity of knowledge.

When a child begins to use his reason, he exercises necessarily the power of abstraction which reason possesses. The outlook upon life of his early years is full of intense interest. A "gee-gee," for example, is especially attractive. The child sees horses of different sizes and colours, and forms automatically the general notion "horse" by abstracting the individualising qualities. Whilst his eye has noted the changing phenomena of colour and size, his intellect has intuitively perceived the underlying "noumenon"—the nature of the horse. But the child has noticed other objects, animate and inanimate. The faculty of abstraction has been busy in every case and thus he forms the most fundamental and universal of general notions—that of "being." The adult mind recognises degrees in the use of this faculty: first degree, the attention of the mind is directed to sensible qualities with abstraction of individual circumstances; second degree, the mind, as in mathematical studies, abstracts all qualities except continuous quantity; third degree, the mind abstracts all qualities of matter, and forms the concepts of "being," "unity," "truth," "goodness," etc.

Concurrently with the implicit cognisance of general notions comes to the child the implicit cognisance of general principles; "that which is real cannot be not real"; "that which begins has a cause"; "the same cause in the same circumstances produces the same effect." The child knows that these principles must be true everywhere and always, i.e. he knows their necessity and universality, though he has as yet but an implicit knowledge and cannot, until he becomes more mature, express the facts explicitly in philosophical form.

But are these primary notions and principles objectively true? It is obvious that, in the case of notions and principles immediately evident, no direct proof can be given. There is no place for a medium of proof between subject and predicate where the connection between them is intuitively cognised to be immediate. But we can have recourse to indirect proof, by showing the absurdity of the results which follow from the supposition of their falsity. One consequence is clear: if the validity of primary notions and primary principles be called in question, knowledge of any kind is no longer possible. All science depends on the truth of the principle of identity used in syllogistic reasoning, of the principle of contradiction which makes possible a "reductio ad absurdum," of the principle of sufficient reason involved in the use of Induction. If our cognitive faculties do not avouch truly, there is no correspondence between the object and the idea of the same. In fact, the object disappears. Nothing is known but the idea. The object of direct thought and the object of reflex thought become one and the same, so that there would be no distinction between (e.g.) Causality and the idea of

Causality. Inasmuch as the idea in the mind has in this supposition no representative (intentional) value it is the idea of nothing. If the ontological value of first principles be doubted, the doubter assents indeed to the mental inconceivability of the absurd, but cannot deny its possible existence *in rerum natura*. A square circle though not only unimaginable but inconceivable (with elements contradictory and mutually exclusive) may exist ! Thus the intellect itself as an instrument of thought is destroyed, unless the ontological value of primary notions and principles be accepted.

From what has been said, the Catholic teaching on the rule and motive of certitude is amply justified. Whatever our cognitive faculties, being in the normal condition and rightly used, declare absolutely to be certain is certain. This is the rule of certitude and the motive is the light of reason which sees the truth of the perception. A distinction, however, of the highest importance must be noted. A stick immersed in water seems bent. The sun seems, and indeed for many centuries was thought, to revolve round the earth. Each of these conclusions has been regarded as certain and yet each is demonstrably false. The objection is easily answered. In the cases just cited, an " undoubting " assent has been given to the seeming facts, but not an " absolute " assent. There is no difficulty, if proof be forthcoming, in passing from belief in the Ptolemaic to belief in the Copernican system. The daily and nightly phenomena of the heavens may be shown to be the natural and exclusive result of the Copernican principle of heliocentrism. But to doubt the truth of primary principles such as that of causation (everything that begins to exist has a cause) would mean the paralysis of the mind and the consequent impossibility of knowledge of any kind. The " influx " too of cause into effect, as contradistinguished from mere antecedence and consequence, is an essential element of the intuition.

The objection may be pressed : is there not a subjective element in human knowledge ? I look, for instance, at an orange and see a distinct and characteristic colour. The opinion of an unphilosophical observer would be that the colour was something inherent in the orange, whereas scholastic writers maintain that the colour is only materially in the orange and is formally as colour in the medium and cognised as such by the perceptive faculty. Before answering this objection, it will help to take another instance. A botanist cuts a very thin section of the stem of a plant, and examining the section with the naked eye notes that there is a certain disposition of parts, a certain arrangement of cells, etc. Thereupon he examines the section under the magnifying power of a microscope, and new and marvellous dispositions and arrangements are revealed. What conclusion may be drawn from this experience? Not that the naked eye gave wrong information, but that it did not give all the details. This fact may be simply and clearly stated by the aid of algebraic symbols. If a represents all the details of the section and the energy involved in their objective reality, and $-b$ represents the limitation of the sense, then the perception is represented by $a-b$; a perception true as far as it goes, but obviously not the whole truth. In this way our knowledge is subjective. Whereas according to Kant, inasmuch as arbitrary mental categories or forms modify knowledge, a positive element of subjectivity is introduced, which, under his successors Fichte, Hegel and Schelling, produced the thoroughgoing systems of German Idealism. Returning to the example of the orange, a certain modification of its structure together with the energy of light playing upon its surface (resulting in the absorption of some rays) produces a compound energy which modifies the visual organ. The objective sensible quality of colour perceived by the sense is a true effect of the outward exciting cause and truly witnesses to its activity, but again no claim is made that the sensation represents wholly and completely the nature and activity of the exciting cause. Human knowledge in truth falls far short of reality! The tiniest grain of sand is made up of an enormous number of atoms, and each atom is, according to recent discoveries in physical science, the theatre of immense activity—activity of electrons in revolution round a common centre of gravity! So that the examination of the commonest and most worthless of Nature's products reveals a complexity of forces, an order, a perfection of design comparable in beauty and grandeur to the vast solar systems, some knowledge of which the science of Astronomy has brought within our ken. Almighty power has left its impress, its hall-mark, upon the indefinitely little as upon the indefinitely great!

Bergson's objection that the dynamic aspect of phenomena is alone correct, that there are no " things " but only " actions " and that " things " and " states " are only mental aspects of continuous activity, fails to grasp the fact that phenomena witness to the substances in which are revealed primary notions and principles universally and necessarily true and not affected by phenomenal change. When M. Le Roy of the same school of " Action " pushes his view to the extent of denying distinctions between " motor " and " moved " (cause and effect), between " act " and " power," asserting that such distinctions are idols of the imagination, he labours in vain in defence of the philosophy of " action," for knowledge of every kind disappears unless the permanent (static) value of primary notions and principles be recognised.

IV

It cannot be denied that the ontological value of primary notions and principles must be accepted, else knowledge of any kind is impossible. The acceptance of this intuition is as imperative as the acceptance of the intuitive truth of the trustworthiness of memory. And as a consequence the falsity of the empiricist philosophy—based on the principle that all knowledge comes from experience—is evident. But another question of the highest importance arises. Have primary notions and principles a *transcendent* value, i.e. may they be legitimately used to reach conclusions concerning not the finite but the Infinite? It will be remembered that Kant found what he regarded as insuperable difficulties (antinomies) in this connection. To him the idea of predicating freedom as a perfection of the Absolute involved a contradiction, as also the idea of Necessary Being in relation to a created universe. Herbert Spencer found, in addition to the Kantian antinomies, special difficulties of his own—the simplicity of God as opposed to the plurality of His perfections, the opposition of Divine justice and mercy, and the coexistence of the infinite power and goodness of God with the evil physical and moral which makes of this world a " valley of tears." These difficulties shall be fully considered as they logically arise.

Père Garrigou-Lagrange states in syllogistic form the claim made for the transcendent value of intuitive notions and principles.

Perfections absolute and analogical are legitimately applied to the Infinite.

Primary notions of " being," " unity," " truth," " goodness," " cause," " end," " intelligence," and " will " may express perfections absolute and analogical.

Therefore they may be applied to the Infinite. Both major and minor premiss of this syllogism require explanation and justification. An absolute perfection is one which contains no element of imperfection. An analogical perfection is one which exists in modes essentially different. The following table of analogical usage shows the variations of mode.

Analogy
- Attribution, e.g. Fresh air is healthy.
- Proportionality
  - metaphorical, e.g. The lion is king of animals.
  - real, e.g. " being " applied to substance and accident.

Regarding the minor premiss, primary notions in their formal signification involve no imperfection except the finite mode in which they exist. " Being " in itself, for instance, implies no limitation of genus or species, i.e. is transcendental. Hence " being " may be applied to a stone, plant, animal, or man without connoting the limitations of each. An " infinite man " involves contradiction (" man " connoting limitation) but not an " infinite being." " Being " therefore may be justly applied to the Infinite, although the infinite or divine mode of "being" can be known only negatively and relatively. The same reasoning applies to the analogical use of "unity," "truth," and "goodness." Or to state the facts in another way, the application of primary notions to the Infinite involves (*a*) the removal of the finite mode and (*b*) the ascription to the Infinite of the idea in its highest formal perfection (*eminentissimo modo*). The other primary notions, "cause," whether efficient or final, and "intelligence," from their intimate association with "being" can be applied in the same way, and "will," closely related to "goodness," falls into the same category.

The foregoing explanation suggests incidentally the fallacy which gives rise to the supposed antinomies of Kant and Spencer. Both these philosophers applied to the Infinite notions of perfection in their univocal instead of their analogical acceptation. If, for instance, the statement be made in the univocal sense that God is good, meaning that He is the cause of goodness, by parity of reasoning it will be justifiable to say that God is material because He is the cause of the material cosmos. When a limited human idea is taken as the adequate symbol of the Infinite, the same contradictions ensue as in mathematical science when the symbols x and y are made to represent zero powers. As Cardinal Newman wrote, the symbols thus unjustifiably applied "stop short and protest by an absurdity." Apart from this direct proof, there are other indirect methods of demonstration which show that the doubt in regard to the transcendent value of primary notions involves doubt of the truth of primary principles and consequent intellectual chaos.

1. If the existence of a First Cause be doubtful, then perhaps the world exists without a cause. The principle of causality disappears.

2. The universe exists neither of itself nor through a cause, i.e. does not exist. The principle of contradiction becomes doubtful.

3. If the doubt regard the transcendent nature of the cause, then perhaps the cause is immanent and pantheism probably true.

The conclusion that follows from the proofs direct and indirect may be thus stated. Human reason aided by its intuitive knowledge of primary notions and principles is justified in its investigation of God's existence and in its claim to comprehend something of His essence, but human reason—a finite instrument—cannot comprehend the Infinite as He is in Himself.

CHAPTER III

PROOFS OF GOD'S EXISTENCE

THE Metaphysical proof of God's existence depends on the law of causality every contingent effect must have a cause. The five aspects of this proof chosen and developed by St. Thomas are well known. Every created being (1) is subject to change; (2) owes its existence to a cause; (3) is contingent; (4) lacks simplicity and perfection; and withal (5) manifests in life and action signs of order and arrangement.

Before proceeding to the exposition of these special points of view, a more general proof may be given, which he who runs can read.

(*a*) In our outlook upon natural phenomena we note the existence of objects classified as inorganic, vegetative, sensitive and rational. They come and they go. Some undergo change, some illustrate the specific change from life to death. All lack a stable specific mode of existence. Whence come they? And even if we allow that the succession of generations has gone on from eternity (a statement at variance, as we shall see, with the physical law of dissipation of energy) the succession is eternally insufficient to explain itself. The conclusion inevitably follows that there must be a First Being, who owes existence to Himself alone, and who gives existence to all contingent creatures.

(*b*) Inasmuch as there are beings endowed with life—an endowment higher than and superior to any quality of inorganic matter—as the greater cannot come from the less—the attribute of life must be referred to the First Being the Fount of Life.

(c) The existence of rational beings cannot be explained as a development from lower forms of animal existence. No animal however capable of adaptation shows the slightest indication of a rational and moral nature. Whence then come intellectual power and the consciousness of right and wrong? From the First Being who is intelligent and good, not in an accidental and contingent way, but necessarily and essentially. "There is no greater absurdity," wrote Montesquieu, "than to suppose that a blind materialistic system should have produced intelligent beings."

(d) A necessary truth is one the contradictory of which is intrinsically impossible. Such truths are significant propositions, i.e. they declare something not expressed in their subject. They are independent of the human intellect, and are not the result of past uniformity in the association of ideas. "All trilateral figures are triangular"; "$2+9=3+8$." The human mind feels the necessity of these truths and of many truths of the same self-evident character. Whence come they? They witness to the Supreme Necessary Being from whom truth proceeds.

(e) Finally the morality, justice, sanctity which we observe exemplified in the lives of some of our fellow-creatures and which have characterised the lives of multitudes in past ages —a morality and sense of justice independent of utilitarian considerations, as witnessed to by the maxim "fiat justitia ruat coelum"—cannot be referred to any contingent reality as to their source. The necessary laws of morality witness to a being who is Supreme Intelligence and Supreme Goodness. Thus the universe which we see postulates as its cause One who is First Being, Fount of Life, Supreme Intelligence, Source of Truth, Absolute Goodness.

The reasoning outlined above suggests the fallacy which underlies materialistic evolution. Matter is not homogeneous, nor is its potency unlimited. The highest scientific authorities are forced to recognise the existence of "enigmas" the explanation of which by natural causes transcends the wit of man. And these enigmas are concerned with the most obvious natural phenomena. Du Bois-Reymond enumerates them as follows: (1) The nature of matter and force; (2) The origin of movement (3) The first appearance of life; (4) Apparent design in nature; (5) The origin of sensation and consciousness; (6) The origin of reason and speech; (7) Free-will.

Nor can Idealistic Pantheism be maintained in view of a First Cause who is sovereignly independent, intelligent and free. These attributes constitute a Divine Personality, who is immanent indeed in power, but transcendent by virtue of His infinite perfection.

I. Proof Based on Moving Bodies

In order to appreciate the force of the argument based upon the movement of bodies, it is necessary to realise that movement is a passage from indetermination to determination, from capability to achievement, or to use the technical scholastic phrase, from "power" to "act." Throughout this argument the movement of bodies is regarded exclusively from the metaphysical standpoint. Wisely so, because of conflicting views of the nature of movement when viewed from the physical standpoint. Modern discoveries regarding the constitution of matter seem to support the hypothesis that matter is composed of inconceivably small elements called "atoms," and that these atoms are spheres of positive electricity within which units of negative electricity ("electrons") are constantly revolving in certain definite orbits—one atom differing from another only in the number and arrangement of its electrons. A microbe so small as to be invisible to the naked eye contains many thousand millions of atoms! And in order to obtain some idea of the relative size of an atom and an electron, if we imagine an atom to be enormously enlarged so that its dimensions measure 160 feet long, 80 feet wide, and 40 feet high, each electron of such an atom, magnified proportionately, would be represented in size by the dot or full-stop at the end of this sentence. Clearly the new conception of matter—a moving mass of electrons—emphasises its dynamic character, and the question arises, does this discovery modify the cogency of the argument upon which Aristotle and St. Thomas based the existence of a First Mover, Himself unmoved. It is satisfactory to know that whether the kinetic theory of matter (which recognises no force in moving bodies except the movement itself) or the dynamic theory (which claims that movement is the effect of some force inherent in the body) be accepted, the argument of Aristotle and St. Thomas, being metaphysical not physical, remains unaffected. The metaphysical conception of movement lies in the momentary passage of a moving body from power to act, from indetermination to determination, from possibility to achievement. And the passage from power to act postulates the influx of an external agent itself in act. A moving body occupies successively positions a, b, c, etc. There is no less change (from the metaphysical standpoint) in the passage from a to b, than in the passage from relative rest to movement. M. Paul Janet in his statement of this argument reasoned thus: all movement is communicated, for matter being " inert " (i.e. indifferent to rest or movement) cannot move itself. His object in stating the argument in this form was no doubt to correct the supposition of Aristotle that matter tended to a state of rest. But once more if moving bodies are viewed from the metaphysical standpoint, the consideration of physical hypotheses (for even the first law of motion is, according to the united testimony of Messieurs H. Poincaré and P. Duhem, nothing more than an hypothesis suggested by the facts) need not detain us. The passage from power to act involves ultimately a Cause, in whom there can be no element of potentiality—a Cause therefore who is " Actus purissimus."

The argument based on movement may be stated in the following syllogistic form. If bodies are in motion (i.e. passing momentarily from power to act) they ultimately owe the continuance as well as the inception of this motion to an extrinsic agent wholly in act. But bodies are in motion. They owe, therefore, their motion ultimately to an extrinsic agent wholly in act.

Example from local movement. A passenger in a sailing

ship moves at the ship's rate of speed : the ship is moved by the wind ; the wind is caused by the rotatory motion of the earth ; the motion of the earth is caused by the sun ; the sun's movement through space is caused by the attraction of some unknown centre and so on. We may, if we choose, suppose an infinite series. But the difficulty is not solved by such a supposition, for each member of the series is *moved*. An infinite number of wheels in a watch will not go without the spring. Hence we come to a First Cause whose being has no potentiality.

Example from metaphysical movement : the fully developed plant comes from the potentiality of the seed. The seed comes from the potentiality of the seed of a previous plant and so on, until we come to the Cause whose being possesses the fulness of achievement, act, or perfection. The words just used, "achievement," "act," and "perfection," have unfortunately a connotation implying progress and so far forth they fail to indicate the unchangeable eternal perfection of the First Cause.

Thus from the contemplation of a phenomenon so familiar as movement, from reflection upon the life-history of the simplest wayside flower finding therein a wayside sacrament—outward sign of invisible power—we rise up to the conception of the Infinite. Just as when an electrified sphere is touched at any point of its surface by a needle, the whole charge of electricity is received, similarly the emergence of the buttercup from the surface of the earth postulates for its production and conservation the agency of Infinite power.

> Flower in the crannied wall,
> I pluck you out of the crannies,
> I hold you here, root and all, in my hand,
> Little flower—but *if* I could understand
> What you are, root and all, and all in all,
> I should know what God and man is.

Two objections will be briefly considered.

First objection. Bodies move owing to certain laws—first law of motion, law of attraction, law of inertia, etc. They require, therefore, no external agent to move them.

Answer. The word "law" represents a fact not a cause. All physical "laws" are only generalisations from experience. To say that bodies move by virtue of the first law of motion is equivalent to saying that bodies move because bodies move! To state that bodies move by virtue of the law of attraction or inertia is to explain a mystery by a greater mystery—*ignotum per ignotius.* No one knows what attraction is. As already stated movement is a passage from power to act, and requires the agency of a cause itself in act. A piece of iron placed in a furnace becomes red hot. It has passed from power to act. It could not possibly have done so itself. There is needed for the transition the agency of an external cause (the fire) itself in act. The same reasoning applies to moving bodies.

Second objection. A cause unmoved is an idea involving contradiction. Creation was a passage from power to act.

Answer. The objection arises, as in the case of Kant's and Spencer's antinomies, from the ascription of human terms, without the necessary correction, to the Infinite. There is the immobility of perfection and the immobility of inertia. A human cause cannot act without vital movement mental or physical. Potentiality is necessarily associated with the finite. But the Infinite has been in act from all eternity. Immobility as applied to the Infinite does not mean quiescence, but the absence of movement from power to act. The creation of the universe was decreed from eternity. We are obliged to think of the world as having been created in time. To God there is no past, no future. Hence God underwent no change when He created the universe—a truth beautifully expressed in the words of the liturgical hymn :

> Rerum Deus tenax vigor
Immotus in Te permanens.

II. Efficient Cause

The metaphysical concept of movement as being a constant passage from power to act—a constant evolution—is aptly described in scholastic phrase as "fieri," or as French metaphysicians name it "un devenir," in contradistinction to the concept of something complete and stable to which the name "ens" is applied. There is a somewhat similar distinction of causes—some are active only for the production of the effect, whilst others remain active in order to secure the continuance of the effect produced. Father and mother are the causes of the generation of their offspring, but the child continues to live after the death of its parents: whereas nourishment, heat, air, etc., are necessary at all times for the life as well as for the production of organisms. This consideration enables us to appreciate the truth that beings necessarily and permanently depend upon efficient causes. But these causes require in turn others to explain their being and activity. And thus we are led back to the Source of being—the First Cause not caused, who dispenses being to all creatures, and continues to conserve the gift conceded.

III. CONTINGENT BEING

Setting out from the standpoint of contingence an *à posteriori* argument establishing the existence of Necessary Being is easy to formulate. Contingent beings come and go. If the successive links of the chain be traced backwards—even if we suppose the links to reach back to eternity—the succession, being eternally contingent, requires ultimately the agency of a being, whose existence is not contingent but essential, i.e. Necessary Being.

Such Necessary Being is not (*a*) the totality of contingent beings as pantheists maintain, for a number however great of contingent beings cannot constitute the Absolute. Nor is Necessary Being (*b*) the law which governs the totality of contingent elements, for a law is dependent upon phenomena. Nor is Necessary Being (*c*) the "noumenon" underlying phenomena and manifesting the "creative force of evolution." Wherever there is evolution, there must be passage from power to act—a change incompatible with the concept of Necessary Being who is in actual possession of all forms of perfection and from whom potentiality must be dissociated.

The cogency of the argument based on contingent being is admitted by Kant: "granted that anything exists, it is impossible to refuse the conclusion that something exists necessarily."

In connection with this line of reasoning, it is curious to note how one of the most momentous of the recent discoveries in physical science strongly confirms the metaphysical conclusion. The so-called " dissipation of energy " is illustrated best by a concrete example. A locomotive is moved by the pressure of steam, the steam is generated by heat ; the energy of heat comes from the potential energy stored in fuel—so that the movement of the locomotive illustrates the change of potential into kinetic energy, i.e. energy of movement. But it is evident that all the potential energy does not pass into kinetic, because the engine becomes heated and some of the heat is necessarily radiated away into space. No scientific authority has been able even to suggest how the energy (heat) radiated away into space can be recovered for any serviceable purpose. Hence the " dissipation " of energy. And the process is at all times going on in every vital and non-vital action. The plant or animal in the process of assimilating nourishment develops heat, a portion of which is radiated into space and " dissipated." It follows therefore that the supply of serviceable energy (source of life, movement, etc.) is gradually disappearing—not indeed " lost," for energy like matter is indestructible, but suffering a transformation into a low form of energy (heat) useless for the maintenance of life. The vital machinery of the Universe, like the machinery of a clock, is running down and this being the case, the question arises, who placed the Universe originally in a position of advantage, who first wound up the clock ?

The objection may be urged that human reason cannot pretend to grasp all the processes of Nature—that the energy dissipated may be in some unknown way restored to its original serviceable form. The answer is at hand. Possibilities are illimitable. The contention here emphasised is that from the scientific standpoint there is no indication of such a process of restoration. Scientists are loud in their condemnation of groundless hypotheses. "Hypotheses non fingo," wrote Sir Isaac Newton. Hence "the greatest discovery of the nineteenth century"—the conservation and dissipation of energy—lends strong support to the theistic reasoning from contingent being.

Though the eternity of matter (possible from the metaphysical standpoint, since God could have created from eternity) seems to be incompatible with the doctrine of energy, yet granted its eternal existence and of course its indestructibility, the argument based on contingent being retains its cogency, because matter, indestructible and even eternal, remains contingent.

IV. Degrees of Being

There are not only repeated instances, but varying degrees of goodness, truth, bravery, etc., amongst rational creatures —a fact which, as we shall see presently, justifies the inference from the multiple to the one, from the compound to the simple. It will be well to develop this line of reasoning (*a*) in its general form, as it points to a First Being entirely simple and perfect and therefore distinct from imperfect and compound entities; (*b*) in the more specific inference from human intelligence to Perfect Intelligence; (*c*) in the inference from truths contingent and necessary to Supreme Truth; (*d*) from the aspiration of the soul towards happiness to the Source of happiness; and (*e*) from the appreciation of the impassable gulf between Right and Wrong, and the binding force of Right and Duty to the Lawgiver who is Supreme Goodness.

(*a*) Relative qualities, which owe their specification to the objects to which they relate, admit of degree both in themselves objectively and as they exist in individuals, e.g. there are higher and lower virtues, there are varying degrees of virtue in individuals. On the other hand absolute qualities possessing specification in themselves (e.g. animality, rationality) do not admit of degree, whether regarded in themselves or as they exist in others. The transcendentals, so wide in extension as to possess universal application, do admit of degree when regarded as existing in others. The transcendental ideas are "being," "unity," "truth," "goodness," "intelligence" in its relation to being, "will" in its relation to good. The transcendentals in themselves imply no limit or imperfection, but regarded as qualities existing in different entities they are capable of degree and are applied analogically. Stone for building purposes is "good" because it is hard; fruit is "good" because it refreshes; a horse is "good" when swift and strong, etc. Bearing these facts in mind, let us examine Plato's twofold principle—the dialectic of the mind and the dialectic of the will. "When a perfection whose concept implies no imperfection is found in different degrees in different beings, none of those beings which possess it thus imperfectly can adequately account for its presence. The perfection must be referred to a superior Principle which is identified with the perfection itself." The application is really twofold inasmuch as the perfection alluded to may be one appreciated by the intellect or one desired by the will.

Examples illustrating the inference from the multiple to one, from the imperfect to the perfect will help towards the comprehension of this subtle reasoning.

(1) Landscape A and Landscape B are both beautiful. But they are not beautiful of themselves, i.e. they cannot be beautiful by virtue of that which constitutes them essentially, for essentially they are different though both have beauty in common. "Multitudo non reddit rationem unitatis." Instances of beauty cannot explain the unity of likeness which exists in different objects. The instances are reflections or echoes of One Superior Principle who is essentially Beauty.

(2) Beauty, greatness, knowledge are associated with imperfection as they exist in Nature. There is a blending of qualities with limitations. The limitation may be contrary to the quality, e.g. Socrates held true and false doctrines; or privative, e.g. Socrates knew some truths and was ignorant of others which he might have known; or negative, e.g. Socrates knew some truths but was ignorant of others in-

accessible to him. Now knowledge of itself does not imply any limitation. If knowledge of itself implied limitation, there would necessarily be the union of contradictory qualities which would be equivalent to a denial of the principle of identity. Therefore the union of a quality and its limitation, not being unconditional, requires an extrinsic sufficient reason. To deny this statement would be equivalent to identifying that which has not in itself its sufficient reason either with that which does not exist (and therefore needs not a sufficient reason), or with that which exists of itself and needs not an extrinsic sufficient reason. The extrinsic sufficient reason is not in Socrates by virtue of that which makes him Socrates, for others possess knowledge. To say that Socrates is learned of himself, although that which constitutes him essentially is different from learning, would be to identify essentially diverse elements. It follows that Socrates owes knowledge to one who possesses knowledge essentially. Thus the blending of qualities and limitations leads to the existence of a Principle who is absolutely simple and perfect.

(b) The application of the foregoing reasoning to the human mind with its varying degrees of knowledge involves the conclusion that Supreme Intelligence is the source of the faculty of thought which is one of man's chief endowments.

(c) Truths, whether contingent or necessary, appeal to a source from which the idea of limitation is removed. The special and striking characteristic of necessary truths (e.g. every trilateral figure is triangular) is their independence of the understanding which grasps them. "If I ask on what basis these eternal and unchangeable truths rest," wrote Bossuet, "I am forced to infer the existence of a Being in whom truth is eternally subsistent." "Such truths are founded on the First Truth—the universal cause of all truth." Such is the judgment of St. Thomas.

(d) Health, pleasures of the body, riches, honours, power, knowledge—finite goods are many and imperfect. The idea of many implies one, the compound implies the simple. The imperfect involves the perfect. Thus Goodness itself—free from admixture of the imperfect—is recognised as the source

PROOFS OF GOD'S EXISTENCE

of finite goods. Or to express the same inference in another form. The natural desire of happiness which all men experience cannot be satisfied by imperfect temporal benefits. " Inquietum est cor nostrum donec requiescat in Te ! " And the thirst for happiness—a thirst as wide as humanity—cannot be in vain, for otherwise it would be an inclination tending at the same time towards something and towards nothing.

> Malgré moi, l'infini me tourmente.
> Au fond des vains plaisirs que j'appelle à mon aide
> Je trouve un tel dégoût que je me sens mourir.
> Malgré moi, vers le ciel il faut lever les yeux.

The testimony of Alfred de Musset, enshrined in these lines, will not be suspected as the utterance of one who is partial.

(e) The idea of goodness implies not only that which is desirable but also that which *should* be desired and which duty enforces. The primary principle of the Natural Law is to do good and to avoid evil. And the " good " here indicated is not necessarily that which is pleasing or useful, but that which is in accordance with right reason. " Fiat justitia, ruat coelum." The law of morality or Natural Law which distinguishes between right and wrong has the same necessary character and the same independence as those axioms of mathematics to which allusion has been made above. And as the inference from necessary truth to its origin in God the First Truth is legitimate, so the recognition of the distinction between right and wrong is a reflexion in human reason of the law of Him who is the Source of moral responsibility—the Supreme Legislator. " Signatum est super nos lumen vultus Tui."

V. Manifestation of Order

St. Thomas notes that beings deprived of intelligence act uniformly in a manner conformable to their end. They do not act by chance, for such action is capricious in its results. They are directed, therefore, by an intelligent cause, as the arrow is directed by the archer. The intelligent being who directs the elements of Nature to their end is God.

The argument, stated in logical form, must now claim our attention.

Major. Unintelligent instruments can be uniformly directed to an end only by an intelligent cause.

Minor. The unintelligent instruments of Nature are uniformly directed to an end.

Conclusion. The instruments are therefore directed by an intelligent cause.

In regard to the major proposition, it is clear that the relation of an instrument to its end—the relation, for instance, of the eye to sight—involves the properties of being which a rational creature alone can perceive. The " sufficient reason " of the eye and of its wonderful apparatus is in the end. If the mere perception of this relationship requires the exercise of reason, much more does the arrangement itself presuppose the action of an intelligent cause.

For the elucidation of the minor proposition, it will be well to distinguish between the two kinds of finality, internal and external—*internal,* i.e. the activity of each instrument taken separately as, for example, the eye, and *external,* which means the subordination and co-ordination amongst agents generally in Nature. Internal finality cannot be denied. We see internal finality in the organs of a viper—organs which secure its conservation and reproduction, but the final end of the viper itself—the utility of its existence—cannot perhaps be satisfactorily stated. Our outlook upon Nature and our comprehension of its parts are subject to limitation. But as science unfolds the marvels of the heavens, the history of the earth enshrined in its rocks, the truths of biology, the constitution of matter, the relations between the inorganic and organic worlds which secure the balance of Nature, the revelation of design is so overwhelming that the denial of external finality seems equivalent to the abdication of reason.

The objection has been urged with special reference to internal finality that Natural Selection accounts for the development of useful organs, inasmuch as only those organs survive which are adapted to the conditions of existence, so that we should say, not that a bird has wings *in order to* fly, but that a bird flies *because* it has wings.

The denial of purpose in Nature is opposed (*a*) to the testimony of mankind ; (*b*) to science ; (*c*) to philosophy.

(*a*) The testimony of mankind recognises the purpose of the parts of an organism so clearly—the co-ordination of parts in the eye and the ear for example—that it is impossible to ignore the certitude of finality to which such co-ordination points. The denial of truths so evident would be equivalent to the denial of the faculty of reason itself.

(*b*) The suggestion that the complex organs of the eye and the co-ordination between them are the result of chance opposes the theory of probability so utterly as to be negligible. Hartmann has calculated that in the case of the eye where 13 main conditions are necessary for vision (neglecting the fact that each condition involves many others) there are 9,999,985 chances to 15 against these 13 conditions being realised. He argues as follows:" Suppose that we assume a tolerably high probability for the development of any of the 13 conditions from the material conditions of embryonic life, say $\frac{9}{10}$ (a probability which but a small portion of our most certain knowledge possesses) still the probability that *all* these conditions follow from the material relations of the embryonic life is only $0 \cdot 9^{13} = 0 \cdot 254$. The probability therefore of a spiritual cause being required for the sum of the conditions $= 0 \cdot 746$, i.e. almost $\frac{3}{4}$. In truth, however, the several probabilities perhaps $= 0 \cdot 25$, or at the most $0 \cdot 5$, and accordingly the probability of a spiritual cause for the whole $= 0 \cdot 9999985$ or $0 \cdot 99988$, i.e. certainty." (" Philosophy of the Unconscious," Introduction Chapter II.)

(*c*) From the point of view of Philosophy, the survival of the adaptations which are " fittest " raises the question of the origin of the adaptations themselves. Apart from the will of an intelligent cause, they can be explained only by chance or necessity. Chance may be defined as the accidental meeting of causes. A man digs a grave and finds treasure. The digging of the grave is intentional. The hiding of the treasure was intentional. The accidental meeting of the causes constitutes chance. Of course the word "causes" means secondary causes, for as regards the Supreme Omniscient Cause chance is impossible. From the definition it is seen that chance is exceptional, accidental, capricious, and cannot be the explanation of phenomena constantly recurring. Hence the following conclusions

1. It is impossible that effects which always or frequently happen should be the result of chance. Uniformity depends on the essential not on the accidental.

2. It is impossible that a large number of causes should by chance constantly produce an effect essentially one and perfect of its kind, e.g. the act of vision.

3. It is impossible that many elements co-ordinated one to another should be evolved by chance from one germ, e.g. the various parts of the oak tree developed from the acorn.

4. It is impossible that an effect essentially one and perfect should proceed by chance from one principle, e.g. an act of thought from the intellect. In such cases the accidental meeting of causes is excluded by the directness of cause and effect.

From the evolution of a sun with its attendant planets down to the arrangements of cells in a plant, the purposive order and harmony manifest in every department exclude the action of chance. The instinct of animals—their wonderful "untaught ability"—such as the ability of a spider analogous to the intelligent work of a weaver, or the ability of the bee which seems to be the outcome of wide mathematical knowledge, postulate the direction of an intelligent cause.

Nor is the orderly development of phenomena—including the origin of "fittest" adaptations—accounted for by Necessity. Indeed "necessity" is no explanation. To say that fire burns because of necessity it must is tautological. The determination to the function of burning comes not from itself but from an extrinsic cause. Moreover the laws of Nature in virtue of which order is evolved and adaptations appear are not absolutely necessary; they are only hypothetically necessary, i.e. if an end or aim be realised, the means to the end are hypothetically necessary, if an action of vision be accomplished, the conditions of sight are hypothetically necessary. Thus the end or final cause, though realised last of all, "ultima in executione," is first in intention, "prima in intentione," and proceeds from an Intelligent Cause.

Résumé

The examination of the phenomena of Nature leads to five conclusions—the existence of:

1. First Mover unmoved.
2. First Cause uncaused.
3. Necessary Being.
4. Supreme Being.
5. Supreme Intelligence.

These qualities involve the existence of One who is (1) Actus purissimus; (2) infinitely perfect; (3) immaterial; (4) intelligent; (5) everywhere present; (6) eternal; (7) not included in any human category, i.e. unique. Thus the invisible attributes of God " are clearly seen, being understood by the things that are made " (Romans i. 20).

VI. Human Opinion

Regarding the existence of God, an appeal is sometimes made to the probative value of the testimony of mankind, and the following syllogism formulated:

The universal testimony of mankind in regard to a belief, upon which it is competent to pass judgment, is a criterion of truth.

But such universal testimony gives support to the existence of God—a belief upon which men are competent to pass judgment.

Therefore God exists.

The major premiss is undoubtedly true. St. Thomas reminds us that an erroneous opinion comes from some accidental defect of intelligence, and cannot, therefore, be universal. Aristotle's judgment is similar: " That which all men instinctively hold to be true is a truth of Nature." But a twofold doubt arises in connection with the minor premiss :

1. With the exception of primary principles intuitively perceived, the statements which universal testimony supports are statements capable of being proved by reason. In face of this fact can it be said that universal testimony has a separate probative value ? Is it not rather the case that universal testimony is the *result* of the fact that human reason perceives the truth of these statements ?

2. Is the question of the existence of God one upon which it is really within the competence of *all* men to adjudicate ? And is the consent really unanimous, i.e. do *all* men attest the *same* truth in the *same* sense ?

These objections, however, disappear if the testimony of mankind be regarded, not as a separate proof, but as confirmatory of the rigorous metaphysical argument. And the confirmation is strong. Rome, Greece, Persia, India, Germany, Scandinavia, in the past—the Kelts, Slavs, Chinese, Egyptians, Ninivites, Chaldaeans, in the heyday of their power, and the races which cover the face of the earth at the present time—all agree as to the existence of God, whatever their differences of view regarding His nature ; " nowhere," wrote Quatrefages in " L'Espèce Humaine," " is there a race, or an important division of a race, without belief in God."

It is time now to consider certain objections raised against the doctrine of God's existence. The assertion has been made, that such belief is due to the prejudices of education, or to the influence of legislators and priests, or to the vague fear which the mystery of life engenders. It is a well-known fact, however, that prejudices change and disappear, and cannot account for a belief which has been and continues to be universal. Nor can any record be found of the imposition of such belief by either legislators or priests. The office of the priesthood is the effect of the belief, and not the cause. To say that the greatest minds of the human race have been actuated by fear in the adoption of religious belief is equivalent to a denial of the value of human thought and character.

But the universality of the belief has been impeached. Certain savage tribes, and many men of science do not believe in the existence of God. The statement as to the atheistical tribes should be met by an unqualified denial. Even the most barbarous—The Mincopies of the Andaman Islands, the Pygmies and Hottentots of Africa—err in this matter by excess and not by defect. When we speak of " men of science," we pass over those who have been justly called " les fanfarons petits-maîtres de la Science "—the blustering coxcombs of Science—and we quote, before giving the full statistics, the testimonies of Lord Bacon, Pasteur, Brunetière, Lord Kelvin and others. " A profound knowledge of Science brings us back to God," is the judgment of him whose name is so honourably associated with the advance of Inductive Science. " C'est pour avoir réfléchi et étudié beaucoup que j'ai gardé une foi de Breton ; si j'avais réfléchi et étudié davantage j'en serais venu à une foi de Bretonne." So wrote Pasteur in the " Revue des Questions Scientifiques " (T. XXXIX, p. 385). Brunetière's witness is not less explicit : " the more I have studied and seen, the longer I live and experience the trials of life, the greater the emphasis and conviction with which I declare myself a Catholic." It is most interesting to note the roads whereby great leaders in Science, Art and Literature have returned to the Church and Faith of their youth : Huysmans by the route of Medieval art ; Coppée by the royal road of suffering ; Pasteur's faith was confirmed by the study of Natural Science ; Brunetière was led back through the study of philosophy and literature ; Bourget, through the investigation of sin, and its consequences. The routes differ, but they all converge to a centre—the home of Unity and Peace. And Lord Kelvin's theistic witness has been expressed in the following words : " Overpoweringly strong proofs of intelligent and benevolent design lie around us . showing to us through nature the influence of a free-will, and teaching us that all living things depend on one everlasting Creator and Ruler." Dr. Dennert's chart records the religious views of the greatest men of Science from the fifteenth to the nineteenth centuries. The class "non-theists" in the chart embraces those authorities in whose works appear no definite theistic views, as well as those who explicitly held atheistic views.

	Theists	Non-theists	Total
XV to XVII centuries	79	3	82
XVIII century	39	16	55
XIX century	124	39	163
	242	58	300

A final objection is drawn from the prevalence at all times of Polytheism. This objection will be discussed later (Chapter XI). It will be sufficient to state here that the testimony of the greatest mythologists emphatically supports the statement that Monotheism was the original belief. Corruption of belief and decadence of nations came later. Such is the contention of Pritchard in his "Egyptian Mythology," of Grimm in his "Germanic Mythology," of Müller in "Orchomenus," of Franck (Oriental studies), and of Darmesteter in his "Aryan Mythology." Thus the testimony of mankind—whether the races be civilised or barbarous—gives strong confirmatory proof of the doctrine of Theism.

CHAPTER IV

ERRORS OPPOSED TO THEISM

ERRONEOUS views opposed to Theism may be considered under three heads :

    1. Positivism and Agnosticism.
    2. Monism.
   3. Attention will be directed to the materialistic and spiritualistic forms of Evolution.

Before enquiring into the principles of these systems, a question may be asked as to variations of meaning which the word " atheist " connotes.

Observe the following classification :

$$\text{Atheists} \begin{cases} \text{Negative} \\ \text{Positive} \end{cases} \begin{cases} \text{practical} \\ \text{theoretical} \end{cases} \begin{cases} \text{by conviction} \\ \text{by persuasion} \end{cases}$$

  1. By a negative atheist is meant one, who, having not the least idea of God, does not trouble about His existence. It is unlikely that many such exist, for Nature proclaims its Maker.

  2. Are there practical atheists, i.e. those who live as if God and His claims do not concern them ? Unfortunately, yes.

  3. Are there atheists by conviction ? No, for the grounds upon which conviction rests are wanting.

  4. Are there men, who, through passion and prejudice, have persuaded themselves that there is no God ? Probably yes, but the genuineness of the persuasion is controverted

I. Positivism and Agnosticism

Positivists and Agnostics agree in maintaining that the knowledge of God and of His nature is impossible. The French positivist leaders were Comte, Taine and Littré. (Littré died a devout Catholic.) The corresponding leaders in England were John Stuart Mill, Bain and Herbert Spencer. Their views may be summarised as follows:

(*a*) All knowledge comes from the senses, i.e. the senses are the *only* source of knowledge.

(*b*) The history of mankind reveals a gradual evolution from the theological phase to the metaphysical phase culminating in the positivist stage.

Refutation.

1. The cardinal principle of the English phenomenist school—" all knowledge comes from sense experience "—can no longer be maintained. The basis of knowledge—the trustworthiness of Memory—is an intuition. Every attempt to prove it involves a petitio principii.

2. Primary Mathematical axioms and necessary truths in the domain of Science and Morality are also intellectual intuitions.

3. The power of abstraction which the mind possesses—the power of penetrating beneath phenomena, and perceiving the abiding principles which form the basis of knowledge—is overlooked.

4. The three stages of Comte are a figment of his imagination. They have no existence either in the general history of the race, or in the lives of individuals. Aristotle was a physicist as well as a metaphysician. Roger Bacon—the true founder of inductive science—belongs to the same epoch as Thomas of Aquin, and Duns Scotus. Helmholtz devoted his attention first to Physiology, then to Mathematics, and finally to Philosophy. Kant was physicist first, and metaphysician afterwards, and Littré, as mentioned above, abjured his positivist errors, and returned to the Catholic fold. Had the principle been true that human knowledge is nothing more than sense experience, the existence of God could not be

established, for that conclusion rests upon the necessary truth " every contingent effect has a cause "—a truth which transcends the experience of the senses, and is perceived through sense impressions by Reason alone.

II. MATERIALISTIC MONISM

Idealistic Monism or Pantheism will be refuted when the question of the personality of God is under consideration. The chief advocates of the idealistic form are Spinosa, Fichte, Schelling, Hegel, Schopenhauer, von Hartmann, and Nietzsche.

The principles of materialistic Monism will be explained in this chapter. Its advocates are Büchner, Tyndall, Huxley, Helmholtz, Haeckel and Metchnikoff.

The principles are:

1. " Experiment is the criterion of truth."

Answer. Yes, in Natural Science.

2. " There is but one substance."

Answer. Whence comes the substance, and its orderly manifestations?

3. " There is no distinction between organic and inorganic matter."

Answer. Eminent biologists agree with Professor Wilson: " an enormous abyss separates the inorganic world from even the lowest forms of life."

4. " Living things come from inorganic matter by the agency of spontaneous generation."

Answer. Tyndall and Huxley, as well as Pasteur, acknowledged that spontaneous generation does not take place.

5. " The human soul is not spiritual."

Answer. The spirituality of the soul will be proved later.

6. " The soul is not immortal."

Answer. As will be shown later, the immortality of the soul is a direct consequence of its spirituality.

7. " The soul is not free."

Answer. The freedom of the will merits the full treatment which it will receive later.

8. An act of intelligence is only a function of a material instrument—the brain."

Answer. Du Bois-Reymond, and many other eminent authorities admit that the attempt to reduce intellectual acts to material conditions of the brain has wholly failed.

9. "Religion is nothing more than social instinct."

Answer. Whence comes the instinct? How reconcile mere instinct with the eternal and necessary distinction between right and wrong which reason recognises?

10. "The supernatural world is a chimæra."

Answer. Undoubtedly so, to those who try to make sense the only criterion of truth.

It is advisable at this stage to examine, and briefly refute the system of Materialistic Evolution which is the logical outcome of Monistic principles. For, if matter be the only substance (hence the name Monism from μόνος alone), development must be purely materialistic. We shall show later that there are immaterial substances (such as the human soul) which for existence and action are independent of matter, whence follows the falsity of the name Monism, and the system it represents.

The word "evolution" means development in a general sense. The Nebular Hypothesis is an instance of evolution on the grandest and most impressive scale. Most students of Science are evolutionists in this general sense.

The word "Transformism" means the evolution of living beings—the development of species. It is well known that the palæontological record reveals a development in the manifestation of living things. The Palæozoic period, though the earliest, yields specimens of vertebrates—namely, ganoid fishes in the Silurian, amphibia in the Carboniferous, and reptiles in the Permian rocks. In the Trias of the Mesozoic period are found remains of the earliest known mammals (marsupials). In the Jurassic, is the first appearance of birds (in the shape of the mysterious archæopteryx) and the first appearance of osseous fishes. In the earliest rocks of the Cainozoic or Tertiary period appear for the first time placental mammals. The presumption is that the latter and more complex types have been evolved from the earlier and simple forms by "transformism," i.e. the gradual change of species and development of new forms. "Darwinism" means a particular method of Transformism, the agencies being "Struggle for existence," "Natural Selection" and "Survival of the fittest." Professor Dwight writes: "the Darwinian theory is not only unproved, but impossible." "Materialistic Evolution" suggests the development of the Universe through the agency of material forces alone, i.e. through mechanical laws; Spiritualistic Evolution, on the other hand, maintains that development is due entirely to Divine arrangement. Spiritualistic Evolution is not opposed either to (1) Scripture.

Scripture does not determine in which one of the two ways, direct creation or evolution, God has produced species.

Nor is it opposed to (2) Catholic Tradition.

Both St. Augustine and St. Thomas use words which suggest their belief in evolution. They both write that God may have created "causaliter," i.e. imposed the law of development on one or more germs.

Nor is it opposed to (3) Catholic Philosophy.

God is recognised, both as efficient and final Cause of all things.

Materialistic Evolution cannot account for the origin of life.

The origin of life cannot be explained by:

1. The eternal germs of Büchner, or by germs from another planet (suggested by Lord Kelvin). These opinions leave the difficulty untouched: whence come the germs?

2. The origin of life does not lie in spontaneous generation, which theory is no longer held.

3. Chemical and mechanical laws cannot produce life. *Omne vivum ex vivo.*

It was in view of the failure of Materialism to explain the Universe that Brunetière felt justified in speaking of "La banqueroute de la science."

Finally, the system of Spiritualistic Evolution which Catholics may hold repudiates a materialistic conception of the human soul. Each soul is created by God directly. Regarding the body of man apart from the soul, there is no clear evidence that it is a development of a lower form of the Primates. In view of the consensus of Catholic opinion against such an opinion, it would be unwise to hold it. It is true that the Church has not spoken. It is true also that if clear evidence appeared of the development of man's body from a lower form, there would be no difficulty in accepting the conclusion. It is equally true that such evidence does not exist, and that a weighty consensus of theological opinion accepts the direct creation of the body of Adam.

In order that the student may have a clearer view of the important subject of Evolution, it has been deemed advisable to give a fuller and up-to-date exposition of the subject.

III. Evolution in Theory and in Fact

The method of discovery is well known to consist of:
1. The observation of facts.
2. The formation of hypotheses suggested by the facts (induction).
3. The verification of such hypotheses (deduction).

Should the hypothesis stand the varied tests of deduction, it becomes Scientific Truth and Law; whilst, on the other hand, if the hypothesis is shown to be false, the facts must be more carefully and more continuously scrutinised, a new hypothesis formed and tested, and so on until truth is attained.

It is quite clear that the second part of the scientific method of discovery—the formation of hypotheses—is the one which in certain cases especially appeals to the student of Apologetics. If the facts of Nature are observed aright, they cannot be in conflict with Revealed Religion. Natural Truth and Supernatural Truth must necessarily be in harmony. But conflict may easily arise between Revealed Religion and hypothesis, and no hypothesis is in sharper antagonism to Divine faith than the now discredited theory of materialistic evolution. On the other hand, the student of Apologetics should bear in mind that when the advocates of organic evolution presuppose the Divine action throughout, and at certain junctures a special Divine interposition, they may hold their opinions with a safe conscience ; " donec Ecclesia hac de re judicium protulerit." The object of the present chapter is to bring to the notice of the student of Apologetics some views recently advanced, as well as modifications of older theories bearing upon the origin of species and the phylogeny of plants.

More than one hundred years ago (1809), the " Philosophie zoologique " of Lamarck was published in Paris. The ability and experience of the author were such as to ensure for the work a sympathetic and respectful reception. Lamarck had studied Botany for many years, and later on in life he devoted time and energy to the more complex problems of Zoology. He was the associate of Cuvier at the Natural History Museum. No opponent could characterise his scientific work as that of an amateur advocating fanciful hypotheses ; his method was largely inductive ; he claimed in support of his views an array of facts drawn from the vegetable and animal kingdoms.

Lamarck's chief contribution to the transmutation theory —i.e. the theory of genetic development—may be summarised in the following propositions : (1) The acquisition of something new in plant life (newly developed organ or newly developed tendency) is due to the action of the environment upon the plant, and the response of the organism to the stimulus. (2) The change in the organism of the plant due to the combined effects of environmental stimulus and reaction is conserved and transmitted by generation.

From this statement of his views, it is clear that one of the characteristic notes of Lamarck's biological teaching is the doctrine of the transmission of acquired characters. A hundred years have passed since the publication of his book, and it is a sure mark of its value that in more recent times a neo-Lamarckian school has arisen, including botanists of distinction—such as Dr. Francis Darwin, the late President of the British Association—and biologists like the late Herbert Spencer. In standing forth as the champion of the Lamarckian theory of heredity Dr. Darwin is not unfaithful to the teaching of his illustrious father, who, in many instances, where the resources of Natural Selection were plainly inadequate to account for facts, was obliged to adopt the Lamarckian hypothesis of the transmission of acquired characters.

It will be well to bear in mind from the outset that there is the greatest possible difference between Organic Evolution itself, and the many theories which have been advanced to explain how Organic Evolution is accomplished. A few examples taken from Lamarck will bring out more clearly the character of the evolutionary process which he defended. The toes of a bird accustomed to perch on trees are supposed to have become longer from the bird's effort to clasp the twig, and the modification thus induced by effort—i.e. the increased length—is transmitted to its progeny. So, likewise, the stilt-like legs of shore birds have attained their development in length from the bird's effort to keep its body above the surface of the water. The long neck of the giraffe has been in its initial stage the outcome of effort on the part of the animal to seek its food on trees in time of dearth, the modification resulting from the effort being transmitted and increased in the transmission. The climbing habit of plants was due originally to effort on the part of the plant to reach the light, the climbing habit being subsequently embodied in the organism.

It has been stated above that the author of "The Origin of Species" was obliged more than once to fall back upon the transmission of acquired characters in order to help out the deficiency of Natural Selection. Darwin's theory of Pangenesis shows the leaning he had towards Lamarck's view. According to the theory of Pangenetic inheritance, each somatic or body-cell of a plant is supposed to give off gemmules which are stored in the pollen cells and egg cells of the organism, and thus changes in the somatic cells of a plant affect through the agency of the gemmules, the germ cells, and consequently affect the offspring. Weismann and Wallace, on the contrary, are strongly opposed to the doctrine of the transmission of acquired characters. The germ plasm theory of Weismann seems to be more in accordance with the facts of inheritance as known at present than the Pangenesis of Darwin. The germ plasm or continuity theory supposes that during the division of the cells which make up the somatic or body structure the germ plasm remains in one cell unaffected by surrounding changes as the organism grows, and finally divides and forms the pollen grains or ovules of the new plant. Many critics feel that the imaginative element enters largely into these two hypotheses. But, whether true or not, the two hypotheses illustrate with admirable distinctness the opposing views of the transmission and non-transmission of acquired characters.

The neo-Lamarckians rely much upon two series of facts to justify their belief. First, the experiments of Brown-Séquard, which seem to show that epilepsy, resulting from injury from the spinal cord, is transmitted. But there is grave doubt as to the agency by which the transmission is effected. Is it effected by inheritance or by disease? More must be known of the pathology of epilepsy before a definite statement can be made. The second set of facts, derived from the geological record, seems to suggest that Evolution has taken place along the lines which we imagine it would follow if the effects of use and disuse were inherited. Again, the evidence is not conclusive, and the verdict in regard to the debatable question of the transmission of acquired characters is the Scotch verdict of " non-proven." This notwithstanding, Dr. Francis Darwin, in his recent presidential address, claims that plant experiences of the past have been inherited to the extent of producing stimuli in many plants of the present day, and that the stimuli produce habits—the transmitted results of ancestral experience. Such habits are styled by him a sort of memory, " a faint copy of what we know as consciousness in ourselves."

About sixty years ago (1859) the interest of the scientific world was aroused by the publication of an epoch-making work—" The Origin of Species," by Charles Darwin. The admiration won for the illustrious author by the revelation of his laborious, painstaking, long-continued series of researches has increased rather than diminished in the succeeding half-century, and no future advance in biological science will release the student from the debt of gratitude he owes to this truly great man. Darwin is the advocate of Natural Selection as the chief agency in the development of new species. The general outline of his argument is familiar. Every plant is differentiated from others by minute fortuitous variations. Variations which benefit the plant, so far forth as they are beneficial, will preserve the life of the plant, and being congenital, will be transmitted. The old species becomes in this way a *terminus a quo*, and as the variations are conserved and increased by generation, the new species is ultimately evolved—the *terminus ad quem*. The action of Natural Selection does not presuppose the transmission of acquired characters, because the variations seized upon by Selection are congenital. An illustration will make this point clearer. The development of the giraffe's neck is accounted for by Darwin differently from Lamarck. Granted that owing to fortuitous variations some giraffes in time of dearth were born with longer necks than others, the accidental advantage would enable them to obtain food from trees which others could not reach. The long-necked varieties would thus survive and pass on the long-necked condition to their offspring, and thus in time the characteristic giraffe neck would be evolved. There is no need here of the inheritance of acquired characters, but, as already indicated, where in the explanation of some difficult cases the agency of Natural Selection was not sufficient, Darwin somewhat inconsequently fell back upon the Lamarckian hypothesis, and thus endeavoured to account for the "arrival of the fittest," since the principle of "survival of the fittest" would not apply.

That Natural Selection has been the sole or the chief agent in the evolution of plants and animals is not now so strenuously maintained as in former years. There are many serious objections to the claim of Natural Selection as the sole agent of development. How can the minute, fortuitous variations on which Natural Selection is supposed to act be in their minute form of any use to the organism? To take a well-known example, flat fishes such as soles, etc., have both eyes on one side of the head, whereas in the immature stage the eyes are normally placed one on each side. Since flat fish lie on their sides, it would distinctly be of advantage to have both eyes on one side (the uppermost); but how could a slight movement of one eye towards the upper side so benefit the organism that Natural Selection should seize upon it and intensify it in succeeding generations?

Another weighty objection arises from the fact that Natural Selection does not explain satisfactorily the coexistence of closely similar structures of diverse origin. The eye of the vertebrate and the eye of the cephalopod are much alike, not only in structure but in origin. The retina and cornea are in both cases derived from the epiblast; the lens in each case is derived from the mesoblast. It staggers not merely the imagination but the reason to conceive how these two closely similar structures belonging to organisms far removed phylogenetically could have been developed independently by the preservation of minute fortuitous variations.

During the lifetime of Darwin, and indeed only six years after the publication of "The Origin of Species," a short paper (fifteen to twenty pages) of far-reaching scientific importance was contributed to the journal of the Natural History Society at Brünn, in Silesia. The author was the abbot of the neighbouring Augustinian monastery, Johann Gregor Mendel by name. His paper gave a résumé of experiments made upon varieties of the Pisum sativum which grew in the monastery garden. For thirty-five years Mendel's discovery was forgotten, until, about the year 1900, Correns (in Germany), De Vries (in Holland), and others drew public attention to it. R. H. Lock, in his book on variation, heredity and evolution, characterises Mendel's discovery as of an importance little inferior to that of a Newton or a Dalton. Perhaps this extraordinary praise may be ascribed to the exaltation of mind—the megalomania—which rejoices in a new discovery. Mendel's law of inheritance is best explained by following his experimental method.

A tall was crossed with a dwarf pea. The progeny (the first filial generation, conveniently represented by F_1) were all tall; and when these were self-fertilised, Mendel found that of the plants forming the second generation (F_2) 25 per cent were pure talls, 50 per cent hybrid talls, and 25 per cent pure dwarfs. Similarly, when the 50 per cent hybrid talls were "selved," the third generation (F_3) appeared in the same definite proportions. The character "tall" was named "dominant," inasmuch as it asserts itself in the hybrid, and the character "dwarf" was called "recessive." If we suppose the first filial generation to number 200, the following table will illustrate the law

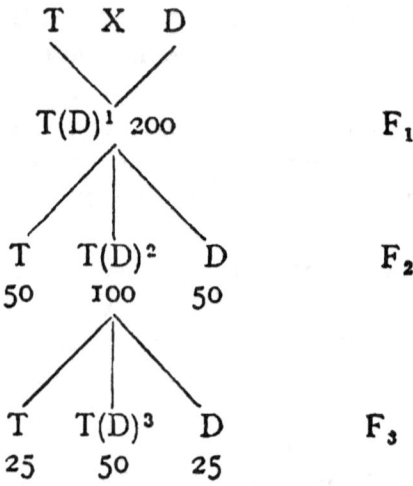

Tall and dwarf are crossed giving progeny $T(D)^1$, so written because though tall in appearance they are proved subsequently to be mongrel talls; the character "tall" because of its dominance asserting itself over the character "dwarf," which, though recessive, is present. The plants $T(D)^1$ upon self-fertilisation give 25 per cent of pure talls (proved to be such because they breed true when self-fertilised), 50 per cent mongrel talls, and 25 per cent pure dwarfs. The 50 per cent mongrel talls upon self-fertilisation give the same proportion of pure talls, mongrel talls, and pure dwarfs. Mendel found the law to hold good for the six generations to which the limited number of his plants restricted the experiment.

But the most interesting part of Mendel's paper was the hypothesis offered in explanation of these results—an hypothesis now widely accepted. When tall and dwarf peas are crossed, the progeny are not intermediate between the two, but are mongrel talls. The characters of "tall" and "dwarf" — the so-called allelomorphs — are each present in the organism; but if we confine our attention to the germ cells of the F^1 generation, we find that 25 per cent of them have the single character of "tall" and 25 per cent the single character of "dwarf." The 50 per cent mongrel talls, which contain both characters (the allelomorphs), will be resolved similarly. This process is known as the "Mendelian disjunction of hybrids," or the "Mendelian segregation of characters." Hence, in the germ cells no fusion of characters takes place; there is only a mingling of them as in a mechanical mixture.

Mendel's hypothesis accounts also very satisfactorily for the proportion of talls and dwarfs. The hybrid produces egg cells and pollen cells, each of which is the bearer of a tall or dwarf character. On the average there is the same number of egg cells and pollen cells. Then, on a random assortment of them, a tall pollen cell will stand an even chance of meeting with a tall or a dwarf egg cell, the resulting being TT (pure tall), and T(D) mongrel tall. Similarly, a dwarf egg cell will stand an even chance of meeting with a dwarf pollen cell or a tall pollen cell, the result being DD (pure dwarf) and T(D) (mongrel tall). Thus we have pure talls, mongrel talls, pure dwarfs, in the proportion of 1 : 2 : 1.

What bearing has Mendel's discovery upon the doctrine of Organic Evolution? A twofold bearing. First, new species can be produced by Mendelian inheritance. For example, a yellow and white Japanese waltzing mouse is crossed with an English albino. The F^1 generation are like the common house mouse. The characters "waltzing" and "albinism" are evidently recessive; the characters "pigmentation" and "normal progression" are dominant. But we know that of the hybrids 25 per cent are albinos and 25 per cent waltzing mice. One mouse in four is therefore an albino, and one mouse in four a waltzer; therefore one mouse in sixteen is an albino-waltzer—a new species. If new species can thus be artificially produced, may we not suppose that in Nature's great museum new species are frequently evolved by the laws of Mendelian inheritance? The second bearing of Mendel's discovery on the doctrine of Evolution flows from the now ascertained fact of the disjunction of hybrids. The opinion formally held that so-called "sports" in plant and animal life are swamped by intercrossing (unless bred *inter se*) is now known to be false. The hybrids which are the result of intercrossing will, if bred out, give the "sport" back again.

Of late years much has been said and written about the "Mutationstheorie" of De Vries. In the year 1886 De Vries found at Hilversum, near Amsterdam, some thousands of specimens of Œnothera lamarckiana. The plant had possibly escaped from a neighbouring park, and is supposed to have come originally from North America. It has received its specific name because one of the types in the Museum of Natural History in Paris was used by Lamarck himself for the description of Œnothera grandiflora in his own herbarium. Upon examination De Vries was able to pick out individuals which differed more or less from their neighbours, and he found from differences in the rosettes of leaves, or in the branching, that new species were being produced. He classified the mutants as follows:

1. Varieties: Œnothera laevifolia, Œnothera brevistylis, Œnothera nanella. These varieties are constant as the best species if kept free from hybrid admixtures.

2. Elementary species: Œnothera gigas, Œnothera rubrinervis.

3. Elementary species (weaker): Œnothera albida, Œnothera oblonga.

4. Inconstant varieties: Œnothera lata, Œnothera scintilla, Œnothera elliptica.

5. Some mutants organically incomplete.

In seven generations 50,000 plants were raised, of which 800 were mutants, the proportion being not quite 2 per cent.

If De Vries is correct in judging these variations to be new elementary species, the discovery is of quite extraordinary interest. Amongst other biologists, Mr. Galton and Dr. Mivart suspected that new species were evolved not by minute fortuitous variations, but by sudden leaps—i.e. by discontinuous variation. Mr. Galton's apt illustration of the many-facetted spheroid, which reposes in a state of stable equilibrium upon one facet, helps us to understand the natural law which conditions the evolution of new specific forms. The sudden development of species had not escaped the observation of Darwin. "It is certain," he writes, "that the Ancon sheep, turnspit dogs, etc., have suddenly appeared in nearly the same state as we see them. So it has been with many cultivated plants." But Darwin regarded discontinuous variation as the rare exception; his own conviction was that continuous variation under the action of Natural Selection was practically the sole agency at work in the formation of new species. A more modern view claims that discontinuous variation is the paramount power in Organic Evolution. The process has been observed not only in Œnothera, but in other plants as well.

In the year 1590 Spenger, an apothecary of Heidelberg, noticed in his garden a new species of Chelidonium majus—a species with leaves cut into narrow lobes. It has never been discovered in the wild state. This species now known as "lanciniatum" is considered to have suddenly appeared as a mutation. The first record of peloric toadflax is assigned to the year 1744. It was discovered by Zioberg, pupil of Linnæus, near Upsala. De Vries began to experiment upon plants of toadflax in 1887; the plants were of the normal type, with one or two peloric flowers. In 1889, he obtained a plant with only one peloric structure; in 1890, a plant with two peloric structures; in 1891, a plant with only one five-spurred flower; then in 1894, suddenly a single plant bearing peloric structures only, which remained true to the type.

But are the mutations in Œnothera lamarckiana described by De Vries really examples of discontinuous variation? There is one serious difficulty in accepting them as such. De

Vries has not succeeded in proving that Œnothera lamarckiana is a natural species. "The fact that it was originally described from a garden flower grown in the Paris Jardin des Plantes," so writes Boulenger in the "Journal of Botany," October, 1907, "and that in spite of diligent search it has not been discovered wild anywhere in America favours the probability that it was produced by crossing various forms of the polymorphic Œnothera biennis." If this is the case, De Vries' Œnothera mutations are only instances of the Mendelian disjunction of hybrids.

But whilst doubt for the time being is thrown upon the mutations of Œnothera, confirmation of the general theory of discontinuous variation comes from another quarter. Professor Kofoid, of California, has made an interesting discovery in regard to the origin of Ceratium furca. Ceratium tripos and Ceratium furca are unicellular protoplasmic bodies showing little morphological differentiation. The organisms are enclosed in hollow shells composed of cellulose impregnated with silica. They feed exactly like a plant—i.e. they absorb the energy from sunlight to synthesise carbohydrate from water and carbonic acid. There is no doubt that Ceratium tripos and Ceratium furca are distinct species. And yet Professor Kofoid has observed that when Ceratium tripos reproduces itself by division (the process takes place always at sunrise) there is sometimes a double change—a sudden leap or mutation—from the form Ceratium tripos to the form Ceratium furca. Thus are we furnished with examples of the mutation from the most complex, and from the simplest of plants.

In summing up the results of recent research the question is suggested—does Organic Evolution (in plant life) take place by continuous or by discontinuous variation, or by both methods? It is somewhat premature to make a dogmatic statement. But the position of importance assigned formally to continuous variation cannot now be claimed for it. Again, does the newest phylogenetic tree carry more authoritative weight than older and more familiar attempts in that direction?

Angiospermæ
|
Pteridospermæ (recently discovered seed-bearing Ferns)
Ferns
|
Ophioglossum (one of the lowest of Ferns)
Anthoceros (one of the highest of Hepatics)
|
Riccia (one of the lowest of the Hepatics)
Coleochæte (one of the highest of the Algæ)
|
Algæ.

May we pass from Algæ to Hepaticæ through the forms Coleochæte and Riccia ? Has the further development been from Hepaticæ to Ferns through Anthoceros and Ophioglossum ? Having reached the Fern order, is the transition legitimate from them to the recently discovered Pteridospermæ ? And finally, by aid of the Strobilus theory, may we advance from Pteridospermæ to the Angiospermous type of flower, and thus link together the past and present in one grand scheme of development ? Theories such as these are not only fascinating but useful. They constitute working hypotheses which encourage research. But the true scientific spirit will always distinguish between assumption and fact, and will always welcome information, from whatsoever quarter it comes, even though it does not square with preconceived ideas and cherished opinions. In the light of the new knowledge which has lately dawned upon us, and which has in some directions materially modified our scientific teaching—knowledge to be subsequently modified by a fuller and deeper revelation of Nature's secrets—we appreciate the import of the words :

> Our little systems have their day ;
> They have their day and cease to be :
> They are but broken lights of Thee,
> And Thou, O Lord, art more than they.

CHAPTER V

A GENERAL VIEW OF THE NATURE AND ATTRIBUTES OF GOD

I

IN order to attain to some knowledge (however inadequate) of the Divine Nature, it is necessary to premise what is meant by the threefold division of distinctions into *real, virtual* and *purely mental*. A real distinction is based upon complete absence of identity, and is illustrated by the difference between the Kaiser of Germany and the King of England. A purely mental distinction, on the other hand, is one made by the mind in regard to a person or thing, when the different mental aspects refer to the same object of thought. Compare for example the two ideas " King of England " and " Emperor of India." They indicate identically the same person, and the distinction is wholly mental. A virtual distinction arises from the fact that the person or object under consideration presents to the mind different aspects, which have objectively a claim to distinct recognition (*fundamentum in re*) in the nature of the being. There is, for example, a virtual distinction between the attributes of rationality and animality in man. Here too, the attributes belong to the same individual, but are not merely mental aspects of the same quality. This example illustrates what is known as a *major* virtual distinction, because one attribute does not include the other, and in point of fact, animality and rationality are found separate in different subjects (e.g. man and horse), as well as associated together in man. A *minor* virtual distinction is illustrated by the Divine attributes of Justice and Mercy.

Formally considered these attributes are distinct, and hence the distinction is virtual and not purely mental, but really, as they exist in God, the attributes of Justice and Mercy are identical owing to His absolute simplicity and perfection.

We attain to some knowledge of the nature of the Deity from the arguments which prove His existence. The First Mover is free from all potentiality—He is Pure Act. The First Cause is uncaused, i.e. has not received existence from another. Necessary Being involves the consequence that existence belongs to its essence. The Supreme Being possesses not a participation of being but being itself, and Supreme Intelligence directs all the multitudinous forces of the Universe and evolves order and harmony from their association and interaction. But we must remember that in ascribing to the Deity any perfection, e.g. wisdom, we not only remove all limitation from the perfection, we not only conceive the perfection (thus free from limitation) in the highest possible intensive degree, but finally in applying the perfection to the Deity, we predicate wisdom in an analogical and not in a univocal sense, i.e. we recognise that between the Divine Wisdom and the highest conception of human wisdom, whilst there is a certain proportion of analogy, there exists withal an essential difference.

But amongst the Divine perfections is there one which seems from our human standpoint to be fundamental? Many answers have been given to this question. Some have argued that the fundamental attribute of the Divine Nature is freedom. But freedom presupposes reason and cannot therefore be ultimate. Others have suggested goodness, but the idea of " being " is logically prior to that of " goodness." Others have maintained that thought is the fundamental attribute of the Deity but surely thought involves an immaterial substance as the principle and source whence it comes. The description of Himself given by God to Moses and recorded in the third chapter of Exodus indicates the fundamental attribute of the Divine Nature. " I am who am," i.e. as scholastic writers point out, God is " Ipsum Esse Subsistens," in regard to whom there is no past and no future, but all things are present to Him, the "pelagus substantiae infinitum" the infinite ocean of substance. All things are made in His "image" the inorganic world resembles Him analogically in so far as He is Being, the animal world in so far as He is the source of life, and rational creatures bear upon themselves the hall-mark of the Divine Image, for God is Supreme Intelligence. The far higher privilege of bearing the "likeness" of God is due to the transcendent gift of Grace which makes us "divinae consortes naturae"—sharers in the Divine Nature.

II

From the perfection of the Divine Nature, reason deduces the Divine attributes which may be defined as "absolutely simple perfections, existing necessarily and formally in God." Some attributes regard directly the being of God, and others His operation. Those which regard His being, are Unity and Simplicity, Truth, Perfection and Goodness, Infinity, Immensity, Immutability, Eternity, whilst from the human standpoint God is invisible, incomprehensible, and withal cognoscible.

1. Composition involves imperfection. The reason of the union of two things $A+B$ is precisely because the compound $A+B$ has some advantage which is not possessed by A or B separately. All such composition of imperfect parts is alien to the conception of God. There are no quantitative parts in God, no constitutive or logical elements, no distinction even between essence and existence.

2. Truth has been defined as "adaequatio inter intellectum et rem cognitam." Truth from the Divine standpoint is the conformity of created natures to the eternal types in the mind of God. His own nature "Ipsum esse subsistens" is so much in conformity with the Divine Intelligence that there is no real distinction between them. Thus God, the First Truth, unchangeable and eternal, is the supreme cause and measure of created truth.

3. That God is infinite Goodness and Perfection follows from the truth that a perfection is a form of being. Hence Sub-

sistent Being possesses all perfections, and God can have no association with moral evil. He does not will it. He permits it, for He is able to draw good out of evil, e.g. to exhibit the patience and heroic charity of the martyr under the trial and torture of persecution. God does not will directly even physical evil. He wills it accidentally as the condition of a greater good.

4. The immensity and ubiquity of God is a consequence of His infinite perfection. He is everywhere, by essence, presence and power. He is immanent in His creation. By His essence He preserves all things in being. By His presence, He is cognizant of all that takes place, "even our most secret thoughts." By His power the countless myriads of agencies in Nature are obedient to His will. But though God is immanent in Nature, He is withal transcendent.

5. God is unchangeable. A change involves imperfection. The ascription of change to God, as for instance " God repented that He had made man," is but a human mode of speech, an instance of anthropomorphism. Nor is the unchangeableness of God an argument against the efficacy of prayer. God foresees from all eternity the prayers of those who appeal to Him. And though His arrangements have been made from eternity, they have been made with the fullest prescience of every prayer and petition.

6. God uncreated is without beginning or end. He is eternal. The definition of eternity adopted by scholastic teachers is that of the philosopher Boëthius who wrote at the end of the fifth century. Eternity is " interminabilis vitae tota simul et perfecta possessio," i.e. the full, perfect, and present possession of life without end or commencement. The " nunc fluens " is the reality of time; the " nunc stans " the reality of eternity. Since the idea of potentiality is inadmissible in regard to God, the fulness of Life and perfection must have existed continuously in the past, and must exist without change in the future. *We* are obliged to recognise a past, and a future, as well as the present time, but there is no past, no future to God. For Him succession of time is replaced by an eternal present.

Owing to human limitations, God is said to be invisible, incomprehensible, and yet cognoscible.

(a) His invisibility is due to two causes. He is Pure Spirit, and cannot therefore be seen by the eyes of the body. Moreover the object of a created intelligence is *created* being. Uncreated being can be perceived only " through a glass darkly." The " lumen gloriae " is needed so that we may see God " face to face."

(b) Aided by the "lumen gloriae" the blessed see the Divine Essence immediately, but no created vision can be comprehensive. To comprehend implies more than to know. God alone comprehends Himself.

(c) Invisible and incomprehensible though He be, there is a reflection of the Divine perfections in the works of creation. The created perfections of being, goodness, wisdom, power, etc., enable the human reason to reach to the conception of One who has analogous perfections in an infinite degree. Thus are known the existence and nature of the First Cause.

III

Apart from the attributes which have a relation to the being of God, there are certain attributes which regard the Divine Operation—Wisdom, Love (with its two characteristics of Justice and Mercy), and Almighty Power.

A. Under the general name of wisdom it is customary to include (a) Divine knowledge ; (b) Prescience of future contingent events ; and (c) Providence.

(a) Regarding Divine knowledge which penetrates the being of God, and extends to all created things, it should be remembered that there is no duality of subject and object. It was the omission of this consideration which suggested to the minds of Fichte and Herbert Spencer the impossibility of reconciling the duality implied in human knowledge with the simplicity of the Absolute. God's knowledge is the cause of things. It is not because things exist that God knows them, but because He knows them they exist. " Scientia Dei est causa rerum secundum quod habet voluntatem conjunctam."

The primary object of Divine Knowledge is the Divine Essence. There is no real distinction between the Divine Intelligence and Essence. The subject knowing, and the object known are one. The secondary object includes all existing creatures which are ascribed to the " vision " of God, whilst possible creatures are cognised by God's " simple intelligence."

(*b*) The infinite perfection of God implies the prescience of future contingent things. Being eternal, God knows them in themselves—not successively but simultaneously. And it is necessary to remember that God's knowledge and God's " praemotio " do not interfere with the freedom of the rational creature. God can infallibly move the human will to come to a free decision, in which case our free will is the cause of the act, but not the first cause.

(*c*) The subject of Divine Providence will be considered at length later. (Chapter VI, II.)

B. The primary act of the Divine Will is love. " God is love." In rational creatures, love is a natural inclination to seek well-being. And from this passion, others spring : Hope is the love of a future good, Joy the love of a present good, Sadness the love of an absent good, and Hatred resolves itself into the dislike of that which is opposed to good. Egoism has been defined as the preference of self to good. Inasmuch as God is Supreme Goodness, God must necessarily love Himself, and yet since God and Supreme Goodness are identical, there cannot be the faintest shadow of egoism in God's love.

Regarding the Divine love of creatures, it is necessary to distinguish between Divine and human love, and to refrain from ascribing to the former the defects of the latter. Human love means that the lover is passively attracted by another. Again human love is subject to rejection. But Divine Love is always active, and so far from being passively drawn by the amiability of the creature, it is God's love which produces the amiability. " Amor Dei infundit et creat bonitatem in rebus." The words of St. Paul are accurate, " What hast thou, that thou didst not receive ? " Does not the human mind tend to spread its enlightenment ? Does not the zeal of the

Apostle, fired by enthusiasm for the cause, explain his labours, journeys, sufferings, martyrdom? And surely Infinite Goodness may, if He chooses, confer upon the creature gratuitous gifts, the most precious of which is the gift of love. And this love is invincible. It is true that by Divine permission some may reject it, but if they refuse the merciful aspect of Divine love they necessarily come under the other aspect—that of Divine Justice.

The properties of Divine Love are threefold:

1. Universality. "He wishes all men to be saved" by His antecedent will. It is only His consequent will that condemns the rebellious.

2. Whilst God gives to all the graces necessary and sufficient for Salvation, to some, according to His pleasure, He gives graces of predilection.

3. God's love is invincible.

The two characteristics of the love of God, Justice and Mercy, claim some words of explanation:

I. Justice has been defined as the virtue which inclines the will to render to each one that which is due to him.

Experience teaches that there is much injustice in this world, and that the more sacred the rights, the more frequent is their violation. The rights of conscience, freedom, of religion, are not recognised in many places. Injustice raises a difficulty regarding God's goodness. It is said that there can be no relations of justice between the Infinite and the finite. Appeal is made to the inequality of natural goods, and the question is asked, how can it be just that for the fault of a moment there should be an eternity of pain?

The answer to these difficulties is at hand. Between God and the creature there is of course no relationship of commutative justice based on equality, but there is and always must be a relationship of distributive justice. And distributive justice may be considered under three heads:

(a) Distribution of natural gifts and graces. The harmony of created things requires a hierarchy of creatures—Angels, men, irrational animals, plants, stones. Amongst men and women living in a state of society, it is essential that there should be inequality—that some should rule, others be subject. Even in the case of men taken individually there are duties which require intellectual power, and other duties which need chiefly physical strength. To one man is given one talent, to another two, and to still another five. More will be claimed where more has been given, but to all is given a sufficiency of graces and gifts to secure salvation. It is the teaching of Catholic Theologians that those who have not heard the Gospel message, those who owing to circumstances have not been able to recognise the claims of the Church, if they live in accordance with the Natural Law and the dictate of Conscience, are regarded as belonging to the soul of the Church, as having baptism of desire and a claim to supernatural reward.

(*b*) The general law regarding recompense is that God gives a natural reward for naturally good actions, a supernatural reward for actions done from a supernatural motive. The measure of the merit is the charity wherewith the act is done. If the same reward be given to those who come to work at the eleventh hour, as to those who bore the heat and labour of the day, it must be remembered that merit is not merely a matter of time or amount of work. The excellence of the intention will raise one hour's work to the value, and more than the value, of hours of work where the intention has not been so perfect.

(*c*) Just as remorse of conscience is the penalty of a breach of the rational order, fine or imprisonment the punishment of disturbing the social order, so God punishes an infraction of the Divine order. God hates sin because it is opposed to His Sanctity, and because it separates Him from His creatures. The hatred of sin is a characteristic of the saints, and especially of her who is the " Speculum Justitiae." And if the objection be raised that there is a want of proportion between a sin committed in an instant and eternal pains, obviously the suggestion of a time proportion is absurd. A murder is the work of a second, and a human tribunal will either decree the penalty of death, or lifelong imprisonment. Blindness is irreparable though the eyes have been destroyed in a second.

The penalty of eternal suffering is pronounced only when innumerable calls and graces have been neglected, only when the will by a last act chooses to be defiant, and becomes fixed in its hatred of God.

And if the just suffer in this life their sufferings are in expiation of the world's sinfulness. The Saviour of Mankind—Source of Sanctity—suffered more than any human creature could endure. Because He loved, He suffered. "Fortis est ut mors dilectio, dura sicut infernus aemulatio." When crucified, He cried out for the forgiveness of His enemies, and, by virtue of that petition, Justice and Mercy are shown to be but two aspects of the Divine attribute of Love. "Justitia et pax osculatae sunt." St. Paul's words reveal the sublime result of suffering supernaturally accepted and patiently borne—"aeternum pondus gloriae," an eternal weight of glory.

II. There are numerous allusions to the Mercy of God, both in the Old and New Testaments. "Quoniam apud Dominum est misericordia et copiosa apud eum redemptio" is King David's hope. The parables of the Prodigal Son and of the Good Shepherd show how Christ emphasised the same idea, and His treatment of the Samaritan woman, of Magdalene, of Zaccheus, of the Good Thief are striking examples of merciful consideration and pardon.

"But 'Mercy' as applied to God is metaphorical, for mercy implies sadness and weakness" such is the common objection.

The Divine attribute of Mercy is only analogous to the human sentiment. God's mercy is a virtue of His beneficent will. If it is a characteristic of the weak to be sad, it is a characteristic of the good and powerful to be generous. Infinite power is infinite generosity, and when human weakness is conscious of want, and appeals to the Divine Goodness, then weakness becomes strength. "Cum enim infirmor, tunc potens sum." And when weakness asks for help in order that the glory of God may shine forth, then weakness becomes the highest strength. To justify the sinner is a greater reach of God's power than to create Heaven and earth, for whilst the creative act produces being without pre-existing material, the greater miracle of Divine Grace evolves good out of evil.

Divine Mercy and Justice are exercised but Mercy prevails. Each work of Justice presupposes a work of Mercy. If God owes anything to His creatures it is by virtue of a preceding gift.

(*a*) It has been said that Justice requires that God should give to His creatures the natural goods and graces necessary for the attainment of their end. But God is not content to give natural gifts. He gives supernatural helps. After the fall, God might with justice have left the human race in its state of weakness and ignorance. He has redeemed us through His Son. In the New Law, He is not content with giving us interior grace; He abides with us in the Eucharist as " the companion of our pilgrimage, the price of our redemption, the food of our mortality."

(*b*) In the apportionment of recompense, Divine generosity has destined us for Himself: " Ego sum merces tua magna nimis "; I am thy reward exceeding great.

(*c*) God, Supreme Judge, exercises His prerogative of granting pardon. Even the pains of Hell are mitigated through His attribute of Mercy.

IV

The attributes hitherto considered relate to Divine operations that are immanent. The attribute of Almighty Power —the immediate principle of the eternal works of God—is also formally immanent, and is identified with the nature of God. But this attribute is virtually transitive, inasmuch as it produces an external effect.

We take in order A, Infinite Power in general; B, Creation and Conservation of Creatures; C, The Divine Concursus; D, The Possibility of Miracles; E, A few words are added regarding the intimate life of God.

A. Infinite Power

There is no passivity in God. He is Pure Act. In created beings, active power (the faculty) is the principle of an action, and of the effect of this action. Divine Activity is the principle of the effect, but not of the Divine Action which is identified with the Divine Nature. God, being infinite, His power is infinite. "Actio sequitur esse." Ockam and Descartes maintained that God's infinite power was compromised by inability to accomplish certain supposed effects, as for instance to make a "square circle." But absurd ideas such as that of a "square circle" have no relation to being; a square circle is a non-ens. The necessary law of thought which the idea of a square circle violates proceeds from the immutable being of God. Leibnitz and his followers have erred in another way by stating that God was obliged to create the "best possible world." God created and disposed all His creatures with infinite wisdom. The animal is not better adapted than the plant, though the animal is higher in the scale of being than the plant. An angel is higher than man, but both angel and man have come from the infinite power and wisdom of God. The "best possible" world is an inconceivable and contradictory idea like that of the "most rapid possible movement."

B. Creation and Conservation

Creation has been defined as "productio totius rei ex nihilo sui et subjecti"—the production of a substantial being without the aid of pre-existing material. The origin of the universe is explicable in three ways only. It is either (*a*) an emanation from God; or (*b*) formed from pre-existing material; or (*c*) created. To suppose that the universe is an emanation from God is to accept Pantheism, which confounds the necessary and the contingent, the finite and the infinite. Moreover Pantheism implies that the world—a contingent effect—has come into being without a cause. For it must be remembered that the indestructibility of matter and of energy does not effect the contingency of the universe. If the second suggestion be considered that the universe has been made out of pre-existing material which must be contingent, it is obvious that such pre-existing material requires explanation itself. No other hypothesis can be held except that of Creation.

The word " creation " is often used in a loose and illogical way. We hear of " creative evolution," creations of the artist and the poet, etc. But in all instances of terrestrial change or of human achievement pre-existing material is necessary. No finite creature can create ; he can but transform mediately that which exists already. Being as being is the most universal effect, and demands the most universal cause. The tiniest grain of sand postulates infinite power for its creation. When an effect is produced, the poorer the material, the greater the power required in the agent. But when the material is so poor as to be nothing, the power needful for the production of the effect must be infinite. An illustration already given is suggestive in this connection. If a globe of steel be electrified, then whenever it is touched by a needle, the whole electrical charge is received. Similarly the production of a grain of sand or of the most familiar organism—the " flower in the crannied wall "—is an effect due to the exercise of Infinite Power.

The end of Creation is twofold :
1. The primary end—the glory of God.
2. The secondary end—the perfection and happiness of creatures.

It is true that some creatures do not, through their own fault, attain their end. But the primary end of Creation—God's glory—is always attained, for creatures will witness either to the goodness and mercy of God or will attest His infinite justice.

The Catholic doctrine which teaches that God has created in time, and not from eternity, is confirmed by physical science. Though creation from eternity has been defended by some writers as theoretically possible, yet the constant " dissipation " of energy to which physical science bears testimony, points not only to the end of the universe as the abode of life, but to a beginning when the vast cosmic machine was like a clock wound up and set going. We can imagine that before the fall, Nature with its hierarchy of being splendidly proclaimed the glory of God. It is true that there was inequality, implied by the harmony and interrelation of parts. All the parts of a tree cannot be flowers. There must be roots, stem, branches, leaves. From inorganic nature to pure spirit, there was manifested wonderful gradation of being—a symphony without dissonance, and all things bore the hall-mark of Infinite Power and Benevolence. The fall has introduced an element of discord. But God by the Divine Redemption has brought good out of evil, so that in the Church's liturgy we hear the startling words: " O felix culpa quae talem et tantum meruit habere Redemptorem."

Conservation. To understand the necessity of Divine Conservation, a distinction should be made between causes that are efficient, i.e. always necessary for the being of an effect, and those which are necessary only for the production of an effect. A father is the partial cause of the passive generation of his son. The father dies and the son lives on. But nourishment, warmth and air are necessary not only for the production of an organism, but for its continuance in being. God is the Supreme Efficient Cause. The creature depends upon God every moment of its existence, and in fact Conservation has been described as " continuata creatio "—a continued creation. Should God withdraw His conserving influence the creature would be instantly annihilated.

Finally, just as the immediate production of matter necessitates the exercise of Divine Power, so also does its immediate transformation. The immediate change of water into wine, the raising of the dead to life, the multiplication of loaves—such direct transformation is beyond the capability of any created agent.

C. THE DIVINE CONCURSUS

Does God move secondary causes to action? The Thomistic answer to this question avoids extremes, both *per excessum* and *per defectum*. The occasionalism of Malebranche, who attributed the action of secondary causes wholly to God, and taught, for example, that the heating property of fire was due to God who acted through the fire, leads to Pantheism. "Actio sequitur esse." If there be but one action—the action of God—all beings are absorbed in God. Being in general is identified with the Divine Being—a pantheistic conclusion which is the direct outcome of the ontologistic realism of Malebranche.

The other extreme (*per defectum*) is that of Molina, according to whom a secondary cause can act without the divine "praemotio," i.e. previous concursus. (The priority connoted by the word "praemotio" is not priority of time, but of causality.)

St. Thomas claims that God is the cause of all created action in four ways:

1. God gives to the creature the power or faculty of action.
2. God constantly supports the faculty.
3. God applies the faculty to action. ("Movet facultatem ad agendum.")
4. God moves the faculty as the principal agent moves the instrument in order to produce the effect which exceeds the power of the instrument, namely, the *being* of the action.

What then does the secondary cause achieve?

The secondary cause is only the instrumental cause of the *being* of the effect, but it is the proper cause of the *individuality* of the effect. Thus the effect produced is wholly the action of the secondary cause in so far as it is this *individual* effect, and wholly the action of the Primary Cause in so far as the effect is *being*. The Thomistic doctrine regards the Primary and secondary causes as two complete causes—the secondary subordinate to the Primary. How to reconcile this doctrine with the freedom of the will does not offer serious difficulty. In all cases God moves the will freely. (*Cf.* Chapter VIII, II.)

D. Miracles

In this chapter miracles are considered from the standpoint of Divine Omnipotence. In Chapter XII, they will be regarded from the Apologetic standpoint.

St. Thomas defines a miracle as an effect which exceeds the power of any created nature. " Aliquid praeter ordinem totius naturae creatae." Miracles fall into one of three divisions according to the manner in which the power of nature is exceeded. The miraculous fact may be (1) essentially beyond nature's power, as for example the resurrection of the just with glorified bodies ; or (2) the effect may exceed nature's power as regard the subject in which it is produced. The resurrection of Lazarus was miraculous, because nature, though it can produce life, cannot do so in the case of a dead body (3) or finally, the effect may be miraculous in *manner* such as an instantaneous cure of a malady which naturally requires time, or an instantaneous change of water into wine.

The statement of the reasons which establish the possibility of miracles may be expressed in syllogistic form.

Major. An all-powerful free Cause, on the free-will of whom depends the application of those hypothetically necessary laws which constitute the order of action of created natures, can act outside those laws.

Minor. But God is a free all-powerful Cause, on whose freewill depends the application of those hypothetically necessary laws which constitute the order of action of created natures.

Conclusion. Therefore, God can act outside the order of action of created natures, i.e. can work miracles. The hypothetical necessity of a fact depends upon its extrinsic causes, efficient and final ; whereas absolute necessity comes from intrinsic causes, formal and material. The order of action of created natures being constituted by causal laws, which are instances of efficient causality and express mode of action, is

NATURE AND ATTRIBUTES OF GOD

only hypothetically necessary. For example, fire, if it acts, heats. But the effect of the fire may be counteracted or modified by a higher cause. Whereas in the case of a triangle, its angles make, under all circumstances and with absolute necessity, two right angles, so that any other hypothesis must be placed in the same category as a " square circle "— the category of non-entia absurdities.

Inaccurate statements in regard to miracles are often made. A miracle is *not* a violation of any law of nature. Suppose that a man holds a stone in his hand. The law of gravitation acts all the time, but the natural consequence of the law (the fall of the stone to the ground) is prevented by the support given to the stone. If the hand be withdrawn, and the stone be supported by God's power, it is clear that the miracle does not affect the law of gravitation—the consequence of the law as in the former case is prevented by support miraculously given. Thus a miracle modifies the effect of a law, but the law itself is untouched.

Regarding the statement of the minor proposition that God is free, and can act outside hypothetically necessary laws, its truth follows from the fact that the created universe has no relation to God's essential happiness and glory. Creation affects His accidental glory alone. God is free to create or not to create, and, if He creates, He is free to create one universe rather than another. God always acts with infinite wisdom. He could not have better created this world, but He could have created a better world. Plants and animals cannot be better adapted to their ends, but the animal is higher than the plant.

The objection which states that as all the powers of nature are not known, certainty as to the miraculous character of a fact is not possible, can be answered easily. We do not know all that nature *can* effect, but we know what nature *cannot* effect. To raise a dead body to life is beyond nature's power. To produce being without the aid of pre-existing material or to modify being immediately—to change, for example, water instantaneously into wine—these effects belong to Infinite Power alone.

E. The Intimate Life of God

The essential attribute of living things is immanence of action—the possession within themselves of a principle of action. A stone is not living, because it has not the power of moving itself. A plant lives because the processes of assimilation, nourishment, growth and reproduction set out from an internal principle of movement. The animal lives a higher life than the plant, because it perceives by the senses the different objects towards which it can move. Man's life is higher still, because, owing to the endowment of reason and free-will, he is able to direct his movements more wisely and effectually. God, Subsistent Being, in whom all principles of action—formal, final, efficient—are present, possesses life or rather is life beyond comparison with created things. To say that God is unchangeable does not mean that God is inert; the unchangeableness of God follows from the fact that He is "Actus purissimus"—Being in whom there is no potentiality, and consequently no change.

The perfections of God are only analogous to those of creatures. The Being of God can be described only *negatively* as "non-finite Being," or relatively as "Supreme and Sovereign Being." Revelation alone can tell us *positive* truth in regard to the intimate life of God, such as the truth enshrined in the words: "go teach all nations, baptising them in the name of the Father, and of the Son, and of the Holy Ghost." Now the mystery of the Holy Trinity seems at first sight to have but small relation to our religious life. The Incarnation and Redemption indeed bespeak the immeasurable love of God for His creatures, but is our faith enriched, our hope aroused, our charity increased by the mystery of the Holy Trinity?

In order to grasp the importance of the doctrine of the Trinity, we shall show (1) that the doctrine strengthens and exalts the knowledge of God derived from reason, and (2) furnishes the supreme object of faith by manifesting the highest reach of the life of intelligence and love.

1. "Summum bonum est sui diffusivum." This princplei manifests itself in the scale of being from the lowest to the highest. The sun diffuses light and heat. The plant and animal pass on their life and powers to their progeny. Man possesses not only material but spiritual fecundity. The artist produces a sculptured form, a painting, a symphony. But the artistic work is exterior to the artist. The teacher communicates knowledge to his disciples, but it is only in exceptional cases—where there is a rare manifestation of genius—that the disciples remain attached to the teacher. Evidently the more perfect a being is the more does he reveal himself intimately, and the more does his action and its results remain intimately united to himself. The apostle, the true friend, are the highest human types of intimate revelation and personal attraction. But in God alone is the ideal realised. The Sovereign Good gives His intimate life, His nature, in the ineffable mystery of the Divine Paternity: " Filius meus es tu, Ego hodie genui te." God communicates His nature without losing it, without dividing or multiplying it. From Father and Son proceeds the Holy Spirit of Love who unites them. The Divine Nature is not multiplied. Absolute diffusion is not incompatible with intimate communion.

2. Highest Manifestation of Divine Intelligence and Love. The human intellect engaged in the pursuit of truth often realises its weakness. How difficult it is to reduce our varied and varying ideas to some sort of order and to arrive at a principle of induction which will give unity and coherence to phenomena. How great is the gulf between knowledge and realisation. The mental concept of man is indeed contingent and imperfect, whereas the Divine " Verbum " is infinite and eternal. " In the beginning was the Word, and the Word was with God, and the Word was God." Perfect, definitive, true Idea adequately expressing the Infinite Nature of God! " Candor est lucis aeternae et speculum sine macula ! Splendor gloriae et figura substantiae ejus ! " And in the Word the Divine Mind sees all real and possible things, even the slightest differences of the temperaments physical, intellectual, and

moral, of those countless members who constitute the great human family!

Moreover, because we are uncertain and vacillating in our conclusions, we seek for confirmation, for guidance in regard to the secrets of the universe in which we live. It is difficult to express our ideas; rare to find a comprehending and sympathetic mind. Whereas the Divine Idea—the Word—is an infinitely intellectual, conscious substance—a Person. There is communication between Father and Son—both sources of truth by one and the same act of thought—the one wholly revealed to the other, essentially related the one to the other. And the bond of association manifests the supreme example of the life of charity. For God is not only Truth and Intelligence, He is also Goodness and Love. The mutual love of Father and Son—a mutual love which is identical—has a term, as thought has a term, and this infinitely intelligent, substantial, loving term is a Person—the Holy Spirit. The three Persons have the same act of thought, the same sentiment of love. Albeit that *Omnis similitudo claudicat*, the example of an equilateral triangle may be used to illustrate—however imperfectly—the doctrine of the Trinity. The angles are (1) really distinct; (2) of the same nature, and constituted by the same surface which belongs to each; (3) equal; (4) essentially relative and distinguished the one from the other by this relation; (5) so related that the position of one indicates the position and character of the others; (6) definitely ordered but not by a priority of causality. But the finite similitude can reflect the Infinite only " through a glass darkly."

In the human soul the three faculties—vegetative, sensitive and rational—constitute an " image " of the Holy Trinity, and if the soul be adorned with grace, there is " likeness " to God. For grace is a participation of the Divine Nature. Grace is (1) light to the mind—a participation in the thought of God; (2) strength to the will—a participation in the power of God; (3) love to the heart—a participation in Divine Charity.

" O the depth of the riches of the wisdom and of the

knowledge of God ! How incomprehensible are His judgments and how unsearchable are His ways ! For who hath known the mind of the Lord, or who hath been His counsellor ? Or who hath given to Him and recompense shall be made him ? For of Him, and by Him, and in Him are all things : to Him be glory for ever. Amen."

CHAPTER VI

SOME SUPPOSED ANTINOMIES

I. Difficulties Arising from the Attributes of Simplicity and Immutability

THE perfections attributed to God, not only in a virtual sense in so far as He can produce them in others, but in a formal sense in so far as He possesses them Himself, seem to be opposed to the Divine Simplicity. Three difficulties arise :

    I. Is the simplicity of the Divine nature compatible with a multitude of formal perfections ?

    II. Is the attribute of simplicity compatible with the duality of subject and object essential to knowledge ?

    III. Is Divine life compatible with immutability ?

It is interesting to notice that, in this as in other instances, the approved teaching of the Schools avoids extreme views on either side. Maimonides and the Nominalists held that perfections, such as "Goodness," existed only virtually (i.e. causally) in God inasmuch as He can cause goodness in others.

But it is easy to see that this opinion makes God unknowable, for if " the things that are made " do not shadow forth in some way (however inadequate) the " power and divinity of God," and give us some idea of His perfections, we know nothing of His nature, and we stand committed to Agnosticism.

Duns Scotus, on the other hand, claimed for the Divine nature an actual and formal multiplicity of attributes—an opinion which runs counter to the idea of Ens Simplicissimum.

The approved teaching of the Schools maintains that perfections exist in the Divine nature formally and eminently, but are only virtually distinct from the Divine essence.

The perfections exist formally, i.e. according to their formal nature; they exist eminently in an infinite way, known to us only relatively and negatively, and the eminent mode of their existence makes their identification possible in the formal nature of God, an identification which, as we shall see, does not imply their destruction. The merely virtual distinction of the attributes from the essence is based:

I. On the eminence of the Deity who can identify in Himself perfections really distinct in creatures; and
II. On the imperfection of our minds, which cannot comprehend the Infinite.

Finally, the perfections of God contain one another actually in an implicit way.

Before we proceed to the consideration of different groups of Divine attributes, an indirect solution of the supposed antinomies may be stated in syllogistic form.

Major. A logically rigorous application of the first principles of reason cannot lead to real contradictions but only to mysteries.

Minor. But such application of first principles leads us to admit the existence of a First Cause, absolutely simple and at the same time possessing perfections such as being, intelligence, goodness, freedom, etc.

Conclusion. Therefore, there cannot be contradiction, but only mystery in the compatibility and identification of these perfections in God.

Coming now to the direct solution of the supposed antinomies, we first ask the question: Can a perfection (e.g. "Goodness") exist formally in God and in a creature? Maimonides answered in the negative, claiming that a formal perfection in a creature exists only virtually in God. Scotus gave an affirmative answer, but not realising the infinite difference between the Divine and human manner of being, he concluded that perfections existed in the same way (univocally) in God and in man, an opinion involving a multiplicity of perfections in God not compatible with the Divine Simplicity.

The Thomist teaching has always been that between a Divine and human perfection there could be only a proportional resemblance, only an analogous relation. Hence a perfection which connotes no imperfection may exist in an infinite as well as a finite way, and therefore exist formally in two beings, one of whom is infinite and the other finite.

It is well to remind ourselves of the distinction between the following three categories:

Univocal qualities are those which have the same name, and whose essence signified by the name is the same, e.g. animality is the same in the horse and in the lion.

Equivocal things have the same name, but their essences or natures are entirely different, e.g. dog, sea-dog, canis major.

Analogous things have the same name, their natures are different, but they are alike from a certain point of view owing to proportionality or analogy between them.

As already noted in Chapter II (IV), St. Thomas distinguishes between analogy of attribution and analogy of proportionality. In the former case an attribute is assigned to one or more things because of their relation to a principal quality. Thus fresh air is healthy because it promotes health, colour is healthy because it proceeds from health. In the second case there is between certain things a proportionality sometimes merely metaphorical as when we say that the lion is king of animals, sometimes not metaphorical but real, as for example, the relation of sensation to its object is proportional to the relation of thought to *its* object, and because of this proportionality the word knowledge is justly applied both to the sense-perception and to the intellectual perception. Similarly the relation of God to His existence is proportional to the relation of man to his existence, and because of this proportionality the word being can be analogously applied to God and man, though God is Necessary Being infinite in all perfection, and man is contingent and finite. And since the concept "being" implies different modes of being, the concept has not the absolute unity which a univocal concept possesses, but only a relative unity—a unity of proportionality.

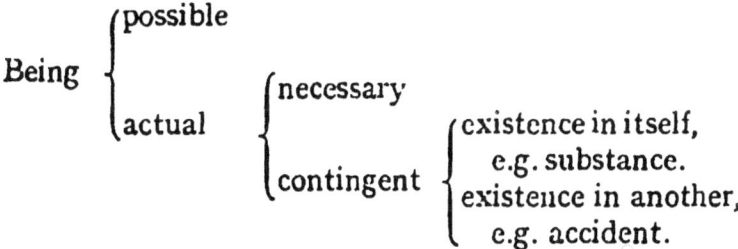

There is a unity of proportionality also in the properties of being, known as transcendentals—unity, truth, goodness. For example, fruit is good in its way, i.e. physically. Man is good in his way, i.e. morally. The applicability to God of the concept of being and its transcendental properties must be extended also to the perfections of Intelligence, Wisdom, Providence, Free-will, Love, Mercy and Justice. Since these perfections are specified by being, or by one of its properties, they have the same unity of proportionality. The formal object of the intellect is "being," the formal object of the will is "good." Wisdom and Providence are perfections of the intellect; Love, Mercy and Justice are perfections of the will.

The Divine perfections though formally present in God are identified with the Divine being. In order to make this fact clear, it will be advisable to group them into three classes:

1. Those perfections which are not virtually distinct one from the other. Consider for example, essence and existence, essence and intelligence, essence and will. If from the human standpoint there is an extrinsic virtual distinction between these perfections, from the Divine standpoint there is no distinction. Essence and existence are distinguished in the creature, because essence is potential existence. In God there is no potentiality, in Him essence and existence are one. Similarly between essence and the exercise of intelligence, between essence and the exercise of will, there

is no distinction in a Being in whom there is no potentiality. But St. Thomas recognises an intrinsic virtual distinction between Intellect and Will of God.

We can now indicate the solution of two difficulties:

(*a*) Is duality of subject and object essential to Divine knowledge? The duality of an act of human knowledge arises from a twofold potentiality—the potentiality of the faculty and the potentiality of the intelligible object. The latter must be divested of its materialistic conditions before it can be understood. Hence our faculty is identified with its object in so far as its object is "*known*," but is distinct from the object in so far as the object is "*being*," and truth is a certain conformity between the intellect and the thing perceived—"adaequatio inter intellectum et rem cognitam." The Divine intelligence cannot be a faculty, for a faculty implies potentiality, but is subsistent intelligence itself and identified with the Divine essence. There is no need of an idea in the Divine mind. The act of intelligence, as well as the intelligence itself, are identified with the Divine essence. Thus there is no duality in Divine knowledge. Similarly, the Divine will and its act of its exercise are identical with the Divine nature.

(*b*) As the duality of subject and object in the acquisition of knowledge is opposed to the Divine Simplicity, so it would seem also that the idea of life involving constant change, is opposed to the immutability of God. Intellectual life in creatures implies change, because the intellect must seek its object outside itself (*ab extrinseco*). Thus the human intellect is potential and imperfect, for the characteristic quality of life is immanence, since life is more perfect in proportion to the perfection of its immanent principle of movement and development. Now God is subsistent knowledge and subsistent love. God—Actus purissimus—has been infinite in perfection from all eternity. God's life, therefore, is absolute stability—not stability in the sense of inertia, but the stability which represents the possession of infinite perfections. And from the answers to these difficulties it will be seen that the difficulties themselves arise from ascribing human perfections with their inevitable limitations to God. But when the perfections are freed from human limitation and potentiality they are seen to become identified with the Divine nature. Intelligence and will are formal perfections in God, and are identified in Him.

    2. Perfections of the second group are those between which there is a virtual distinction by reason of the different relations of creatures to God.

According to the different relations of created beings to God, we can distinguish between the science of simple intelligence which concerns possible beings, the science of vision which relates to actual beings, and the action of Divine Providence which directs all things to their last end. The distinctions are of course but virtual, and constitute no objection to the truth of the Divine Simplicity. Again the virtual distinctions between the love of God wherewith He necessarily loves Himself, and the love wherewith He freely loves creatures, between the Divine mercy and Divine justice —these difficulties arise merely from the human standpoint. The infinite goodness of God pours out benefits on His creatures. Herein is His mercy: " Summum bonum est sui diffusivum." He has a right to be loved in return. Herein is His justice. And if love is unjustly withheld Mercy becomes Justice to the rebellious creature. The change of relation is due to the attitude of the creature, and does not imply a twofold perfection in God. The Divine Victim of Calvary— the most moving manifestation of Divine benevolence—is love to the obedient and justice to the wicked. " Misericordia et veritas obviaverunt sibi, justitia et pax osculatae sunt " (Psalm lxxxiv. 12).

    3. Perfections of the third group, Intellect and Will, involve (according to St. Thomas) a virtual distinction independently of creatures. But as Divine Intelligence is not virtually distinct (intrinsically) from the Divine essence, nor Divine love virtually distinct from the Divine Essence, the identification of these perfections is not an antinomy but a mystery, and of this mystery it has been possible to give some explanation, but of

course only negatively and relatively. We can now estimate the value of the reasoning whereby Scotus pleads for an actual and formal distinction (a distinction neither *virtual* nor *real*) between the attributes of God. Otherwise, he argued, the Divine Justice would be the same as the Divine Mercy, and it could be said that God punishes through mercy and pardons through justice. The source of error in the teaching of Scotus springs from the univocal sense in which he understood the concept "being," fearing that unless the univocal sense be taken, the word "being" could not be applied to God and creatures, with the result that God would remain unknowable.

The objections to the univocal sense are overwhelming:

(*a*) The actual-formal distinction for which Scotus pleads is not compatible with the simplicity of God. Scotus' example of this distinction—the distinction between the human soul and its faculty—is wholly inadmissible as applied to God.

(*b*) The adoption of the univocal sense of the concept "being" implies that being as such is not essentially varied. Hence the danger of confounding God and creatures, and of pointing the way to Pantheism.

(*c*) The univocal sense of "being" compromises the essential distinction between the natural and supernatural orders. According to Scotus "being" is the object of human intellect, "being" in its univocal sense embracing God and creatures, and if we have not a conscious intuition of God such deprivation, according to Scotus, is not natural, and may be due to original sin.

(*d*) Finally, the fear entertained by Scotus that, unless the concept of being be used in a univocal sense, a syllogistic argument proving the existence of God would be impossible, is met by St. Thomas, who shows that an analogous concept can be chosen, as the middle term of a syllogism: "ad hoc autem commune analogum quaedam consequuntur propter unitatem proportionis sicut si communicarent in unâ naturâ generis vel speciei."

Père Garrigou-Lagrange gives the following example:—

Major. Origin has priority as compared with that which proceeds from it.

Minor. The source of a river is its origin.

Conclusion. Therefore the source has priority as compared with that which proceeds from it (i.e. the river).

II. Difficulties Arising from the Existence of Evil, Physical and Moral

One difficulty in connection with the proof of God's existence is veritably the crux of Apologetics—the problem of the existence of evil, physical and moral. How can the presence of suffering and sin in the world be reconciled with the providence of God who is infinitely powerful and infinitely loving? " Si Deus undè mala ? "

Theologians mean by Divine Providence the action of Divine Intelligence and Will whereby God preserves, governs, and directs His creatures to the end for which He has created them. That God should have created beings and left them to their own devices is unthinkable. " Deus non creavit et abiit," to use the words of St. Augustine. The denial of Divine Providence would be equivalent to the denial of the infinite perfection of God. Apart from this à priori necessity, there is the plain inference in regard to the Providence of God derived from the order observed in the harmonious working of the physical world, the order in the domain of the moral world with its laws of Right and Wrong manifest to human judgment and conscience, as well as the incradicable belief in Divine Providence—the belief extensive and intensive—of the human race. There is no need to labour the point. If God exists His Goodness, Justice, Sanctity and Wisdom postulate providential care for the creatures dependent upon Him.

Why then the prevalence and intensity of physical suffering and mental agony? Earthquakes, shipwrecks, railway accidents, disease, war—the tragedy which began in 1914— how many and how ruthless are the agents of destruction? The earthquake of Messina and Reggio involved the death of

100,000 inhabitants. The horror of the *Titanic* disaster is still fresh in our memories. From time to time we are startled by the details of railway accidents involving agonising deaths. We stand aghast at the prevalence of cancer, to mention but one of a host of diseases. We know how often it happens that death comes to shatter the joys of family life, leaving the bereaved to mourn with desolate hearts. Truly is this life a sad pilgrimage. We send up our sighs " mourning and weeping in this vale of tears." Why should this suffering be ? Why, above all, should there be the presence amongst us of moral evil—of sin—with its polluting influence upon life, and its sequel in the shape of eternal loss ? Some answer to this question is due to men " of peace and goodwill " who enquire not captiously but earnestly—who desire to know the truth.

I. Let us suppose then that the man who asks the question " Why does evil exist ? " is one to whom the grace of Divine Faith in Revelation has not yet come. He begins to enquire into the existence of a Personal God who is infinitely powerful and loving, and he asks the question which Boëthius framed twelve centuries ago, " Si Deus unde mala ? " To meet his objection, Evil, its origin and consequences, must be considered from the standpoint of Natural Reason alone, leaving aside for the moment the further light which Revealed Religion affords. From the standpoint of Reason, then, how can the existence of evil be justified ?

In the first place some allusion must be made to answers which are quite inconclusive. It is often said that the evil of sin exists because of the endowment of free-will. Free-will, it is alleged, implies the possibility of moral evil, i.e. of sin. But surely it is not true to say that free-will in its essence implies the possibility of moral evil. Free-will in God is free-will in absolute and infinite perfection, free-will without the possibility of the slightest moral defect. Nay, Catholic philosophy insists that man's power of sinning is a defect of free-will which does not belong to its essence. The angels possess free-will and do not sin. Our Blessed Lady was free and at the same time immune from moral defect. If it is possible for the angels, if possible for the Blessed Virgin, why not possible for man to exercise freedom without the unfortunate capability of disobeying the moral law and involving himself in the dreadful consequences of such disobedience?

It is not difficult to indicate the cause of the confusion of ideas which underlies the statement that the possibility of sinning follows from the endowment of freedom. It is often said that free-will consists in the " potestas eligendi," the power of choice. The statement is not quite accurate. The more enlightened a rational being becomes, the less will he exercise the power of choice. Is it not a fact that a man chooses now in one way, now in another, because of the varying and imperfect light which reason gives? The intellect of an angel is free from the disturbing influences which beset our human nature in its present state, and therefore the course to be followed by the will stands out clearly and definitely, yet so as not to compel assent, so that the will freely but without doubt or hesitation follows the rational course revealed by reason.

In truth the essence of free-will seems to consist not in the power of choice, but in the free acceptance of the light furnished by the intellect. Unfortunately, in the case of man, the intellect often gives false lights that are coloured and obscured by human passion, and consequently our frailty should be ascribed to the darkness of the intellect quite as much as to the vacillation of the will. And if the objection be urged, does not this view of the nature of freedom tend to eliminate responsibility, the answer is at hand. No, for will and intellect act and re-act the one upon the other. The sphere of responsibility is merely extended to the intellect. I am to some extent responsible for the light which my intellect gives, for though that light is confessedly obscure and uncertain in its directive influence I can make the intellect revise its decisions, I can bring new motives into the intellectual field of view. I can compare its decision with the steady light of the moral law, the universal acceptance of which secures for it the force of an objective external standard.

Another reason is sometimes put forward to explain the existence of evil. God, it is said (and truly said), has left an impress of His Divine Nature upon created beings. Hence the element of opposition in creation from which evil comes is claimed to reflect in some mysterious way the element of contrast in the Divine Nature—contrast of Unity of Essence and Trinity of persons. This mode of reasoning may easily degenerate into mere juggling with words, and has no apologetic value.

Again, it is said, and justly said, that much of the sum of human suffering is due to excess in some way or another on the part of individuals, and therefore attributable not to God, but to the abuse of the freedom which God has given to His rational creatures. Granted. Doctors assure us that a high percentage of disease is due to preventible causes. On the other hand, many diseases are not due to individual excess, and in this discussion it is not a question of the amount of suffering. A single instance of pneumonia, for example, which is contracted, precautionary measures notwithstanding, is sufficient to raise the objection against a First Cause and Ruler who is infinite Benevolence. Is it possible then, to throw any light upon this difficulty? Some light is attainable, though that light is necessarily " per speciem in aenigmate "—light that reaches us through the dark medium of human limitation.

(a) An example which suggests an erroneous inference may be taken from Mathematics. Those who are acquainted with Algebra know that it is possible in two or three lines to arrive at startling conclusions. The procedure is as follows:

$$\text{Let } X = 3 \text{ and } Y = 4$$
$$X^\circ = 1$$
$$Y^\circ = 1$$
$$\text{Therefore } X^\circ = Y^\circ$$
$$\text{i.e. } 3^\circ = 4^\circ$$

Now it is well known that if the symbols X and Y are used to represent definite numbers, no matter how great, and if the rules of Algebra are observed the results will be correct. In this example the suggested erroneous deduction (3=4) shows by its absurdity that some mistake exists in the chain of the argument. Whether the reason perceives the exact position of the fallacy or not, the example may serve to suggest the difficulties which surround conclusions based upon the use of symbols.

What are our ideas on the subject of the Divine Nature or Divine action ? Surely our ideas are symbols, true as far as they go, but necessarily inadequate to the reality they represent. Hence, if we attempt to regard our limited ideas as adequately representing the Infinite, we shall be at once face to face with paradox. When St. Thomas defined truth as the " adaequatio inter intellectum et rem cognitam " he was careful to point out that the word " adaequatio " does not imply the grasp of the totality of objective qualities, but merely a true aspect of the objective reality " secundum modum cognoscentis." The analytic mind of St. Paul realised human limitations, and his comment thereon is not only a devout expression of humble Faith, but also an expression informed with the deepest and truest principles of philosophy : " O the depths of the riches of the wisdom and knowledge of God. How incomprehensible are His judgments, how unsearchable His ways. Who hath known the mind of God ? Who hath been His counsellor ? " A rigorously demonstrative proof can be given that God is Infinite Benevolence and Power. On the other hand, we see the ravages of sin, and of suffering in God's creation. Here is a tremendous paradox, feebly illustrated by the erroneous deduction 3=4. The difficulty in each case is due to the limitation of the symbol and does not exist objectively.

(*b*) In the second place it is a truth of Reason that man's sense of justice and sense of sympathy come from God. If man feels sympathy with his brother in the hour of need, if he is moved to alleviate pain, moved to pour the balm of consolation into a suffering heart, à fortiori does the Infinite Source of compassion and tenderness sympathise with human sorrow. And if the alleviation does not come, there must be a factor in the problem which escapes human scrutiny. This is the veriest common sense. Human love is but a drop in comparison with the boundless ocean of Divine compassion of Him who is Subsistent Love.

(c) Again, the conclusion is forced upon us that finite life of necessity implies impermanence. Impermanence implies death. Death imports separation. Separation of the physical parts of a sentient creature, separation from possessions which belong to its environment carries with it bodily pain and, in the case of rational creatures, mental pain also. In connection with the suffering of animals, it is interesting to contrast the differences of view held by scientific authorities. Mr. Winwood Reade writes: " Pain, grief, disease, death, are those the inventions of a loving God ? That no animal shall rise to excellence except by being fatal to the life of others, is this the law of a kind Creator ? It is useless to say that pain has its benevolence, that massacre has its mercy. Why is it so ordained that bad should be the raw material of good ? " On the other hand, Alfred Russel Wallace has the following : " Given the necessity of death and reproduction—and without these there could have been no progressive development of the organic world—it is difficult even to imagine a system by which a greater balance of happiness could have been secured."

But if pain is a necessity in the scheme of creation—in any scheme of finite existences—why has God chosen to create ? To which question the answer is—we may not attempt to make our finite minds the measure of Divine arrangements. The solution is beyond the power of human speculation. Natural faith and natural humility have their trials, as well as the supernatural forms of these virtues. The impotence of human speculation recalls the touching act of Faith spoken by one whose paternal heart was wrung with grief : " I believe, O Lord, do Thou help mine unbelief." We know not why God has chosen to create a system of which pain is a necessary part, but we do know that God is infinite in power, infinite in love. We hold the two ends of the chains (to use the figure of Bossuet), though we cannot see the intermediate links which, if visible, would reveal to us the connection, the coherence, the compatibility of the whole.

(*d*) Finally, if finite existence implies impermanence and imperfection the human intellect shares in the imperfection. Human reason is vacillating in its decisions. We see through a glass darkly. Hence the duty incumbent upon us of revising the decisions of the intellect, of bringing them into harmony with the Natural Law, and here comes in human responsibility. Sin becomes possible owing to the vacillating light of reason and the instability of the will. In this statement of the fact, we avoid the superficial dictum that sin is the concomitant of free-will. No; Our Blessed Lady enjoyed the endowment of free-will in its integrity. Our Blessed Lady was sinless. The sinfulness of man cannot be attributed to the Freedom of the Will, but to the imperfection of both Will and Intellect—an imperfection flowing from their finite natures. And in regard to responsibility, the Intellect must be associated with the Will, " Nil volitum nisi praecognitum." Even the clearer light of the Angelic mind was subject to defection. Either God elects to desist from creation altogether, or if He creates, then the beings thus brought into existence shall experience the consequences of their finite nature by being subject, in the physical order, to impermanence, to pain, to death ; and, in the moral order, to the possibility of sin.

II. The half light which Reason sheds on natural mysteries is reinforced by Divine Revelation. Man does not belong to the Natural order alone. He has been elevated to the supernatural order with its final end of the intuitive vision of God and the means for the attainment of that end—reason aided by Divine grace. Brief, indeed, and insignificant therefore is the passage through life in comparison with the never-ending life of weal and woe which awaits us beyond the grave. " Cette vie n'est pas la vie " was the theme of Lacordaire's conferences upon Divine Providence. What opinion should we form of a critic who would judge the merit of a dramatic representation from the first act alone ? Nature herself by her inability to satisfy the needs of the human heart constantly recalls to our minds the fact that our true happiness is elsewhere. " Inquietum est cor nostrum donec requiescat in Te," wrote St. Augustine. " Thou hast made us for Thyself, and our hearts are restless until they find their rest in Thee." Unhappily we are prone, notwithstanding repeated disillusionments, to rest satisfied with the things of earth and time, and therefore we need to learn again and again, however painfully, the lesson of detachment from attractions that have no permanency, so that we may wisely fit ourselves for the life to come.

(a) To help in the achievement of this design Divine Providence makes use of the gospel of pain. In the liturgy of the Office for the Dead the words of Job are chanted: " Miseremini mei quia manus Domini tetigit me ! " God in His mercy touches us at times with but a slight pressure. A friend, for example, whom we have loved, in whom we have trusted, begins to weary of our companionship. Anon a stronger pressure is felt. One who is strongly and deeply loved, with whose personality are bound up the tenderest associations of years, disappears in death ! Other calamities may follow, so that our frame of mind is comparable with that of the Apostle : " I wish to be dissolved and to be with Christ ; who will deliver me from the body of this death ? " Surely from the touch of God here described it is possible to draw the greatest spiritual good—detachment, resignation, desire of Eternal Life, appreciation of God as of One whose friendship will never fail. This supernatural gain is immeasurably more beneficial, more conducive to abiding happiness and peace, than the lost possession however dear. The touch of God is a source of light.

(b) Consider, too, the expiatory character of suffering. Suffering, from the supernatural standpoint, is the antithesis of sin. The creature who sins is disobedient, is rebellious ; whereas the man stricken with disease is obedient, even to his nurse. The creature who sins has perhaps been influenced by sensual enticements, whereas in the privations which disease entails there is room for the meritorious acceptance of suffering as an expiation for the offences of former days.

The creature who sins is proud, whereas the sick man, appreciating his bodily weakness, is encouraged to utter the prayer of the humble and the needy, " O God, be merciful to me a sinner." St. Augustine's aphorism finds in such a case a notable illustration " God judged it more wise to bring good out of evil, than not to allow evil to exist." " Where sin hath abounded, grace will much more abound." The touch of God is a remedy for sin.

(c) Significant also is the fact that the best specimens of our race do not reach to excellence of character—to heroism —by means of genius, or glory, or success. The lives even of those who have claimed to be philosophers, who have, in fact, been men of undoubted genius, reveal the sad truth that genius is compatible with moral turpitude. If we understand the word "glory" as meaning the adulation of men, then some glorified mortals have been the most despotic and cruel of tyrants. Success has often been attained by means which no moralist can justify. Who have been in truth the real heroes of our race ? On this question one will not find enlightenment, though possibly one will find amusement in the perusal of such books as " Heroes and Hero-worship." For the true heroes of humanity are those who have purified themselves in the fiery ordeal of pain from the gross tendencies of nature, who have conquered in the battle waged against themselves and have become to their fellow men for all time examples of manliness and virtue. Contrast Francis of Assisi, the soldier of the Cross, with Bonaparte or Cromwell ; contrast Vincent de Paul with Martin Luther ; contrast the author of the " Spiritual Exercises " with the author of " Paradise Lost " ; compare Thomas Aquinas with Nietzsche. No man will hesitate to whom to assign the laurel of genuine heroic achievement, either in the world of practical affairs or in the realm of thought. And thus the experience of life witnesses to the truth of the familiar illustration. In the block of marble lies hid potentially the human form divine. But there is need of the blows and the chiselling of the artist before the form of beauty is evolved from the shapeless material. To evolve the form of spiritual beauty in man, there is need likewise of the touch—the chiselling—of the supreme Artist.

(d) And finally, if Revelation, and Revelation alone, throws a new light on the problem of evil, does not that fact constitute an additional claim for the acceptance of Revelation? In physical science, for example, the undulatory theory of light is accepted because it explains phenomena—notably the phenomenon of interference, which is regarded as a crucial test. The problem of evil is surely a crucial test of the validity of supernatural Revelation. And thus even the principle of Pragmatism, now so much in vogue, is in accord with the time-honoured principles of Catholic Philosophy, all true principles being so many converging rays which reach their focus in Divine Faith. In this brief review of the Problem of Evil, judged from the standpoint of Revelation, it must not be forgotten to mention that millions of rational creatures in successive generations have not enjoyed, and do not enjoy, the light which comes from Faith. True. But Divine Grace and Divine Consolation are as wide as humanity. The old axiom of the schools, " Facienti quod in se est, Deus non denegat gratiam," is a sufficient answer to this objection. If the lily of the field is the object of God's providential care the help will not be withheld whereby the rational creature outside the Christian Fold may attain the happiness for which he was created.

A brief résumé of the line of reasoning given in this section will perhaps be useful.

1. From the standpoint of Reason.

(a) Reason demonstrates the existence of God, infinite in Power and Love. Reason recognises also the presence of evil in our midst, evil physical and moral. We cannot, therefore, infer the incompatibility of these two truths.

(b) The sense of justice and sympathy in man is but a trace, an echo, of the infinite Justice and Sympathy of God.

(c) Physical evil is essential to finite being.

(d) Moral evil is also possible to the finite faculties— faculties of Intellect and Will—of a rational creature.

2. From the standpoint of Revelation.
(a) Evil is a source of enlightenment.
(b) Evil is a remedy for sin.
(c) Evil is a discipline which builds up character.
(d) Evil, so far from being an argument against Revelation, is, in fact, one of the strongest arguments for its truth, for it is Divine Revelation alone that shows how " good will be the final goal of ill."

III. Difficulties Arising from the Consideration of the Divine Nature as seen from the Standpoints of Reason and Revelation

It has been shown that God is " Ens simplicissimum." His attributes are only virtually distinct from His Nature, and as a consequence there is no composition in God. Even such attributes as Justice and Mercy are identical with the Divine Essence, and differ only one from the other by an extrinsic virtual distinction. Justice and Mercy are in reality identical. But when we leave the domain of Natural Religion and come to Revelation, we at once remember the further light given to us in regard to God. He is not only one in Nature, but threefold in Personality. He is God the Father, God the Son, and God the Holy Ghost. This revealed doctrine seems to be opposed to the philosophic meaning of the word person, opposed to the equality of the Divine Persons, and seemingly fails to harmonise with the absolute simplicity of God which is a fundamental characteristic of the Divine Nature.

First in regard to the meaning of the word " person."

The philosophic meaning of the word implies a complete rational nature subsisting in itself, and master of its own actions. Hence, in our experience, there are always as many natures as there are persons. As we have already seen, human perfections are ascribed to God only in an analogical sense, because of His Infinitude. It is clear that the meaning of the word " person," as applied to God, differs somewhat from its human meaning. The three persons in God do not involve three distinct natures; there is only one nature—one generically, specifically and numerically. How then should we understand the word " person " as applied to God ? The word in this higher sense signifies the subsistent relations which distinguish the Father, Son and Holy Ghost. The person of the Father is the relation of paternity, as the person of the Son is the relation of filiation. From the fact that there are three Divine persons, we justly conclude that there are three subsistent relations but not three distinct natures. But " person," both in its Divine and human sense, indicates that which is distinct and incommunicable in the respective natures, and this essential meaning is preserved in the connotation of person as applied to God and man.

The well-known Unitarian objection directed against the doctrine of the Trinity may be thus formulated :

The property which distinguishes the Persons from one another is either an imperfection or a perfection : not an imperfection because incompatible with the Infinite perfection of God, and not a perfection, for a distinguishing perfection possessed by one would involve the imperfection of the other two persons. A twofold answer is given :

(a) The paternity of the Father as the Filiation of the Son, and the Spiration of the Holy Ghost—these three subsistent relations are only *virtually* distinct from the Divine Essence. It is true that there is a *real* distinction between Father, Son and Holy Ghost, but the perfections which distinguish the Persons and which are formally in the Persons to whom they individually belong, are *radically* in the Divine Essence, so that all three Persons are equal in dignity and power. The same dignity which in the Father is paternity is filiation in the Son.

(b) Other theologians merely say that the relations which distinguish the Persons are of equal dignity, so that there is not greater perfection in paternity than in filiation. To give and to receive, being both infinite acts within the Godhead, are equal. But this equality is not opposed to the real distinction of the Persons. Perrone suggests an illustration length is the same as the space which it affects, breadth is the same as the space which it affects, and the superficial area which arises from length and breadth is the same as the space which it affects, but length, breadth and superficial magnitude are all really distinct.

Finally, regarding the difficulty arising from Divine Simplicity, inasmuch as the subsistent relations which constitute Father, Son and Holy Ghost, though *really* distinct in themselves, are only *virtually* distinct from the Divine Essence, they do not affect the essential simplicity of the Divine Nature.

CHAPTER VII

POLYTHEISM AND PANTHEISM

I. Unity of God: Polytheism

WHEN the statement is made that God is infinitely perfect, the usual connotation of the word "perfect" must be modified, inasmuch as one who has reached perfection is supposed to have attained the *term* of his development and there is the implication of advance, slow or rapid, towards the plenitude of being. Fortunately we can use the word "perfect" to indicate a state without reference to the manner of its acquisition, and only in this sense can perfection be predicated of God.

When we say that God is infinitely perfect we mean:

1. God possesses all perfections.
2. He possesses them in an infinite degree.

The infinite perfection of God follows as a consequence from the fact that He is "Necessary Being." For every perfection is a form of being. The words we use in speech or writing witness to this profound truth, e.g. when we say that "he *is* good" or "he *is* beautiful" we assert that these attributes belong to the individual, in so far as he exists. God who is Necessary Being—Being itself—must possess all these perfections. The lack of any perfection would imply potentiality which is incompatible with the nature of Necessary Being.

The cogency of this reasoning is supported by the natural tendencies of the human intellect and will. The intellect seeks after truth, and the object of its search is an object without any shadow of obscurity, without limitation of any kind. The will seeks after "happiness in general." And the quest of this happiness is incessant, is necessary. The daring and beautiful poem entitled "The Hound of Heaven" sets forth in splendid imagery the untiring pursuit of the redeemed soul by the Good Shepherd of Redemption, but there is correlatively on the side of the soul the constant seeking after happiness, the gradual realisation of the vanity of earthly pleasure, and in many cases the consequent appreciation of the truth enunicated by St. Augustine: "Inquietum est cor nostrum donec requiescat in Te."

If this tendency in human nature were illusory, then man, the king of creation, would be a monstrosity, an anomaly.

The infinite perfection of the Supreme Being involves the unity of the Deity. Suppose that two Supreme Beings exist. If one depends on the other he who depends cannot be supreme. If both are independent neither is the Supreme Being, for each has no power over the other. Moreover, two infinitely perfect beings would be identical, for both by supposition possess all perfections, and could not be distinguished one from the other.

The unity of the Supreme Being is manifested also in the uniformity of law observed in the universe. One of the most interesting hypotheses of Modern Science is that known as the Nebular Hypothesis. By aid of the wonderful optical instruments now at the command of the astronomer and the physicist it has been possible to trace the steps in the evolution of solar systems, and the stages of development are so well marked as to win universal acceptance for the theory. A brief statement of such stages will suffice:

1. Nebula in Orion ; nebula widely diffused.
2. Nebula in Andromeda ; more condensed.
3. Spiral nebula (Canes Venatici) ; partly solidified.
4. White stars ; e.g. Rigel, Sirius.
5. Yellow stars ; e.g. Sun.
6. Dark stars ; existence revealed by the attractive influence exercised.

DAYS OF CREATION

GENESIS		GEOLOGY	VEGETABLE WORLD	ANIMAL WORLD
6th. (b) "Let us make man." (a) "Let the earth bring forth the living creature, cattle and beasts of the earth."	Q.* { C. {	Recent Pleistocene Pliocene Miocene Oligocene Eocene	Dicots and Monocots	Man First true Monkey Mammals
5th. "Let the waters bring forth the creeping creature and the fowl that may fly."	M.	Cretaceous	Dicots and Monocots	First typical Teleostei Bird—Archæopteryx Reptiles on land: Megalosaurs, Dinosaurs Reptiles (flying): Plesiosaurs, Ichthyosaurs Reptiles (aquatic): Pterodactyls
		Jurassic	No new Forms	Reptiles much advanced
		Triassic Permian	No new Forms	{ Synthetic type, Microlestes { Reptiles
		Carboniferous	Trigonocarpon—First Gymnosperm	Amphibians—Labyrinthodonts
	P.	Devonian	Many plants related to ferns —Lycopods	Fishes of every class except typical Teleostei
		Silurian	First undoubted plants (Alga Psilophyton—Lycopod ?)	Fishes with cartilaginous skeleton
		Ordovician	No Record	Higher developments of early forms
	Latest {	Cambrian Pre-Cambrian		All invertebrates represented Crustacean—Beltina

Day	Scientific Description	Fossil Record
4th. "Let there be lights made in the firmament; and let them be for seasons and days."	Dispersal of Clouds, appearance of Sun.	Tracks and burrows possibly of lowly organisms.
3rd. (b) "Let the earth bring forth the green herb." (a) "Let the dry land appear."	Later Pre-Cambrian, many rocks of which are indisputably of sedimentary origin. Early Pre-Cambrian, i.e. oldest known rocks. They are unfossiliferous, of igneous origin and show evidence of great disturbance. Further cooling—Partial solidification and contraction, resulting in great earth movements and the formation of elevations and depressions.	No Record—but aquatic plants and lowly terrestrial ones which rarely or never appear as fossils throughout geological time most probably throve here.
2nd. "Let there be a firmament amidst the waters and let it divide the waters from the waters."	Further cooling, accompanied by condensation. Formation of dense clouds above earth and of the waters upon its surface.	
1st. (b) "Let there be light." (a) "The earth was void and empty and darkness was upon the face of the deep."	Coming together of particles under influence of gravity—heat, incandescence, vaporisation, rotation of nebulous mass. Earth thrown off as cooling proceeded. Beginning of REIGN OF LAW. Meteoric condition; widely diffused solid particles, molecules or atoms. CHAOS.	

Here we have the various stages in the life history of solar systems.

As regards our own solar system we find that:

1. Jupiter, Saturn, Uranus and Neptune are still in a state of intense heat, of which the impenetrable clouds which cover their surfaces are the witnesses. They are in the stage of planetary youth.
2. Venus and the Earth have attained full development.
3. Mars is in the decadent stage. The oceans are almost dried up and the atmosphere rare.
4. The Moon is dead; there is no moisture, no atmosphere. Finally as regards the past history of the planet on which we live the "days" of creation have their scientific equivalents as follows:

1. As contraction of nebula advanced there was light—1st day.
2. When the temperature had decreased down to the degree of heat known now as 100 C. the seas were formed—2nd day.
3. The Earth was still surrounded by clouds of vapour. Hence the probable luxuriance of shade vegetation of which, of course, there is no record—3rd day.
4. The clouds of vapour broken so as to admit Sun's rays —4th day.
5. Animal Life:
   Fishes. ⎫
   Amphibia. ⎬ Primary Age. ⎫
   Reptiles ⎭   ⎬ 5th day.
   Birds.   Secondary Age. ⎭
   Mammals. Tertiary Age. ⎫
6. Appearance of man in the present ⎬ 6th day.
   Quaternary period.   ⎭

The foregoing chart gives these facts in greater detail.

The reign of law throughout the Universe, the identity of elements in the composition of Suns and planets, the analysis of the phenomena of Light, Heat, and Sound, and their resolution into modes of motion—innumerable instances in Natural

Science point to the unity of the Supreme Power upon whom all beings and physical processes depend.

In face of these arguments which demonstrate the unity of God, how explain the error of Polytheism? Unfortunately it is clear that the intellect of man has been darkened and his will weakened. Hence the domination of evil passions and the power of Satanic suggestion. Moreover, there is a tendency in human nature to make the Deity visible and present—whence the worship of Sun, Moon, and Stars. There is a tendency also to idealise the lives and achievements of national or racial heroes, and finally to give them Divine honours. But the testimony of mythologists quoted in a former chapter and developed more fully in Chapter XI is emphatic as to the original belief of the Egyptian, Germanic, Oriental, and other races. Monotheism was the most ancient and primitive belief, and Polytheism a later corruption. In Chapter XI religious belief viewed from the historical standpoint will be carefully considered.

II. Pantheism

One of the most curious facts in the history of philosophy has been the tendency of every system of thought to end in Pantheism. From Buddha to Bergson examples are frequent. The philosophic movement in Germany which began with Kant, and was carried on by Fichte, ended as the Oriental systems ended in pure Pantheism. The one notable exception has been the philosophy of the Catholic Church, which systematised in the thirteenth century by Albert the Great and his illustrious pupil, Thomas Aquinas, has taught that whilst God is everywhere present in the Universe by "essence, knowledge, and power," everywhere immanent and energising throughout creation, withal He is transcendent. The forces of Nature are but the ministers of the Divine will. He is apart. The Earth-Spirit of Goethe's "Faust," in a passage already quoted, claims with profound truth and significance that the phenomena of Nature are but the vesture of the Deity.

The scholastic conception of person may be defined as "a

complete rational nature subsisting in itself." Obviously the angels are persons. Obviously also the human nature of Christ, though a complete rational nature, never for one moment subsisted in itself, and therefore was never a human personality. The human nature of Christ from the first moment of its being subsisted in the Word, the second person of the Blessed Trinity, and inasmuch as the human actions of Christ belong to the Divine Person ("actiones sunt personae") it follows that His actions and sufferings were of immeasurable dignity and merit.

From the definition of personality just given, it is seen at once that God is a Person, and indeed the Supreme type of that as well as of other perfections.

Pantheism, the negation of Divine Personality, offends (1) against Reason. (*a*) Pantheists must admit that the same cosmos is necessary, infinite and simple in so far as it is identified with God, but contingent, finite and compound in so far as it is cosmos. (*b*) If God is not really distinct from the world, the world is an effect without a cause. But the world being contingent postulates a cause.

(2) Pantheists misunderstand and contradict the testimony of consciousness. Our intimate sense attests that we do not naturally share in the Divine Nature.

> Etrange vérité, pénible à concevoir,
> Gênante pour le cœur comme pour la cervelle,
> Que l'Univers, le Tout, soit Dieu, sans le savoir !
> (Sully-Prud'homme.)

(3) Pantheists destroy by their doctrine the foundations of religion and morality, for the weaknesses and crimes of mankind may be justified from the pantheistic standpoint as being divine.

The objection is sometimes raised, if God is infinite and distinct from the Universe (i.e. transcendent) it follows that God and created beings are greater than God alone, i.e. greater than the Infinite, which is absurd. The answer is at hand: God, Necessary Being, cannot be associated with the analogous and contingent beings who constitute the Universe. Even if we make the absurd addition suggested, it follows that there are more beings, but not more being, seeing that contingent beings depend absolutely for their existence and conservation upon the Necessary Being from whom they proceed. It is instructive, too, to examine the substitute which Pantheists give for the God of Theism. Taine writes: " le monde forme un être unique, indivisible, dont tous les êtres sont les membres. Au suprême moment des choses se prononce l'axiome éternel, dont le retentissement prolongé compose, par ses ondulations inépuisables, l'immensité de l'univers " (" Philosophes français," p. 364).

The reader will make his choice between the God of Theism and the eternal axiom of Taine. The compatibility of the Divine immanence and transcendence, as has been pointed out above, should offer no serious difficulty. Thus the infinite power of God energises throughout the Universe, revealing itself in the growth of a flower as much as in the evolution of a Solar system, and that infinite power, though immanent, is at the same time distinct from the Universe, i.e. transcendent.

CHAPTER VIII

THE NATURE OF MAN

I. The Spirituality of the Human Soul

The existence and nature of God have been discussed, and the subject which next claims our attention is man, his nature, origin, and destiny. The consideration of man and his powers will show that he has three endowments, spirituality of the soul, freedom of the will, and knowledge of the moral law.

No one denies that man is made up of a body and a vital principle. The lower animals are similarly composed. But the claim is made, and will be presently justified, that the human vital principle has specific and exclusive endowments, which differentiate man from all other animals. The first of these endowments is the spirituality of the soul. A spiritual substance is defined as one that is simple, and subjectively independent of material organs for its existence, and for some of its actions. Hence spirituality implies (1) the power of existing and acting without the aid of material organs, and (2) the absence of physical parts both integral and constitutive.

The spirituality of the soul is proved : (1) from the object of our knowledge. (a) The soul perceives immaterial concepts totally inaccessible to the senses, e.g. God, truth, beauty, goodness. As already stated the idea of God is acquired by the synthesis of perfections from which finite limits have been removed, and which are conceived to have reached the highest degree. Truth is the " equation between the intellect and the object perceived." The concept of beauty implies (1) completeness, or integrity ; (2) order, proportion, harmony, " Unitas in Varietate " ; (3) clearness or brilliancy, so that the unity and order may shine forth. Goodness is the realisation of an ideal perfection beyond the power of sense to perceive.

(*b*) The soul perceives material objects in an immaterial way. The power of abstraction is coextensive with human nature.

Even the child, when its mind has been stimulated by experience, forms general notions or concepts of material things, by neglecting the concrete materialising conditions which constitute the individual. But "actio sequitur esse," the action of a being follows its nature and is proportioned to it. The soul, therefore, from its spiritual mode of action must be in its essence spiritual.

(2) The spirituality of the soul is proved from its power of making reflex acts.

The soul can make itself the object of its thought. No extended material object is capable of a reflex act. One part of an extended body may be applied to another part, but it is impossible to superimpose the whole upon itself. One part of a body may act upon another part, but the whole body cannot act wholly upon itself. This property is exclusively characteristic of spiritual substances.

(3) The spirituality of the soul is proved from the will. Our will has for its object not particular concrete goods, but happiness in general. Moreover, as we shall see, the will is free, whereas material natures are ruled by absolute determinism. If the will, a faculty of the soul, acts in a spiritual way, it follows that the essence or nature to which it belongs is itself spiritual.

Two consequences follow from the spirituality of the soul :

A. The soul is simple, i.e. it is not composed of physical parts either integral or constitutive.

   1. The soul has not integral or quantitative parts :
      (*a*) because of its power of abstraction which eliminates local extension and sensible properties ;
      (*b*) because of its power of making reflex acts.
   2. The soul has not constitutive parts, i.e. is not composed of matter and form. The endowment of spirituality shows that the soul is independent of matter.

In what sense do scholastic writers admit that the soul is composite? It is composite metaphysically, for it consists of essence and faculties, which are *really* distinct from the essence. It is also in a certain sense composite physically, for as the actions of the faculties are accidents, there is a composition of substance and accidents. But the soul is absolutely free from the physical parts which are known as quantitative and constitutive.

B. The second consequence of its spirituality is that the soul is essentially distinct from the body with which it is united to form a complete human nature.

Materialistic Objections

The vogue of materialism is on the wane. Recent discoveries in physical science, e.g. the resolution of atoms into electrons—has given strong emphasis to the dynamic aspect of matter. But it is profitable to give a brief answer to the objections which materialists advance against the spirituality of the soul.

1. Force is a property of matter therefore the soul is material.

Answer. Forces belonging to the physical and material order are associated with material substances. But spiritual and immaterial forces—power of abstraction, determination of will, appreciation of the ideal—have their bases in immaterial substances.

2. The mental activity of man is found in an inferior degree in the lower animals. But animals are admittedly material; therefore man is material.

Answer. Animals acquire sensitive knowledge, make use of the internal senses, imagination, memory, and appetite. But man, and man alone, can form an abstract idea. Hence between man and the lower animals there is a difference not of degree but of kind.

3. The power of thought varies with the size and quality of the brain. The brain is, therefore, the cause of the thought.

Answer. We might reason à pari: The light in a room varies with the size and number of the windows, therefore the windows are the cause of the light. The brain is the condition, the occasion, the instrument of thought, not the cause of thought. Moreover, the connection between the size of the brain and mental ability requires careful examination and cautious statement. "The increase of brain, which is directly due to increase in size of body, gives no increase of brain power; hence tall and bulky men are not necessarily more able than short and small men. Thus, although we cannot argue that because a man has a big brain he is a man of great capacity, yet the fact remains that many of the world's famous men had large heads and big brains. In the average Englishman the brain weighs 1,360 grammes (48 ounces); in Cromwell it is said to have been 2,231 grammes, and in Byron 2,238 grammes. In Gambetta, the French statesman, it weighed only 1,294 grammes. Still, if size of brain is not a certain index of capacity, it must be taken into account. Broca found when he compared the brains of a group of eminent men with those of men of ordinary ability that the average eminent man had a brain 80 grammes above the ordinary. When the sexes are compared, it is found that the brain in man is 130 grammes more than in woman on the average. Woman's smaller brain is due chiefly to her smaller body, for we have seen that the size of body has a direct influence on the size of brain." So writes Dr. Keith in his book " The Human Body," and in a private letter he sums up thus: " There is a real relationship between potential (and actual) intelligence and brain size. But just as the size of a country and the number of its inhabitants are no index of its military power, so brain size may be no index of mental ability." This subject comes up for discussion in the next chapter in connection with prehistoric man.

II. The Freedom of the Will

It is necessary to emphasise certain facts, and to distinguish clearly between different kinds of freedom.

A. An act may be necessary owing to physical compulsion, and this compulsion may be:

(a) from without (e.g. a prisoner confined to his cell), or;

(b) from within (e.g. all men are compelled to seek after "happiness in general").

B. An act or abstention from an act may be obligatory owing to moral compulsion, e.g. the acts enjoined or forbidden by the moral law.

Consequently there are different kinds of liberty :
1. Physical liberty
    (a) freedom from external compulsion called technically "liberty from constraint";
    (b) freedom from internal compulsion called "liberty of indifference."
        Liberty of indifference may be :
        (1) Liberty of contradiction, e.g. to love or not to love.
        (2) Liberty of contrariety, e.g. to love or to hate.
        (3) Liberty of specification—the choice of performing specifically different acts, e.g. to walk or to sing.
2. Moral liberty, i.e. the power of performing or omitting an act which is forbidden or enjoined by the moral law.

In claiming for a man free-will we do not claim for him complete "liberty from constraint." There are physical necessities which are obvious. Nor do we claim "Moral liberty," inasmuch as a rational being is always bound by the moral law. We claim for man "liberty of indifference," i.e. we maintain that though man is compelled to seek after "happiness in general" he is free in the choice of the means (particular goods) which he judges to be conducive to this end. How then should we define free-will? "An endowment in virtue of which the will can, in presence of a particular good, which is presented as a means of attaining an end 'happiness in general,' choose it or not choose it."

Proofs

(a) The first proof is an appeal to consciousness. Every man is swayed by different motives of action. To the average man the materialistic or sensualistic appeal is in itself stronger than the spiritual or supernatural appeal. And the reason is not far to seek. The materialistic appeal comes from a present concrete object, whereas the supernatural appeals to many only in a dim, misty, far-off way. But consciousness testifies that a man can, if he chooses, shut out from his thought the seductiveness of the materialistic appeal, and can by concentrating his thought upon and realising the cogency of the supernatural appeal make it immeasurably the stronger.

Hence, I *know* that I can give or not give alms to the poor (liberty of contradiction), I *know* that I can devote money to relieving a poor man's needs or use it to procure personal enjoyment (liberty of specification), I *know* that I can employ my money in procuring legitimate pleasure or culpable indulgence (liberty of contrariety). Obviously the liberty of contradiction—to act or not to act—is sufficient to justify the claim of freedom.

(*b*) The second proof rests upon the absurd consequences of the denial of free-will. If man is not free, there is no difference of worth or merit between the good and evil acts which he performs, and the " still small voice " of conscience has no spiritual significance, no objective value.

Certain results follow from the examination of the endowment of freedom and its conditions.

Corollary I. Freedom of the will can be prejudicially affected in its exercise by :

1. Ignorance. It is obvious that unless there is advertence of the mind in its normal state there can be no freedom, because there is not the requisite exercise of reason. " Nil volitum nisi precognitum." The actions, for example, of somnambulists are not imputable. Prayers said with distractions, to which advertence is not given, are not blameworthy.
2. Fear. If one is compelled to act in virtue of an overmastering fear the action is not free. Hence " Fear " is one of the diriment impediments of matrimony, which make the contract null and void.
3. Tyranny of passion. It is conceivable that an action which follows sudden and great provocation, even

though the action has serious results, may be devoid of moral culpability. Even the law of the land recognises that, in some cases of the taking of human life, the provocation has been so great that the verdict of "wilful murder" is reduced to one of "homicide."

Corollary II. One of the most important results in connection with the study of Free-will should be the recognition of fact that the power of sinning is an imperfection of the endowment, and does not belong to its essence. Consider free-will in God, in the human nature of Our Blessed Lord, in the angelic nature, in the human nature of Our Blessed Lady—in all these cases there is no question of sin, and yet there is perfect freedom of the will. Unfortunately, apologists sometimes attempt to explain the presence of moral evil in the world by saying that it is a consequence of the exercise of free-will. In this crude form the statement is incorrect, and has no apologetic value. Free-will in its essence may be defined as the free adoption by the will of the truth revealed by the intellect. Inasmuch as the human intellect is darkened, and will weakened, the intellect is often unable to give clear light, and we exercise the power of choice with insufficient knowledge. The power of sinning comes from the darkness or the false light which the mind gives, and from the weakness of the will—both faculties having been prejudicially affected by Original Sin—and not from the endowment of free-will as such. It is also clear that the more the mind is enlightened the less necessity there will be for the exercise of choice.

Corollary III. The essence of moral evil lies in a negation. Moral evil is a "non ens." Hence the prohibition of the moral law, which forbids the doing of evil, is no detriment to the exercise of free-will. If I claim the right to believe that $2+2=5$, I do not exercise free-will, for I resist a truth which is intrinsically evident, I oppose reason, and the result issues in a perversion of freedom. Similarly the claim of the right to contravene the moral law is not a legitimate exercise of freedom, but a perversion of the gift. As Auguste Nicolas has written: "to be free is to do what one wishes in doing what one should."

Corollary IV. Since we have the power of self-direction, it is easy to see how absolutely our characters and dispositions depend upon the wise use of the endowment of freedom. A man, for instance, may naturally be of a hasty and irascible temperament. Using the power given him by free-will, he may on a particular occasion suppress the manifestation of his anger, and the suppression may have cost a considerable effort. On a second occasion he also conquers and as the victories are multiplied, the effort becomes easier, until owing to the help of the psychological power of habit (restricting ourselves to purely natural agencies) the irascible disposition gives way to one of patience and gentleness. The inspired writer truly says that a man who conquers himself is greater than one who takes a city, and assuredly the saints who have conquered themselves are the most heroic and splendid types of humanity. No matter, therefore, how unfavourable environment may be, how powerful certain hereditary tendencies, how serious the want of wise moral education, there is still left in the human soul the mysterious self-originating power of freedom, the exercise of which can correct faults, weaken the power of inherent tendencies, develop the growth of virtues, so that under the influence of Divine grace the light of sanctity will be able to disperse the darkness of vice.

DETERMINISM

The doctrine of free-will is denied by various schools of Determinists.

1. Mechanical Determinism.

The argument adopted by mechanical determinists is based upon the indestructibility of energy. The sum of energy in the Universe is constant, and, as the will is a material force, it is subject to the law of Conservation of Energy.

Answer. (1) The faculty of the will is not material.

(2) The exercise of the will merely changes the kind of energy but does not affect the sum. If one wills to move his arm, there is a change from potential to kinetic energy, but the law of Conservation is untouched.

2. Psychological Determinism.

The chief protagonist of this school was Leibnitz, and he and his followers claim that the will is determined by the strongest motive.

Answer. We can by the exercise of free-will make the weaker become the stronger motive. Some writers (e.g. W. G. Ward in the " Philosophy of Theism ") maintain that the will can act from a motive whilst it remains the weaker. It is sufficient for the vindication of the doctrine of Free-will to know that we can determine the strength of the motive as already explained.

3. Physiological Determinism.

Our course of action, it is objected, is due to temperament.

Answer. That heredity, environment, education, or want of education are largely responsible for the character and action of an individual no psychologist will deny. But there is a power of resistance in the will which can and does rise superior to these untoward influences.

4. Theological Determinism.

Free-will, it is said, is incompatible with the providential arrangements of God and with the Divine prescience.

Answer. To God the future and the past are present, and He has foreseen, or rather He sees, from all eternity the free determinations of the human will. Hence the exercise of free-will is not in conflict with the providence or prescience of God. Even man who exists in time, notes on a fine night the scintillation of α Centauri, of Sirius, and of Arcturus—actions which took place respectively 3, 8, and 200 years ago. And man's capability is but " broken light " as compared with Infinite Wisdom.

III. THE BINDING FORCE OF NATURAL LAW

The natural law, echo in the human soul of the Eternal Law, may be defined as a " Divine Command, manifested by the light of reason, binding us to do good and to avoid evil." As the object of the natural law is to furnish guidance to man so that he may attain his last end, the morality of an action depends upon its influence and power to help us to reach the end for which we have been created.

The distinction between good and evil is essential and objective. It cannot be explained as springing from the pleasure or pain which an action entails, nor from the utility which results from an action, nor can it be based upon convention ; the distinction is absolute and universal.

That the Natural Law exists is proved by :

1. Conscience which witnesses to the essential distinction between good and evil.

2. The testimony of mankind.

Races, in accordance with the degree of civilisation to which they have attained, differ in regard to what is right and wrong, but all recognise the essential difference between the two ideas of good and evil.

(*a*) There is universal agreement regarding the truth and the binding force of the first principles of the moral law, such as :

Good should be done.

Evil should be avoided.

The Deity should be worshipped.

Benefactors should be honoured.

Do not to others what you wish not done to yourself.

(*b*) Regarding the precepts which flow directly and immediately from the first principles, e.g. the Commandments of God (excepting the determination of the Sabbath) there cannot be for any length of time invincible ignorance.

(*c*) With reference to the precepts, which are derived remotely and mediately by study and thought from the primary principles, there may be and are differences of opinion. Hence the necessity of a sound and safe system of moral teaching, the possession of which is one of the glories of the Catholic Church.

A necessary condition of the binding force of a law is its due promulgation. The Natural Law is promulgated through human reason. As soon as a child comes to the years of discretion he or she by the natural light of reason sees the distinction between things good and bad, but, of course, at that

early stage the power of discernment, radically present, needs instruction and guidance. The sanctions of the Natural Law are :
(1) interior sanction—praise or blame of conscience.
(2) natural sanction—health or sickness.
(3) public sanction—esteem or contempt of man.
(4) legal sanction—recompense or penalty established by positive law.

But it is clear that these sanctions are not sufficient. A hardened criminal, for example, has no remorse of conscience, and may escape the penalty of the law. Without the sanction which is based upon a future life of eternal recompense or eternal expiation, the sanctions enumerated are not sufficiently strong to help man so that he may withstand the power of passion and practise virtue.

Independent Morality

Independent Morality or Morality without God is :
1. An error, because,
    (*a*) morality has a necessary relation to man's last end which is God, and,
    (*b*) the obligatory character of morality is based upon the Divine Will.
2. A disaster.

It has been shown again and again in the histories of individuals and of nations that morality divorced from religion has no binding force.

CHAPTER IX

ORIGIN AND DESTINY OF MAN

No one denies that between the soul and body of man there is union. Is the union accidental like the union of rider and steed, or is it an essential, substantial union by virtue of which soul and body, two incomplete substances, are so intimately associated as to form one complete substance?

The substantial union of body and soul is proved:

1. From the testimony of consciousness.

Each one is conscious of the fact that it is the same ultimate principle which thinks, feels and is affected by vegetative needs. The sensitive and vegetative faculties are material, and the faculty of reason is immaterial. Hence the unity of consciousness and diversity of faculties can only be explained by the existence of one and the same ultimate principle compounded of spiritual soul and matter in which the faculties material and immaterial inhere.

2. This truth is confirmed by the common relationship of the faculties. Vegetative, sensitive and rational powers conspire together to attain the well-being and due development of the individual.

Man is made up of body and soul. Enquiry should be made into the origin of each. The theory of the evolution of the human body from a lower form has been already considered. Here it will be useful to give a résumé of the present state of knowledge in regard to prehistoric man.

I. THE OLDEST HUMAN RELICS

Sir Arthur J. Evans, in his address as President of the British Association delivered at Newcastle-on-Tyne in

September, 1916, alluded to the labours of a band of brilliant archæologists, aided by geologists and palæontologists, whereby such a striking mass of materials regarding prehistoric times had been brought together as to place on a higher level the evolution of human art and appliances during the Quaternary Period. Some years ago a résumé of data then known bearing upon the antiquity of man and the nature of his appliances appeared in the " Irish Theological Quarterly." But research has been steadily at work during the intervening years, so that now a chart of Post-Tertiary times may be presented, with an assurance that it is fairly accurate. The chart given below has been constructed from information derived from various sources British and foreign. The reader will notice that the first column furnishes the names of the epochs, the English titles being for the most part chosen. But the foreign nomenclature, in some cases added, is necessary for purposes of comparison and identification. The second column sets out the cultures of the Pleistocene period in chronological order, the typical fauna are added in a third column, whilst the " notes " record salient geographical and climatic conditions. Of supreme interest to the student of Theology are the human remains which the zeal and perseverance of anthropologists have uncovered. And as we study the characteristics of prehistoric men beginning with Neolithic times and going backwards to the oldest Pleistocene cultures, we shall have an opportunity of forming an opinion as to the probable truth or falsehood of the once popular view that man has been evolved from an ape-like ancestor.

The duration of the Neolithic period, as indeed of all geological periods, cannot be even approximately estimated. Let us suppose that Neolithic times came to an end about 2000 B.C. But when did they begin? Did they extend to 10,000 B.C., or even further back? Frankly we cannot say. But we have most fortunately in the case of the find at Tilbury in 1883 human remains which can be certainly ascribed to the Neolithic period. A trench was cut across the marshland at Tilbury 40 feet deep with the object of form-

EPOCH	CULTURE	TYPICAL FAUNA	NOTES
Present	Iron	Existing Forms	
Recent	Bronze	" "	
6th Glacial: Upper Turbarian	Neolithic	" "	Human remains at Oban: Kitchen-middens of North-West Europe. Slight elevation of land.
5th Interglacial: Upper Forestian	Neolithic	" "	British Isles separated from Continent: Kitchen-middens of North-West Europe.
5th Glacial: Lower Turbarian	Neolithic	" "	British Isles united to Continent.
4th Interglacial: Lower Forestian	Azilian	Stag (Cervus elaphus)	Sea 130 feet above present level. Beautiful engraving, sculpture, and animal painting.
4th Glacial: Mechlenburgian: Würmian	Magdalenian	Reindeer	Willow leaf implements.
	Solutrean	Reindeer	Implements of bone: drawings at Altamira.
	Aurignacian	Reindeer	Not so warm as 2nd interglacial period.
3rd Interglacial: Dürntenian	Mousterian	Mammoth	
3rd Glacial: Rissian	Mousterian	Rhinoceros tichorinus	Britain not part of Continent: Ice sheet to English Midlands only.
2nd Interglacial: Tyrolian	Acheulean	Mammoth & R. tichorinus	Surface lowered between 50 and 100 feet. English Channel and North Sea dry land; land bridges across Mediterranean; river drift implements belong to this period; warmest and most protracted interglacial period.
	Chellean	Hippopotamus, R. Mercki & Elephas intiquus	
	Strepyan		Implements of the type which M. Rutot discovered at Strepy (Belgium).
	Mesvinian		Implements obtained by M. Rutot in Belgium.
2nd Glacial: Mindelian: Saxonian	Maffian	Mammoth, R. tichorinus	British Isles not joined to Continent: epoch of maximum glaciation. Ice sheet down to Thames Valley; lowering of temperature of not less than 20°.
1st Interglacial: Norfolkian	Mafflian	Elephas meridionalis, E. antiquus, Hippopotamus	Britain joined to Continent: human mandible found in sand beds of Mauer: Piltdown skull perhaps of same date.
1st Glacial: Günzian: Scanian	Reutelian		According to M. Rutot the first and oldest Pleistocene cultures.

ing a dock. The Neolithic valley-bottom was met with at a depth of 32 feet, and 3 feet beneath the surface of the valley was found the skeleton of the "Tilbury man." A minute examination of the skull revealed the fact that it was of the "river-bed" type, in no respect different from the modern European, and that the cranial capacity (1500 cubic centimetres) was slightly above the modern European (male) average of 1450 c.c.

In passing from Neolithic to Palæolithic times, I should like to emphasise a fact first of all which is of interest from the Catholic point of view. Just recently I have had the opportunity of paying a visit to Kent's Cavern at Torquay. It was there that nearly 100 years ago the first glimpse was obtained of Palæolithic times, and the fortunate individual who by his patient labour discovered the association of man with that remote age was the Reverend Father McEnery, at that time chaplain at Tor Abbey. From 1825 to 1828 he worked the cavern at his own expense, and finally induced the Natural History Society at Torquay to give their attention to the matter. Subsequently the British Association provided funds for its thorough investigation.

Another circumstance in connection with the passage from the New to the Old Stone Age is of great interest. Geologists speak of a "hiatus"—a break in the continuity of human occupation at the end of Palæolithic times. And it is very doubtful whether the discoveries at Mas d'Azil in the Pyrenees —known as the Azilian culture—bridge over the hiatus long recognised. It has occurred to me, and I throw out the suggestion for what it is worth, that the termination of the 4th glacial period (known also as the "Mechlenburgian" and the "Würmian") synchronised with the Deluge, or rather was (under Divine Providence) the chief contributory cause of that event. The breaking up of vast sheets of ice in Europe and Asia as well as in North America, the atmospheric disturbance occasioned, the opening of "the floodgates of Heaven," the swollen state of the great rivers, the fact that the sea rose 130 feet above its present level—these circumstances point to the catastrophe recorded in Genesis whereby "all flesh was destroyed." It would seem as if we had independent scientific testimony to the effects of the Deluge in the non-continuity of human occupation at this period. An allusion has just been made to the Azilian culture. It is interesting to know that in this culture M. Piette found rounded pebbles marked with coloured hieroglyphics, which seem to be the letters of a script. If so, its antiquity is far greater than that of the Egyptian writing or the cuneiform inscriptions of Babylon. Sargon is modern in comparison! But there does not seem much chance of finding the key which would unlock and reveal the meaning of these mysterious symbols, and thus unfold the views and sentiments of the men of those far distant times.

The closing stages of the Palæolithic period—the Magdalenian, Solutrean, Aurignacian—constitute what is known as the Reindeer Age. As the Reindeer Age synchronised with the 4th glacial period (indeed the relation was that of effect to cause) men were driven to live in caves where shelter might be found from the severity of the weather. And in these caves evidences still remain of the wonderful artistic excellence to which the cave-men had attained. Many specimens of sculpture, of drawing and even of painting, which have survived on the walls and roofs, show a life-like realism that cannot be excelled. We turn with the deepest interest from the artistic work to the artists themselves, and fortunately the human remains are sufficiently abundant to enable us to form some idea of their intellectual calibre. Without professing to give an exhaustive enumeration, the following are the chief finds arranged in the chronological order of their discovery.

Later Pleistocene Period

(1) 1833. At Engis on the Meuse a skull was found by Dr. Schmerling. The culture was Aurignacian. Just as the honour of discovering the Palæolithic Age, and man's association therewith, belongs to Father McEnery, so the honour of finding the first relics of Palæolithic man belongs to Dr. Schmerling.

(2) 1868. At Cromagnon, near Les Eyzies in the Vésère valley (Dordogne), M. Louis Lartet uncovered four skeletons evidently Aurignacian, but not of the river-bed type. They were tall men about 6 feet in height with a cranial capacity of over 1600 cubic centimetres—a capacity notably above that of the modern European. Thus the Cromagnon type does not support evolution in an upward direction, but points rather to a subsequent degenerate tendency.

(3) 1878. Professor Rolleston described the skeletons of two individuals found at Cissbury (Sussex). In his opinion they were Aurignacian.

(4) 1891. At Brünn, the capital of Moravia, a skull was uncovered—a variant of the Cromagnon type.

(5) 1895. The caves at Grimaldi, near Mentone, are well known. Remains of about 16 individuals were disinterred there. The Prince of Monaco formed a committee of investigation, consisting of Canon Villeneuve as historian, M. Cartailhac as judge of the articles of culture, Professor Boule as geologist, and Dr. Verneau as anthropologist. As the result of an investigation extending from 1906 to 1911, two magnificent volumes have been published. The human remains were identified as of the Cromagnon type, and of a second type negroid in character. As the Bushmen in the Kalahari desert make the nearest approach in their art and in other characteristics (e.g. steatopygy) to the representatives of the Aurignacian Age, it is not an unlikely hypothesis that the Negroid Aurignacians, driven out of Europe and forced southwards, were the progenitors of the Bushmen.

(6 and 7). 1899 and 1902. Aurignacian types were disinterred at Trenton and Lansing in the United States. In glacial periods ingress to the North American Continent was possible by Behring Strait and the Aleutian islands.

(8) 1903. The skull of Langwith cave (Derbyshire).

(9) 1903. The skeleton of Cheddar cave (Somerset). Magdalenian.

(10) 1909. Discovery at Combe Capelle (Dordogne). A skeleton of the Aurignacian type, found at the junction of Aurignacian and Mousterian cultures.

(11) The uncovering of the Halling (Kent) skeleton brings the list of the later Pleistocene relics of Ancient Hunters to a close. Thus, as far as our present information goes, the Reindeer period was peopled by men of three types: (1) Cromagnon; (2) Brünn (a variant of the former); and (3) Riverbed (e.g. the Engis skull). The cranial capacities were, as a rule, equal to or above the modern average, and what has been said of the English Aurignacian—the Halling man—may be applied to all the representatives of this period; " there is not a single feature of the skull which one can say is primitive or ape-like."

Mid-Pleistocene Period

It cannot be said that the men of the Mousterian Age (Mid-Pleistocene) had not a single ape-like feature. Whilst in certain respects this striking and startling type approached the simian, in other respects it was widely different. The chief anatomical peculiarities were:

(1) Platycephalism, suggesting a likeness to the gorilla and chimpanzee.

(2) The supra-orbital torus—a projecting bony ridge extending across the forehead over the eyes.

On the other hand, the teeth and palate were widely different from the simian type, and the cranial capacity in the case of the La Chapelle-aux-Saints skull was 1600 c.c., although the man's height did not exceed 5 feet 4 inches.

But how account for the extraordinary fact that during Mousterian times Europe from Gibraltar to Weimar, from Croatia to Jersey, was populated by this very distinctive race? Whence came they? Why did they disappear? And the mystery is still further increased if we appreciate the fact (to be detailed later) that in Pre-Mousterian days the predominant type was not " Neanderthal " (the technical name of Mousterian man), but the " river-bed " type, differing little, if at all, from the modern European. Professor Huxley maintained that Neanderthal man was only an extreme variant of modern man, notwithstanding the low retreating forehead, the enormous brow ridges, the large round eye-orbits, the massive jaws, the feebly developed chin. Another opinion in opposition to that of Huxley is in favour at the present time, viz. that "homo neanderthalensis" is specifically distinct from modern man.

For the convenience of the reader, a list of the chief Neanderthal relics is appended :

(1) 1848. The Gibraltar skull—but it was not till 1901 that Dr. Gustav Schwalbe established the separate identity of the Neanderthal race.

(2) 1857. Discovery of a skeleton in the Neanderthal cave near Düsseldorf. Hence the name of the type.

(3) 1866. Mandible of Neanderthal woman found at Naulette, in the valley of the Lesse (Belgium).

(4) 1886. Skeletons of two men uncovered at Spy, eight miles east of Namur. The culture was early Aurignacian.

(5) 1899-1906. Remains of about ten individuals, of all ages and both sexes, were disinterred at Krapina and identified as Neanderthal by Professor Kramberger.

(6) 1907. The Heidelberg mandible was found at Mauer, 10 miles south-east of Heidelberg, by Dr. Schœtensack. The interest of this relic centres round the claim of M. Rutot that the Heidelberg mandible goes back to the dawn of the Pleistocene era, and belongs to the culture which he has named Mafflian.

The diagrammatic illustration on the opposite page will make clear the reasons upon which the conclusion of M. Rutot rests.

The mandible discovered at A' was covered by a series of deposits amounting to 78 feet. In the deposits over the mandible Dr. Schœtensack recognised 24 different strata. They fall into three series (1) Recent loess (D) the debris of the Würmian (4th glacial) ice-age ; (2) Ancient loess (C) the debris of the Rissian (3rd glacial) ice-age ; (3) Mauer sands (B) in which occurs the chalky boulder clay (A) known as the "Glaise moreen," and due, as is supposed, to the floods which marked the close of the Mindelian (2nd glacial) glaciation. Thus the mandible is referred to the 1st interglacial period to a culture called by M. Rutot the "Mafflian."

(7) 1908. It is curious to note how prominently Catholic

clergy have been identified with anthropological discovery. Allusion has already been made to Father McEnery of Tor-

FIG. 1.

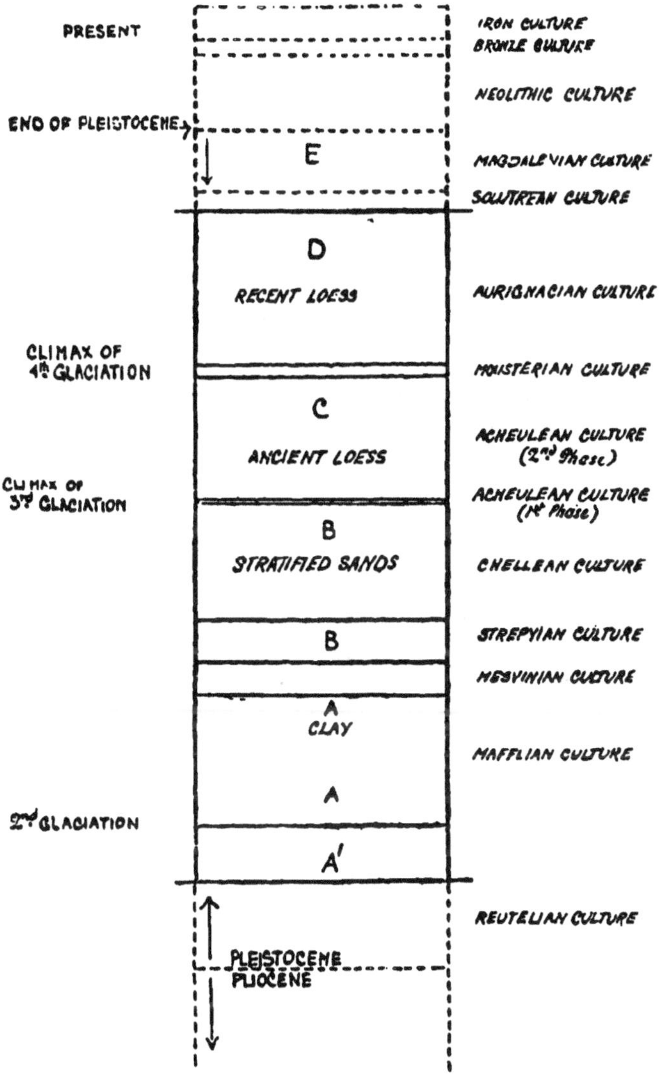

```
PRESENT                                  IRON CULTURE
                                         BRONZE CULTURE

                                         NEOLITHIC CULTURE
END OF PLEISTOCENE
                        E                MAGDALENIAN CULTURE
                                         SOLUTREAN CULTURE

                        D
                    RECENT LOESS         AURIGNACIAN CULTURE

CLIMAX OF                                MOUSTERIAN CULTURE
4th GLACIATION
                        C                ACHEULEAN CULTURE
                    ANCIENT LOESS          (2nd Phase)
CLIMAX OF                                ACHEULEAN CULTURE
3rd GLACIATION                             (1st Phase)
                        B
                   STRATIFIED SANDS      CHELLEAN CULTURE

                        B                STREPYIAN CULTURE
                                         MESVINIAN CULTURE
                        A
                       CLAY              MAFFLIAN CULTURE

                        A
2nd GLACIATION
                        A'
                                         REUTELIAN CULTURE
                   PLEISTOCENE
                   PLIOCENE
```

DIAGRAMMATIC SECTION OF THE STRATA OF THE SAND-PIT
AT MAUER.

quay, and the discovery of the La Chapelle-aux-Saints skeleton was due to the labours of the Abbés A. and J.

Bouyssonie and Bardon. One of the most eminent present-day authorities on Prehistoric Man is the well-known Abbé Breuil of the Fribourg University.

(8) At Le Moustier (Dordogne) the skeleton of a boy (Neanderthal) about 16 years of age.

(9 and 10) 1909, 1910. At La Ferassie skeletons (2) were uncovered, and finally

(11) 1911. At La Quina (Charente) Dr. Martin brought to view the skeleton of a Neanderthal woman. The brain capacity was 1350 c.c., and the height 5 feet.

Professor Sollas is responsible for the suggestion that just as the Aurignacians and Solutreans may be the remote ancestors of the Bushmen of South Africa, just as the two types of Magdalenians—the Chancelade and the Cromagnon—may have given rise to the Eskimos and the Red Indians respectively, so the Neanderthal race of Mousterian times may have been the progenitors of the aboriginal Australians.

Early Pleistocene Period

The most recent discoveries of human relics has revealed an extraordinary fact—already alluded to—a fact which does not seem in accord with Darwinian Evolution as popularly accepted. The fact is this. Long before Mousterian times, nay even at the beginning of the Pleistocene Age, the type of man predominant in Europe did not differ materially from the modern European. If, as Evolutionists suppose, Pleistocene times began 500,000 years ago, or according to some geologists more than a million years since, surely that enormous stretch of time has afforded sufficient scope to evolutionary agencies for the manifestation of recognisable results. And yet the Dartford skull, which is pre-Chellean, had a cranial capacity of 1470 c.c.,—a capacity notably greater than the modern average.

It is usually said that intellectual power depends (1) on the mass of the brain; (2) on its surface area; and (3) on the number of its association tracts. Dr. R. Gladstone of King's College, London, an expert in regard to cephalometric data bearing upon the relation of the *size and shape* of the head to mental ability, has taken the measurements of 457 students personally known to himself and 88 members of the staff of King's College, London, and the Middlesex Hospital. The students were divided into three classes A, B, and C. Class A comprised medallists, scholarship and prizemen ; Class B students of average intelligence ; and Class C students below average intelligence. Dr. Gladstone writes : " the figures show that there is a small correlation between large size of head and a high degree of intelligence . the more intellectual have both actually and proportionally to the size of their bodies larger heads than the less intellectual."

If, in accordance with this conclusion, pre-Chellean man was more highly endowed than his modern representative, the fact does not fit into the scheme of Darwinian evolution.

Indeed the prepossession in favour of Darwinian evolution has been so great as to prevent students of anthropology from accepting results because they could not be made to square with preconceived theory. Surely an unscientific attitude.

The human remains assigned to pre-Mousterian days are given in the chronological order of their discovery.

(1) 1863. The Moulin Quignon mandible of the Somme Valley was uncovered by Boucher de Perthes from the lower gravels of a pit. The culture was Acheulean. The genuineness of this relic was long questioned because, according to evolutionary principles, a human relic older than the Mousterian Age ought to be more primitive than the Mousterian type.

(2) 1863. The skull found at Olmo (Arezzo) by Signor Cocchi is assigned to the Chellean Age, but in this case there is some doubt as to its genuineness.

(3) 1868. At Clichy, M. Eugène Bertrand found a skeleton which belongs to the Chellean Age.

(4) 1882. The fragment of skull found at Bury St. Edmunds by Mr. Henry Prigg is referred to the Acheulean period.

(5) 1888. The Galley-Hill (London) skeleton is Chellean.

(6) 1902. The Dartford skull is presumably Acheulean.

(7) 1911. The Ipswich skeleton is probably Mesvinian.

(8) 1912. The Piltdown (Sussex) skull found by Mr. Charles Dawson belongs probably to early Pleistocene times. Though there is no identification of the Mafflian culture in Sussex, yet we cannot be far wrong in classing (from the time-standpoint) the Piltdown skull with the Heidelberg mandible, and regarding both as the oldest human relics hitherto discovered. A second skull more recently discovered by Mr. Dawson at the same spot raises the question to which skull belongs the mandible of somewhat simian type found close by, and invalidates the assumption that the original skull and mandible constitute the " missing link," to which the high-sounding title of " Eoanthropus Dawsoni " has been given. Professor Keith's reconstruction of the skull gives a cranial capacity of 1500 c.c., which points to present-day mental powers rather than the less developed brain of the " missing link." Moreover, if Keith's cautious judgment be true that the Piltdown remains are those of a woman, it is absurd to regard such a well-marked development as belonging to a lower type. In the original reconstruction of the pieces of the skull by Mr. Woodward, it was claimed as evidence of its primitive state that the articulation of the skull to the backbone was so close as to preclude the possibility of speech, but Professor Keith pointed out that if " Eoanthropus Dawsoni," as thus reconstructed, could not speak, neither could he eat nor breathe.

I reproduce on the opposite page with Dr. Keith's permission and that of his publishers a portion of an illustration which attempts to indicate the genealogical tree of man's ancestry. Needless to say it is confessedly hypothetical. But if hypothetical from the evolutionary standpoint, it is useful as affording a résumé of some of the salient facts dwelt upon in this chapter.

The reader will note that the origin of the Neanderthal type is ascribed to a branching from the " human stem " during Pliocene times. The oldest Neanderthal relic is of course the Heidelberg mandible, and the spread of the race is proved by the many specimens of the Mousterian period. " Eoanthropus Dawsoni " (doubts and difficulties notwithstanding) is referred back for its origin as a distinct type to a branching at the same period. Of the varieties " Homo sapiens," African, Australian, Mongolian, European—no relics have been found as yet either of the Australian or of the Mongolian, and only one of the African variety at Oldoway (German East Africa) by Dr. Hans Reck in 1914—a human

Fig. 2.

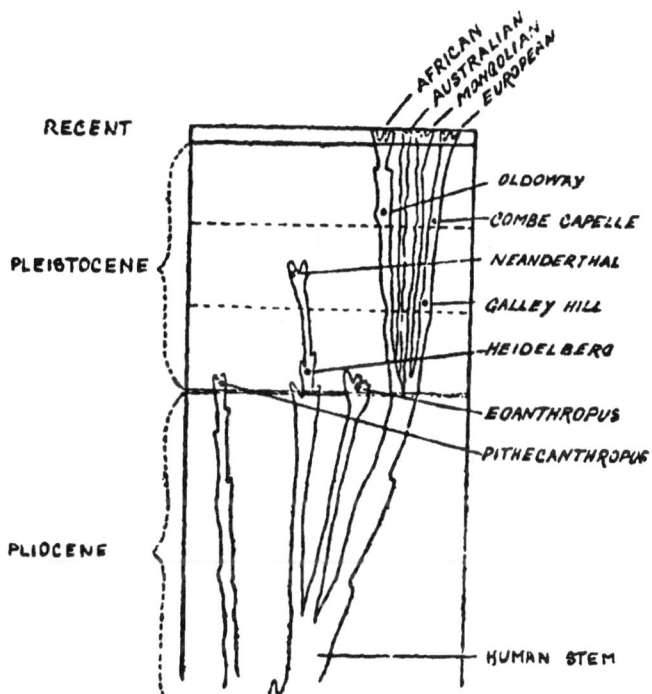

Pleistocene Human Relics.

skeleton with negro characters. Of the European variety, on the other hand, we have remains from early Pleistocene to the Neolithic Age—from the Galley-Hill specimen representing the earlier phase to that of the Combe Capelle at the dawn of the Reindeer period and onward to the Tilbury man of the New Stone culture. But there is no indication of the supposed evolutionary advancement. Regarding the geological periods antecedent to the Quaternary and the supposed "eoliths," Abbé Breuil's judgment is emphatic: "not a trace of unquestionable evidence of man's existence has been found in strata admittedly older than the Pleistocene." Even "Pithecanthropus erectus," whether ape-like man or man-like ape, is undoubtedly to be classed as Quaternary. The important question arises: are we free to accept the great antiquity of the Human race which some geologists claim? Professor Sollas, for instance, argues that the deposits laid down during the Pleistocene period would, if superimposed, reach a thickness of 4000 feet. Allowing that one foot a century has been the rate of growth, we have 400,000 years for the age of the Pleistocene period, and consequently for the antiquity of man. M. Rutot's estimate is only 140,000 years. Professor Penck claims anything between 500,000 and 1,500,000 years. Dr. Frederick Wright, on the other hand, influenced by Sir G. Darwin's mathematical treatment of Astronomy, and his conclusion that the birth of the moon took place between 50 and 100 million years ago, maintains that the whole of the Post-Tertiary period up to the present time is not of longer duration than 30,000 years.

How stands the case from the standpoint of the Catholic Theologian?

It has long been recognised that the genealogical tables of the ancestry of Our Lord have been compressed. Hence there is no difficulty in assuming that the ante-diluvian and ante-Abrahamic lists have been similarly shortened. The Hebrew words "to bear" and "to beget" are used in the Old Testament in a wide sense without necessarily indicating immediate offspring. "Enos lived 90 years and begot Cainan." The meaning can be that when Enos was 90 years old he begot one from whom Cainan sprang. Again it is clear that long periods of time are passed over without any attempt being made to give even a summary of events. The years of exile in Egypt (430) are silently included between some incidents at the beginning and at the end. All these circumstances point truth that the Scriptures furnish no data for a chrono-computation prior to the time of Abraham. There is iculty therefore from the Catholic standpoint in accepting a great antiquity for man. But in fairness it should be pointed out that the hundreds of thousands of years claimed by Sollas, Penck, and Geikie are based upon an unproved and unlikely assumption, viz. that geological changes have taken place in the slow and uniform way with which *we* are familiar; whereas a glance at the Chart of the Glacial period given above shows that mighty catastrophic agencies were then at work. We note successive glacial and interglacial periods, successive elevations and depressions of land and sea, revolutions of fauna and flora. May not the epoch-making forces which produced these results have been much more active and effective than in our quiescent days? Surely the uncertainty of the data of time-calculation shows itself in the divergent estimates formed. And in view of this hopeless divergence, our answer to the question how long has man inhabited the earth shall be given in the words of the well-known couplet:

> I cannot tell, I do not know,
> But 'twas a long long time ago!

II. Origin of the Soul

The human soul is contingent and consequently owes its existence to an external cause. Its existence is due to the creative act of God, because a spiritual substance can be produced only by creation. For the proof of this statement it will suffice to recall the natural relation or proportion that exists between origin and being—the origin of a being is in necessary relationship with its mode of existence. Since the spiritual soul is independent of matter for its existence and action, its origin must have been equally independent of matter. Creation being the technical term which means the production of a substance without pre-existing material, it follows (1) that the soul has been created, and (2) created by God, since the miracle of creation exceeds all finite power. A notable modern theologian holds that the creative act necessary for the production of a human soul is one of the most cogent proofs which testify to the existence of God. From the standpoint of science, it is generally agreed that all human types belong to the same species. "Homo primigenius"[1] is but a variety of "Homo sapiens." May one conclude that unity of origin as well as unity of species is established? No. Many anthropologists allow that the unity of origin is not only possible but likely. They cannot, however, from examination of the data which they possess lay down as certain that the different races past and present derive their origin from a single pair. We owe the knowledge of that truth to Divine Revelation.

III. Destiny of Man

From the spirituality of the soul, which renders it subjectively independent of matter, we may legitimately infer that the soul is naturally immortal. But inasmuch as God could annihilate the soul, the question arises as to the *reality* of the soul's immortal life.

The aptitude of the soul to survive the body is an endowment given to it by God. The infinite wisdom of God precludes the possibility of such an endowment having been given in vain. Moreover, God's sanctity and justice require that a sufficient sanction should be given to the Moral Law. We have seen the insufficiency of the sanctions of time and must infer the reality of a future life, so that the practice of virtue may be duly recompensed, and indulgence in vice suitably punished. In order that the sanction of the Moral Law may be truly and absolutely efficacious, the future life of the soul must be a life without end. Indeed the prospect of annihilation would render the deterrent effect of any sanction inefficacious. Again the desire to live for ever implanted in the soul owes its origin to God who gives to each being the privileges for which its nature essentially craves. From the standpoint of human reason, apart from the light of Divine Faith, we can only conclude that the Moral Law must have an efficacious sanction and that the just will be recompensed and the wicked punished. That God will punish eternally *in a*

[1] Homo primigenius, i.e. the Neanderthal type.

specific way cannot be *proved* by reason though it may be *defended* by reason. The doctrine of eternal punishment of Hell is a revealed truth.

Belief in the pre-existence of souls, and belief in metempsychosis or the reincarnation of the soul in a series of existences are both so utterly opposed to reason and experience that no formal refutation is necessary.

CHAPTER X

RELATIONS BETWEEN GOD AND MAN

I. THE NECESSITY AND UTILITY OF RELIGION FOR THE INDIVIDUAL AND FOR SOCIETY

Religion is the tie which binds man to God—the creature to the Creator.

The derivation of the word "religion" is ascribed by Cicero to "relegere," i.e. to reflect; St. Augustine and Lactantius derive it from "religare," to bind.

The divisions of Religion from one standpoint into dogmatic and moral, and from another standpoint into natural and supernatural need no explanation.

Worship consists in the fulfilment of the duties which man owes to God, and may be exterior, interior, private or public.

A. NECESSITY OF RELIGION FOR THE INDIVIDUAL

1st Proof. God is our Creator, Providence, Legislator, and Judge. Therefore homage, thanks, obedience and virtuous conduct are due to God.

2nd Proof. The world's greatest men have recognised the justice of God's claims, e.g. Plato, Cicero, Augustine, Aquinas, etc. "To be religious," writes Aquinas, "is to give to God that which is His due."

B. UTILITY OF RELIGION FOR THE INDIVIDUAL

Whatever secures for men peace of mind and heart (i.e. happiness) is most useful. But religion secures these benefits, therefore religion is most useful. Proofs must be given of the minor proposition, viz. that religion secures peace of mind and heart.

1st Proof. From Reason.

God alone—Infinite Truth, Infinite Beauty, Infinite Goodness—can satisfy the faculties of the soul, i.e. give them peace and happiness. No earthly good satisfies, because all earthly goods are impermanent. " Inquietum est cor nostrum donec requiescat in Te."

2nd Proof. From Experience.

Experience teaches that Religion alone explains the fundamental problems of our origin and destiny. Without the elucidation of these problems there cannot be peace of mind or heart.

But the objection may be raised that peace of mind and heart can be secured by the study of Science and Philosophy. Indeed Science cannot solve even natural, much less supernatural, mysteries Science does not enlighten us as to origin and destiny. Du Bois-Reymond, than whom there is no greater authority in the domain of Natural Science, has declared in his well-known lecture on "the impassable limits of the experimental sciences" that there are seven enigmas upon which Science has thrown no light. They have been already enumerated. And he further states that of these enigmas the "Nature of matter and force," the "Origin of movement," and the "Origin of sensation and consciousness" are beyond possibility of solution, i.e. are transcendental. M. Duclaud, director of the Pasteur Institute, has spoken emphatic words in regard to those who exaggerate the power of science. "I have never been inclined to say that Science furnishes the solution of social problems. Science has not promised to do so—has in fact promised nothing. And those who accuse Science of having failed to fulfil its promise have confounded science with the vapourings of mountebanks" ("ont pris pour de la science des boniments de tréteaux").

Has the theory of evolution explained man's origin? Has Philosophy thrown any light upon these problems? No clear light. " Pythagoras, Epicurus, Socrates, Plato are but torches ; Christ is the Day " (Victor Hugo).

Honours, Riches, Pleasures of the world do not give peace to the human heart. Religion alone gives peace, puts order into thoughts and affections, reveals the origin of man, his present duty and future destiny. Death to the religious man is but the moment of deliverance ; " la vie de l'âme sincèrement religieuse est une fête continuelle " (Guyot).

> Novembre approche ; assis au coin du feu
> Malade et seul, j'ai songé tout à l'heure
> À cet hiver où je croyais en Dieu—
> Et je pleure. (Paul Bourget.)

C. Necessity of Religion for Society

The association of human beings which is named " Society " is not an arbitrary arrangement, or a " free contract " as Rousseau and Hobbes maintained, but a law of Nature, and therefore the will of God.

Proofs.
1. Men have always lived together.
2. The endowment of human speech presupposes mutual association.
3. Natural sentiments demand this association, e.g. pity, generosity, affection, etc.
4. The needs of men in the physical and moral orders require association: the babe and the old man need assistance.

Hence God is the author of Society, and Society owes to Him homage as to the author of its being.

D. Utility of Religion for Society

1st Proof. The testimony of Philosophers and Legislators.

Plato " The ignorance of the true God is the greatest calamity for states. He who overthrows religion overthrows the foundation of all human society " (" Laws ").

Cicero: "I doubt if trustworthiness, human society, or justice, the first of virtues, could persist if reverence towards God be not maintained" ("De Natura Decorum").

Rousseau: "Never has a state been founded of which religion was not the support" ("Contrat Social").

Hume: "Find a people without religion and be sure that they will differ but little from brutes" ("Natural History of Religion").

Legislators give a like testimony, Minos, Solon, Lycurgus, Numa Pompilius, Mahomet, Franklin, etc.—all regarded Religion as the safeguard of society.

Portalis, one of the greatest lawyers and statesmen, wrote: "When the influence of religion is removed, there will be neither country nor society for mankind."

2nd Proof. In order to secure the well-being of society it is necessary that there should be (1) Reverence for authority; (2) Obedience to the laws; (3) Stability; (4) Just and efficacious laws; (5) Morality.

But without Religion these benefits cannot be secured. Religion, therefore, is most useful—indeed essential—to Society.

The minor proposition is proved thus:

1. Authority implies "right," and right is based upon the eternal law of God.

2. Obedience is the corollary and the correlative of "right." Obedience for God's sake is free and noble submission; obedience without relation to God is servitude.

3. The foundation of stability is respect for authority, but respect cannot operate as a principle of protection unless based upon Religion. Without Religion all agreements and decisions can be cast aside.

4. Laws suppose authority and submission, and both these principles can be based effectively and securely only on the Divine will.

5. No motive, except the Divine will, can secure the observance of the moral law.

(*a*) The motive of "general interest" will not appeal with sufficient strength to subdue passion.

(b) The motive of "honour" is based upon the idea of duty, i.e. of submission to the Divine Will.
(c) The sentiments of Patriotism and Altruism cannot quell the power of passion.
(d) Conscience is unmeaning, unless as the echo of God's eternal law in the human soul.
(e) Private interest, even if its importance is fully realised, fails to control the impulse of passion.

3rd Proof. From History.

"The history of humanity is in truth the history of religion." Max Müller ("Essays," Vol. I).

"The one absorbing theme of universal history is the conflict of incredulity and faith." Goethe ("West-östlicher Divan").

Objection. Catholic are not so prosperous as non-Catholic countries.

Answer. It is necessary in the first place to emphasise the truth of some general principles.

1. The true well-being of a country does not consist in its material prosperity alone. The claims of morality must be considered.
2. The direct aim of Religion is not to secure material prosperity. But Religion helps indirectly, because of its influence upon the character of the citizens. Material prosperity depends largely upon geographical position, nature of soil, etc. Compare the Swiss cantons of Le Valais and Thun. Le Valais, mountainous and barren, is Catholic; Thun, a rich pasture land, is non-Catholic. On the other hand, Rhenish Prussia (Catholic) is much more prosperous than Eastern Prussia (non-Catholic).
3. Many so-called non-Catholic nations are not wholly so. One-third of the inhabitants of those countries which constituted the German Empire are Catholic. Many so-called Catholic nations are falsely named Catholic. Only five millions of the thirty odd millions of France are even nominally Catholic.
4. When Spain, Austria, and France dominated the world

they were really Catholic. But their declension in political importance has gone on *pari passu* with their declension in Religion. " Les grandeurs ou les chutes des nations sont à la mesure de leur religion " (Felix, " Le progrès par le Christianisme ").

Having emphasised these principles, we proceed to answer the objection :

I. Let us grant for a moment that Catholic nations are decadent.

(a) Is the decadence due to Catholicism ? Is the superiority of non-Catholic nations and the inferiority of Catholic nations a constant factor ?

(b) It is impossible to find any Catholic Doctrine or disciplinary rule which interferes with temporal prosperity. The fundamental principle of Catholicism (reverence for authority) is a principle which protects religion and opposes social disruption.

(c) History proves that for centuries Spain, Austria, and France were devotedly Catholic, and brilliantly prosperous ; that Sweden, Norway, and Denmark have been and are non-Catholic and *not* prosperous. For two hundred years after the Reformation Germany was stagnant agriculturally, industrially, and commercially. Singularly great was the commercial prosperity of the Hanseatic League and the wealth and influence of Venice.

II. But the superiority of non-Catholic nations does not exist.

(a) Compare Belgium (as it was) with Holland from an economical point of view.

(b) From the moral point of view the natural tendency to corruption finds a powerful antidote in the Catholic Sacramental System.

(c) From the social point of view, there have been more true liberty and real prosperity in Catholic than in non-Catholic countries. Recall the history of La Vendée, Brittany, Belgium, Westphalia, Tyrol, Bavaria, Silesia and Austria.

II. THE NECESSITY AND UTILITY OF WORSHIP

Inasmuch as man is dependent on God for the needs of soul and body, he is bound to give to God (1) the homage of his soul, i.e. interior worship; (2) the homage of his body, i.e. exterior worship; and (3) the homage of his social relations, which constitutes social worship.

A. INTERIOR WORSHIP

It is obvious that the homage of mind and heart is the essence of worship. God should be worshipped in spirit and in truth (John iv. 24), and external worship without the interior homage would be a base hypocrisy. It would be a lip-worship, the heart being far away (Matt. xv. 8). Moreover, in itself, interior worship is most salutary, as it raises the mind and heart to God so as to recognise His majesty, power, justice, and goodness, and furnishes man with the strongest motives to do good and to avoid evil.

B. EXTERIOR WORSHIP

Owing to the substantial union of soul and body, it is natural that man should express outwardly the interior sentiments of mind and heart. The child who loves his parents manifests outwardly the affection which he feels. A sympathetic man shows by his words and actions the genuineness and depth of the compassion aroused by the sight of sorrow and suffering. Moreover, the external act supports the interior sentiment. To clothe our ideas in words gives a precision and emphasis to the idea which previously was vague and indeterminate. The student realises how much his geometrical or algebraical reasoning is helped by the use of diagrams and symbols. And if a respectful posture of body, if pictures, if statues, in a word, all the external instruments of piety, be neglected, piety itself will quickly languish and disappear.

It is clear that the duty of external worship may be performed in private or in public. As man naturally tends to communicate his sentiments to his fellow-man, the performance of exterior worship privately does not satisfy human aspirations. Again, if each member of society ought to contribute to the well-being of the whole, and if the well-being of society is measured by the extent and genuineness of religious practice, each one should, by his own example, i.e. by exterior acts of worship, help the cause of Religion.

C. Social Worship

As society is dependent on God, the duty of social worship follows. Again, public worship unites round the altar the king and his subjects, the noble and the peasant, the rich and the poor, and the effect upon the individual makes for encouragement and perseverance. The well-being of society depends upon the well-being of the individual. Hence the duty of public worship is emphasised by its utility.

But is not the prayer of petition, public or private, mental or vocal (*a*) an injury to God and to man, implying as it does that God has not sufficiently provided for the creature, that man is not content with God's arrangements?

Even from the standpoint of reason, it is to be expected that God should make the giving of His benefits conditional upon our asking and our rendering thanks, else we should forget our dependence on Him. From the standpoint of Revelation, the doctrine of elevation to the supernatural order and the subsequent fall explains the urgency of human needs for which God is not responsible, and explains also that the prayer of petition does not convict the suppliant of cupidity.

(*b*) Is not the prayer of petition inefficacious because God's decrees are unchangeable?

The eternal decrees of God have been made with the prescience of future events. It may well happen that God has decreed an event from all eternity because of the prayer of petition which He foresaw.

But finally (*c*) is not the prayer of petition presumptuous? Is it not equivalent to asking God to work miracles?

Monsabré defines prayer as a " moral force eternally predestined to concur with a physical cause which produces naturally its effect." We do not then pray to God to perform miracles, but even if the creature should ask of the Creator His miraculous interposition the petition would be, from every point of view, reasonable and commendable. God is omnipotent. God is Father of His creatures and loves them with infinite tenderness. He has performed miracles in the past, being touched by human grief, and why not therefore make appeal to the Divine compassion in these days of urgent need ? The dignity of the father is not compromised by the request of his child, and our Heavenly Father has encouraged His children to pray : " Ask and you shall receive ; seek and you shall find ; knock and it shall be opened unto you."

CHAPTER XI

RELIGION FROM THE STANDPOINT OF HISTORY

IN physical science the method of discovery involves a threefold process: (1) enumeration of instances, i.e. an accurate and really representative collection of facts bearing upon the subject under review; (2) the collation of these facts, and the determination of the hypothesis which they seem to support; (3) the testing of the hypothesis formed. It has been suggested by Count Goblet d'Alviella of Brussels that the study of the science of Religion may be conveniently divided into: (1) "Hierography," the aim of which would be to secure an accurate account of various religious beliefs; (2) "Hierology," an attempt to explain how the different forms have developed; and (3) "Hierosophy," an appraisement of values. In the present chapter we shall be content with noting very briefly the more important manifestations of religious belief, and the results which a careful examination and comparison suggest.

I. FROM EAST TO WEST

(a) China and Japan.

"There is something true and divinely revealed in every religion, overloaded as it may be and, at times, even stifled by the impieties which the corrupt will and understanding of men have incorporated with it." Such was the judgment of Cardinal Newman, and the history of Eastern religions bears witness to the accuracy of his opinion. From a study of the religious history of China, one principle seems to emerge—the more remote the period, the purer becomes the religious belief, and indications are not wanting that hundreds of years before the advent of the Chou dynasty (which lasted roughly from 1100 to 300 B.C.) the Chinese were in a broad sense monotheists, offered sacrifices to the Supreme Being, and believed in the immortality of the soul. References to the Supreme Being are numerous both in the Shu King (book of historical documents) and in the Shi King (ancient poems). Subsequently corruption grew apace—astrology, fetishism, metempsychosis, etc.

K'ung Fu-tze, known in latinised form as Confucius, lived from 550 to 478 B.C. His teaching was purely secularist—the service of mankind. He encouraged the cultivation of such domestic and social virtues as loyalty, kindness, and the sacred ties of family interest. Amongst his aphorisms occur the two following, the first of which is one of the primary precepts of the moral law and the second enunciates an educational truth of the deepest import " What you do not like when done to yourself do not do to others." " Learning undigested by thought is labour lost ; thought unassisted by learning is perilous." Confucius wrote a preface to the Shu King, and a book of philosophical speculation " Ch'un Ch'iu," i.e. Spring and Autumn.

It is said that Lao-tsze (the words mean " Venerable Philosopher "), who was born 604 B.C., met Confucius in the year 517 B.C. Lao-tsze's composition—the Tâo-Teh-King, in size about half the gospel of St. Mark, witnesses to belief in a Supreme Ruler. His moral system is elevated, inculcating simplicity, humility, self-abnegation, and rising even to the idea of recompensing injury with kindness. His book was translated in 1842 by M. Stanislas Julien, under the title " Le livre de la voie et de la vertu "—a literal rendering of the words of Tâo-Teh-King.

Taoism degenerated later, and it seems unfair to regard Lao-tsze as the founder of corrupt and superstitious belief.

In A.D. 65 Buddhism was introduced into China, and inasmuch as Buddhism emphasises the binding force of certain precepts of the Natural law its influence was beneficial, though its indifference to dogmatic truth led later to the spread of Taoism, Mazdeism, Mohammedanism, etc. The Neo-Confucianism of which Chu-hsi (A.D. 1200) was the chief leader degenerated into a lower form of Pantheism.

The earliest type of Japanese religious belief is known as Shintoism and lasted till A.D. 600. It was a form of nature-worship blended with the worship of ancestors. About the beginning of the seventh century of our era Buddhism was introduced, and spread rapidly. There are now several sects of Buddhism. Since the beginning of the eighteenth century there has been a revival of Shinto worship. The extraordinary way in which the Japanese have assimilated the culture and ideals of western civilization makes it unlikely that certain tenets of the Shinto faith will be revived, as for example the divine origin of the Mikado.

(b) India. Brahmanism and Buddhism.

The sanskrit word Brahmā (neuter) means Supreme Cause. Brahmā (masculine) indicates the first of three hypostases of the Trinity, Brahma, Vishnu, and Siva, the creator, preserver, and destroyer respectively. The Veda literature containing the earliest religious aspirations of the Indian Aryan race dates back more than 1000 years B.C. It is thus the oldest and most authoritative document of Brahmanism. The collection (Samhita) consists of (1) the Rig Veda, i.e. Veda of hymns; (2) Samaveda, i.e. the Veda of chants; (3) Yagur-veda of prayers; and (4) Atharva-veda referring to the priestly family of Atharvans. The word "Veda" means knowledge, and each veda has its corresponding Brahmana or books of ritualistic precepts. The Upanishads were treatises on metaphysical subjects often inclining to mysticism, as in the famous precept "Know thyself," which is interpreted to mean "find thyself in the Eternal Being who underlies the world"—an interpretation recalling the well-known poem of St. Theresa. The Sutras—treatises on religious topics—appeared from 800 to 500 B.C., and Brahmanistic philosophy assumed the pantheistic tendency visible in the Vedanta. Puranic Brahmanism—so called from the 18 Puranas, the oldest not antedating the fourth century of our era—developed a large and by no means attractive company of gods and goddesses, and prevails throughout India to-day. The two epic poems: (1) the Mahabharata, which chronicles the contests of two families, the Kauravas and Pandavas, ending in the victory of the latter; and (2) the Ramayana, which describes Rama, an incarnation of Vishnu, belong to a later period than that of the Vedas.

The early Brahmanical religion was a species of nature-worship, but often there are indications that behind natural phenomena a living presence—a Supreme Being—was recognised. And many outpourings of the Vedic hymns have the ring of monotheistic fervour. About 550 B.C. Gotama, son of the Raja of Sakyas (an Aryan tribe), was born. Hence his name Sakya-mouni, the Sakya sage. Having spent six years in the desert meditating in solitude, he became "Buddha," i.e. enlightened. There is no dogmatic teaching in Buddhism, not even in regard to the existence of the Supreme Being, but its ethical and spiritual teaching is not unlike that of Christianity. The chief precept inculcated was the elimination from the spirit of all desire, and the acquisition of calmness and content which constitute Buddhist sanctity—"Arahatship"—a species of Nirvana-on-earth. The reward of sanctity was the absorption after death of Karma (i.e. character) into the Nirvana as a drop of water is lost in the great ocean. Such is the Buddhist ideal of the "peace which surpasseth understanding." It is interesting to note that the Buddhist commandments against theft, lying, murder, adultery and alcohol show that in all ages human reason attains to the knowledge of the Natural Law.

The conversion of Asoka, king of Magadha, the Constantine of Buddhism, is mentioned as one of the causes which favoured the spread of the cult. This event took place 250 B.C. Much later still Buddhism developed in China and Japan.

The chief characteristics of Buddhist doctrine are:
1. Transmigration of Souls.
2. Human existence a curse.
3. Four sublime truths:
    (a) pain exists.
    (b) pain due to desire.

(c) pain ended by Nirvana.
(d) Way to Nirvana.
4. Cenobite and Celibate life, the practice of confession of sin, the invocation of saints are points in harmony with Catholic practice, but the resemblance does not mean more than the parallel development and independent evolution of the ascetic ideal.
5. The characteristic virtue of Buddhism is charity—a fact which no doubt helps to explain its propagation.

The three Pāli Pitakas (triple basket), which contain authoritative Buddhist doctrine, received their present form about the beginning of the Christian era, but were not reduced to writing for two or three centuries afterwards. Three treatises are included

1. Sutras, discourses for the laity.
2. Vinaya, discipline for the monks.
3. Abhidharma, a metaphysical treatise.

(c) Persia, Babylonia, Assyria and Syria.

The Parsees of Bombay are the only representatives now left of a cult at one time widely diffused—the cult of Zoroaster (Zarathustra) who was born about 660 and died about 580 B.C. The first explorer who succeeded in giving to Europe authentic information in regard to Zoroastrianism was a Frenchman, Anquetil Duperron, born in 1734. He went to India when he was twenty-one years of age, and, difficulties notwithstanding, devoted seven years of study to the religion and sacred book—the Avesta—of this cult. In the year 1764, he gave to the Bibliothèque Royale the whole of the Avesta, and in 1771 published the first European translation of the same. Further light has come since then showing that many truths of the Natural Law were cherished by the disciples of Zoroaster. It is now known that Zoroastrians were not fire-worshippers. It was not the material element but the elemental force which they revered. They believed in the existence of a Supreme Being—Ahura Mazda or Auramazd'ı —who possessed attributes of omnipotence and omniscient, To him they directed their prayers and intercession their views on matters spiritual and moral were in many instances reasonable and elevated. It may be stated here that exception is justly taken to the term "Zend-Avesta," inasmuch as the prefix "Zend" indicates a commentary rather than the revelation itself. The Pahlavi commentary was written in Persian in the first centuries of the Christian era.

There are indications that in the dim past the people of Babylonia and Assyria worshipped Marduk as supreme. But polytheistic beliefs soon supervened, and the religious history of Babylon is useful as affording so striking a contrast to the neighbouring Monotheistic creed of Israel. The student of Comparative Religion finding that corrupt and superstitious beliefs inevitably appear in the course of time to the detriment of an older and purer faith, is led to admire the transcendence of the people of Israel, due to the Supernatural revelation and protection vouchsafed to them.

In the Syrian language, the word "El" (mighty) points to the original monotheism of the Semites. Most religions of which the history has been traced give distinct indications of a primitive period in which idols were unknown. Witness the Vedic hymns for India, Herodotus and Strabo for Persia, Plutarch (in his account of Numa) for Rome, and Tacitus for the Germanic tribes.

(*d*) Arabia.

Previous to the appearance in the seventh century of Islamism in Arabia, the Arabs worshipped local deities under the forms of stone and wood. Sacrifices of sheep, oxen, and camels were offered in a sacred enclosure, but there was no temple, nor were the stones and wood hewn into human or any other shape. In the south of Arabia temples and images had replaced the worship of unhewn stones, and in the fourth century of our era Monotheism prevailed, borrowed probably from neighbouring Judaic or Christian sources. Mohammed was born in 570, and in 622 took place the Hegira or ·migration to Medina. He died in 632. The Korān (Qurān ·ns "reading") was the name given to the collection of ·ations supposed to have been made to the prophet.

Hence, the book was, and is, regarded as the work of God. It was officially recognised in the year 660. In the Koran there are 114 suras, i.e. discourses or chapters. Besides the revelation made (as supposed) by God, and recorded in the Koran, the Mohammedans recognise officially the " Hadith " which contains sayings of the prophet and traditions. Six such collections have obtained official recognition.

The five pillars of Islām (the word means " resignation ") are (1) Faith ; (2) Prayer (five times daily) ; (3) Almsgiving ; (4) Fasting ; (5) Pilgrimage. The visitor to the East cannot help being profoundly impressed by the manifest fervour of Mohammedan devotions due, no doubt, to a lively and unwavering faith. The fasting during the month of Rhamadan is most strictly observed. The precept of Almsgiving is generously interpreted, and the pilgrimage to Mecca involves privations and hardships, to face which a robust faith alone can give the necessary courage and determination. The Sufis or Mohammedan saints have written some spiritual works of great beauty and elevation. The Pend-Nama— book of counsels—of 'Attar bears resemblance both to the Imitation of Christ and the Spiritual Combat. The following extract from the Mesnevi composed by the Muslim saint and doctor Jelalu-d'-Dîn (" Majesty of the Faith ") might have come from the writings of approved Catholic mystics. The author lived in the thirteenth century (1207–1273) being thus, curiously enough, a contemporary of St. Francis, St. Dominic, and St. Thomas of Aquin.

" One knocked at the door of the Beloved, and a voice from within said : ' Who is there ? ' Then he answered : ' It is I.' The voice replied : ' This house will not hold me and thee ! ' So the door remained shut. The lover retired to a wilderness, and spent some time in solitude, fasting and prayer. One year elapsed when he again returned and knocked at the door. ' Who is there ? ' said the voice. The lover answered : ' It is thou.' Then the door was opened."

In one of his odes which has been translated into English verse the same writer shows the advantages of detachment, and concludes :

> Thus when self-abased, man's spirit
> From each earthly tie
> Rises disenthralled t'inherit
> Immortality.

Amidst many errors and corruptions " something true and divinely revealed " characterises the faith and worship of Islām (cf. " Many Mansions," by W S. Lilly).

(*e*) Egypt.

The earliest records of Egypt point to belief in one Supreme Being, of whom the Sun was the symbol, and who was worshipped under various names: Atum at Heliopolis, Phtah at Memphis, Thot at Hermopolis, Amon at Thebes, and Horus at Edfu. Mr. E. A. Wallis Budge writes " The Egyptians believed in the existence of One Great and Almighty God, who created the world and everything in it. They seem to have thought just as modern African tribes think, that He was too exalted to concern Himself with the affairs of men and the governance of this world, and therefore He committed all such things to a large number of spirits or ' gods,' some of whom were benevolent and some malevolent. Both classes of gods could be propitiated with offerings, and hence arose worship by means of offerings, which plays such an important part in Egyptian religion." It is now an accepted truth that Heliopolis was a seat of learning about 4000 B.C., but the decadence observable in the history of other countries may be traced in that of Egypt. It is true that the legend of Osiris and Isis teaches the recompense of the good in a better world, the final triumph of justice over iniquity, and the immortality of the soul. The pyramids and mummies bear witness to belief in life after the death of the body. About 700 B.C. the degeneracy from a purer faith was marked by the spread of totemism and the cult of animals.

(*f*) Greece and Rome.

The earliest " gods " of Greece dwelt in Olympus, and do not owe their cult to an evolutionary development through animism and nature-worship. Subsequently some of the philosophers broke with the conventional religious traditions. Protagoras writes " As to the gods, I can say nothing as to whether they exist or not." The great poets of tragedy were also somewhat sceptical, though words of Sophocles on the moral law are some of the finest in literature : " It (the moral law) is from everlasting and no one knows its birthplace " ("Antigone," ll. 456 and 457). The intellectual gifts of Plato and Aristotle enabled them to reach with surprising accuracy and great beauty of expression the truths of monotheism, of immortality, and of the binding force of the moral law. Plato writes : " The real and proper object of human desire is Infinite Beauty," a truth expressed later by St. Augustine in memorable words " Inquietum est cor nostrum donec requiescat in Te." Plato's illustrious pupil Aristotle was supremely gifted as a thinker. His philosophical method was adopted by Aquinas in the thirteenth century and made the basis of that system of Christian Apologetics known as Scholasticism. As an illustration of Aristotle's subtlety and cogency the theistic argument drawn from " motion " and " contingent being " may be instanced. Both Plato and Aristotle saw the moral necessity of a divine revelation whereby " the journey may be undertaken with greater safety and fewer hazards " (" Phaedo ").

The Roman mind was averse from religious speculation and little is known of their early religious history except that they worshipped "numina," i.e. influences rather than individuals. The Etruscans, said to be of Greek origin, influenced the Romans towards the adoption of a mythology which in many ways resembled the Grecian. But the intensely practical nature of the Roman people paid but scant attention to questions which others have discussed with the deepest interest : " Whence do I come ? " " Whither do I go ? " We note, however, in Roman literature occasional expressions which manifest the hunger of the human soul for some authentic information in regard to the mysteries of life :

Tendebantque manus ripae ulterioris amore.

(g) So-called Primitive Races.

It has been truly said that man cannot be caught in a

primitive" state. His intellectual beginnings are far distant in time from the state of culture in which we find the lowest known races. Of late years we are in a better position to examine the religious views of so-called primitive races, inasmuch as valuable books have been published by authors who have an intimate knowledge of those of whom they write. Thus books on the Northern tribes of Central Australia, on the Arunta, and on the native tribes of South-East Australia give valuable information. There is recent and trustworthy information, too, in regard to the primitive races of Africa and America.

1. The Supreme Being worshipped by Australian tribes has different names in different localities, e.g. Baiame, Darumulum, Pundjel, Cagn, Mungan-ngaur (Our Father). The Being indicated by these names is in all cases Supreme Master and Lord, inculcates the practice of the natural virtues and punishes trespasses. He is represented as without beginning or end.
2. The Fijians regard Ndengei or Degei as Lord of Heaven.
3. The Polynesians reverence Taa-roa as eternal.
4. African tribes.
   (a) The Yaos of Central Africa pay worship to Mulungu or Mtanga as containing in himself all power and excellence.
   (b) The Bantus are Monotheistic in belief, though their views are disfigured by deism. A Bantu tribesman is reported to have said to a priest : " there are more wonders above than are described in all the books of the white men."
   (c) The Dinkas of the Upper Nile reverence Dendid who created the Sun, stars and man.
   (d) The Bakwains' monotheism is vouched for by Livingstone.
   (e) The Fangs of the Congo (cannibals), believe in the existence of "Anyambi," who made all things. His worship began to wane as Ghost-worship arose.
   (f) The Tshi-speaking tribes of the Gold Coast worship

Nyan-Kupon as Creator. Mr. Andrew Lang maintained that this deity was not a loan-god borrowed from missionaries.
- (g) The Zulus worshipped Unkulunkulu, but now worship Amatongo, a deity who may be won over by bribes. Animism has supplanted Theism.
- (h) Mr. Wilson, who has written on the inhabitants of North and South Guinea, assures us that belief in one Supreme Being is universal.

5. The Negritoes of the Andaman Islands worship Puluga, whom they regard as creator, eternal, immortal, and judge.
6. American tribes.
   - (a) The Hurons of Virginia worshipped Ahone, creator of Sun, Moon, and Stars.
   - (b) The Pawnees of Nebraska regarded Ti-ra-wa as Spirit-Father and Creator.
   - (c) The Blackfoot Indians reverence Na-pi as Supreme Creator.
   - (d) The Zunis pay worship to Awonawilona, maker and container of all things.
   - (e) The Incas of Peru worshipped Pachacamac, sustainer of the world.
   - (f) The people of the Guianas worship the "Great Father."
   - (g) The Chonos have faith in Yorri Yuppon, author of all good.
   - (h) The Fuegians reverence a magnified non-natural man who punishes evil deeds.

II. THE COMPARATIVE METHOD

It is customary nowadays from a comparison of the resemblances and differences of the various religious systems to evolve theories concerning the origin and progress of Religion. And whilst writers are agreed in regard to the *terminus ad quem*, i.e. Monotheism, there is much difference of view in regard to the *terminus a quo*. Mr. Tylor finds the origin of Religion in Animism; J. G. Frazer in Magic; Max Müller in the perception of the Infinite; Herbert Spencer in Ancestor-worship; F. B. Jevons in Totemism. But notwithstanding his belief in Animism, Mr. Tylor, in his valuable book " Primitive Culture," records two important judgments: that there is not sufficient justification for belief in the existence of wholly non-religious savages and that " there are in barbaric theology shadowings quaint or majestic of the conception of a Supreme Deity." Mr. Payne, though a believer in the Animistic theory, naïvely writes that " the idea of a creative spirit is one of the earliest efforts of primitive logic."

From the survey given in this chapter certain conclusions emerge

1. Belief in a Supreme Being, eternal, immortal, rewarder of the good and punisher of the bad, seems to have been, and to be, universal, and this monotheistic belief was purer and less obscure the more remote the record.

2. Belief in the continued life of the soul after the death of the body was also practically universal. Dr. Livingstone in his " Missionary Travels " writes of the Bakwains: " there is no need to tell the most degraded of these people of the existence of God, or of a future state, the facts being universally admitted."

3. There is evidence too of wide acquaintance with the primary and secondary precepts of the Moral Law.

4. Strong cumulative proof is forthcoming that the tendency in religious belief has been from a purer form to a form disfigured by spirit-worship, ancestor-worship, totemism, fetishism, and other superstitions. Mr. Andrew Lang writes: " beyond all doubt savages who find themselves under the watchful eye of a moral Deity whom they cannot ' square ' will desert Him as soon as they have evolved a practicable ghost-god whom they can square."

5. Evolution from Animism, ancestor-worship, etc., to Monotheism is beset with the gravest difficulties:
   (a) Belief in a Supreme Being which, from the current anthropological standpoint, should be latent and most

potent is, amongst many savage tribes, shelved and neglected, whereas animism is in full vigour.

(b) Belief in a Supreme Being is found though the social conditions for the cult of ancestor-worship are not present. M. Réville—a weighty authority—writes: " it was not the first ancestor who became God in the belief of His descendants, but much rather the Divine Maker and Beginner of all, who in the creed of His adorers became the first ancestor."

6. The process of degeneration took, in all probability, the following course

(a) The idea of a Supreme Being became localised or nationalised.

(b) When tribes were conquered and united to the conquering race they brought with them *their* conception (localised or nationalised) of the Deity. Hence the rise of Polytheism.

(c) In Polytheism, the idea of a Supreme Being sank to the low level of president of the Immortals, e.g. Zeus.

7. The value of "civilised" and "non-civilised" races requires readjustment. The so-called civilisation of the twentieth century has resulted in the greatest tragedy in all history. William Watson's appraisement of that civilisation is truly and beautifully expressed:

> O, Thou that with a gesture canst control
> All seas that roll:
> O, Thou that with a whisper canst assuage
> All winds that rage:
> Behold how softer than the human breast
> The wild bird's nest,
> Behold how calmer than the world of men
> The wild beast's den.

8. Finally, the anthropological doctrine of St. Paul covers all the facts of the " Science of comparative Religion," and points out the basis of true civilisation in the unity of the human family.

" The invisible things of God from the creation of the world are clearly seen, being understood by the things that are made, His eternal power also and Divinity." Romans i. 20.

"They (i.e. nations) changed the glory of the incorruptible God into the likeness of the image of a corruptible man, and of birds, and four-footed beasts and creeping things." Romans i. 22.

"God that made the world and all things therein hath made of one blood all nations of men that they should seek the Lord if haply they might feel after Him, and find Him, though He is not far from each one of us; for in Him we live, and move, and have our being." Acts xvii. 24-28.

9. The following is an approximate estimate of the religious tenets of the 1560 millions in the world . It is that given by Father Krose in the "Catholic Encyclopædia," Vol. XIV, p. 281 (1912).

1. Catholics, 292,787,000.
2. Ancestor-worshippers and Confucianists, 240,000,000.
3. Hindus, 210,100,000.
4. Moslems, 207,067,000.
5. Protestants, 186,055,000.
6. Orthodox, 127,541,000.
7. Buddhists, 125,270,000.
8. Heathen and Fetish-worshippers, 91,604,000.
9. Taoists, 49,000,000.
10. Jews, 12,989,000.
11. Eastern Schisms, 8,974,000.

Thus 618 millions are Christians, i.e. 39·6 per cent.

CHAPTER XII

REVELATION AND ITS CRITERIA

I. Divine Revelation

THE foregoing chapters on Natural Religion prepare us for an all-important question has God vouchsafed to man a Divine Revelation embodying Supernatural truths, and what are the criteria whereby it may be recognised?

It is necessary to define what is meant exactly by the terms "natural" and "supernatural."

The word "natural" is applied to

1. The elements which constitute a nature, e.g. senses and reason in man.
2. All that flows from a nature thus constituted, e.g. sensations, ideas, volitions, etc.
3. All that a being requires for the use of his faculties, e.g. an end, means toward the attainment of the end, general Divine concursus, etc.
4. All that a being can accomplish by his own powers.

The word "supernatural" implies superiority over nature. The superiority may be

1. Relative: when for instance a perfection is given to a nature without raising the nature beyond its own sphere, e.g. the immortality and freedom from concupiscence accorded to our first parents. Such gifts are termed "preternatural."
2. Absolute: when the perfection surpasses all created nature, e.g. sanctifying grace, the vision of God.

Instances of the Supernatural in its absolute sense may be either in substance or in manner. Sanctifying grace is supernatural in substance, the raising of Lazarus to life was supernatural only in manner, as Nature can produce life, but not in the case of one who is dead. The following example will elucidate still further the distinction between the supernatural and the preternatural. " A king gives to his ambassador certain powers necessary for his diplomatic duties. These powers are natural. If the king gives him further powers increasing his dignity and influence, but not superseding ambassadorial functions, these powers are ' preternatural.' Finally, should the king share with him his royal prerogative, and make him adopted son and heir to the kingdom, such privileges would be ' supernatural.'" It is possible now to differentiate between the Natural and Supernatural Orders.

When God created man He appointed as his end the *knowledge* of Himself, as seen through the veil of finite perfections, and the *love* of Himself proportioned to this knowledge. God also gave to man the means to attain to the end—intellect seeking truth, and will seeking goodness. Man created for this end and endowed with these means constitutes the Natural Order.

But God has raised man to the sublime dignity of sonship. He has given man a supernatural end—intuitive vision of God. He has given also means for the attainment of this supernatural end—intellect illuminated by faith, and will strengthened by Grace. Hence man raised to a supernatural destiny, aided by Divine grace, and destined for the vision of God, constitutes the Supernatural Order.

The possibility of the Supernatural Order is plain from the fact that there is no obstacle either as regards God or man. God is all-powerful, infinite in goodness, and absolutely free in His external work, and man, though limited in faculty, is capable of receiving this perfection. But the raising of man to the Supernatural Order is not only possible but congruous. Such a benefit would be in keeping with God's infinite goodness : " Summum Bonum est sui diffusivum," and would confer on man supreme advantages in the extended knowledge of Divine truths, in conferring peace of heart, and in furnishing the support of Divine Grace to face the difficulties of life. The advantages to society are seen by the comparison of the pagan and Christian ideals.

Allusion has been made to the "extended knowledge of Divine truths"—truths beyond the reach of human reason. Such knowledge is called Divine Revelation, and may be defined as the act of God whereby He manifests to man certain truths. Revelation may be made (1) immediately by God Himself; or (2) mediately by one divinely authorised.

That Revelation is possible is shown by the fact that there is no obstacle to this Divine benefit on the part of God or man, and no obstacle arising from the revealed truths themselves. It is consonant with the Divine Nature to reveal to His creatures truths which are advantageous. So far from lowering human dignity it is an immeasurable honour and advantage to man to have Supreme Wisdom for his teacher. God's revelation does not destroy human reason, but extends its power and scope, as the telescope enables the eye to see stars invisible to unaided vision. Moreover, truth, revealed as well as natural, is always truth, and therefore the proper object of the human intellect. The universality of the belief that Revelation has been made is witnessed to by the sacred books of nations—the Avesta of Zoroaster, the Vedas of Brahmanism, the Korān of Mohammed, as well as by the unwritten traditions of more uncivilised nations.

Since Revelation includes truths which are beyond the reach of human reason, there is neither hardship nor absurdity in the fact that mysteries should form a part of Christian belief. If a wayside flower—an outward sign of almighty power—be in many ways incomprehensible, if natural phenomena such as light, heat, gravitation, etc., are mysteries, surely it is à priori reasonable to suppose that, when the mind of man fixes its attention upon the Infinite as manifested in Revelation, there will be truths which are incomprehensible. Our knowledge of God is analogical. The depth of the infinite ocean of being cannot be gauged by the short plumb-line of human scrutiny. The real injury to reason is not belief, but disbelief in mysteries when the evidence for the truth of the mystery is from every point of view unexceptionable. The trinity of persons in the Godhead is taught by the true Church of Christ, a church infallible in itself and in its chief pastor. It is no derogation to human reason to believe the doctrine of the Unity and Trinity of God, since human reason is directed by an infallible guide.

The reader's attention is now asked for the consideration of a most important truth—the necessity of Revelation—a necessity based upon a twofold inability of reason

1. *Absolute inability* when the truths cannot under any circumstances be reached by the natural light of reason.
2. *Moral inability* in this case the truths are accessible to reason, but owing to difficulties the acquisition of them is morally impossible.

It is clear that there is absolute inability to reach :
1. Mysteries and truths of the Supernatural Order.
2. Positive precepts imposed by God, inasmuch as such precepts depend on His free-will, and cannot be known apart from revelation.
3. Supernatural belief in the truths of the Natural order. Supernatural belief or Faith is the acceptance of a truth, because of the infallible authority of God.

The absolute necessity of Revelation in regard to these truths is so obvious that it cannot be questioned. The moral necessity of Revelation implies certain restrictions which should be carefully noted

1. The statement (of the necessity) does not regard *each* man, but men generally, hampered by conditions of life and work.
2. The statement (of the necessity) does not refer to *each* truth of Natural Religion, but to the whole body of such truths.
3. The statement (of the necessity) is not intended to apply to any kind of knowledge, but to prompt, certain, accurate knowledge.

Hence the following thesis :

" Revelation is morally necessary so that all men may

know promptly and with certitude the dogmas and precepts of Natural Religion."

This proposition is a "via media" between the extreme claim of Traditionalism on the one hand and the extreme attitude of Rationalism on the other. Traditionalists hold that *no* truth of Natural Religion can be known without Revelation. Rationalists claim that *all* truths of Natural Religion can be satisfactorily known by all without the aid of Revelation.

1st Proof. From Reason.

(a) Without Revelation but few men could acquire the knowledge of these truths owing to indifferent health, the exigencies of work or want of energy.

(b) Without Revelation these truths would be known only after a long time, because of their difficulty, and the special mental powers necessary, and owing to the passions which darken the mind.

(c) Without Revelation the knowledge would not be free from error owing to defects of both intellect and will.

Thus Revelation is morally necessary both to enlighten the mind and strengthen the will.

2nd Proof. From History.

No nation has, without the aid of Revelation, professed a Religion worthy of God.

(a) Educated pagans despised the ignorance of the masses. "Odi profanum vulgus."

(b) Educated pagans—even the philosophers—were in many cases quite as much in error as the common people. "There is no absurdity which has not been held by some philosopher" (Cicero). "What damned error but some sober brow will bless it and approve it with a text?"

(c) At the time of Varro there were 300 sects amongst the philosophical schools.

(d) The teaching of the philosophers had no authority and carried no weight.

Objection. If Revelation be morally necessary why has God left the human race so long without it?

Answer. (*a*) It was man himself who through disobedience forfeited the helps which God had originally provided.

(*b*) After the fall God constantly instructed the chosen people and prepared them for the fuller revelation to be made later.

(*c*) The recognised inability of reason to attain to the fullness of truth turned the eyes of men towards the Orient, whence the Sun of Justice was expected to appear.

The necessity of Revelation raises at once the question of its cognoscibility. What are the criteria upon which Revelation depends for the assertion of its claims?

Some truths are intrinsically evident, e.g. every trilateral figure is triangular. Other truths depend upon extrinsic motives of credibility, and of such kind are the truths of Revelation.

The criteria of Revelation may be tabulated in the following way:

$$\text{Criteria} \begin{cases} \text{Negative} \\ \text{Positive} \end{cases} \begin{cases} \text{intrinsic} \\ \text{extrinsic} \end{cases} \begin{cases} \text{miracle} \\ \text{prophecy} \end{cases}$$

Negative criteria of Revelation require that the revealed truths should not be opposed to reason, the Divine perfections, or the well-being of mankind. It is clear that the presence of these criteria indicates merely that the truths *may* be divine.

The extrinsic criteria—miracles and prophecy—are supernatural facts which prove with certainty the Divine origin of Revelation. The intrinsic criteria have reference to the sublimity and excellence of the doctrines involved. But as the subjective element enters largely into a judgment of this sort, reliance is placed on the extrinsic criteria alone.

II. MIRACLES

A. NATURE OF A MIRACLE

A miracle, taken strictly in its apologetic sense, may be defined as "an extraordinary fact observed by the senses, and surpassing the power of any created being."

Three conditions are therefore necessary to constitute a miracle

1. The fact must be of such a nature that it can be observed by the senses, either in itself or in its effects. The raising of Lazarus from the dead was directly perceived by his friends. The miracle of Pentecost was visible in its effects.
2. The fact must be extraordinary—not explicable as an instance of the customary laws, natural or supernatural, which prevail. If, for example, a stone remain suspended in the air without support, the occurrence would be an extraordinary fact of the natural order. The change of the substance of bread into the body and blood of Christ is not a miracle in this apologetic sense for two reasons (*a*) the change cannot be perceived by the senses, and (*b*) the change is in accordance with the ordinary supernatural law ordained by Christ. But if Christ appeared in visible form under the sacramental veils such an occurrence would be miraculous.
3. The fact must exceed the power of any created nature.

A miracle may belong (1) to the intellectual order, e.g. prophecy, or (2) to the physical order, e.g. the sudden calming of the tempestuous waves, or (3) to the social order, e.g. the rapid spread of Christianity in face of overwhelming obstacles.

Regarding a physical miracle, it may surpass natural powers (1) in itself, or (2) as exercised upon a particular object, e.g. the giving of life to one dead, or (3) as regards its manner, e.g. the healing of an organic malady by a single word.

B. Possibility of a Miracle

It has often been said that a miracle is impossible because it is a violation of one or more of Nature's laws, and human testimony witnesses to the uniformity of Nature's laws. This conception of a miracle is radically false. The following illustration will be of use. A man (let us suppose) holds a stone in his hand. The attraction of gravity is acting all the time upon the stone, but the law of gravitation is not violated, its effect is suspended by another force (the supporting power of the man's hand). Now if the man remove his hand, and if the stone be suspended miraculously, the case is the same precisely as regards the law of gravity, which continues to act, only its effect is suspended by Divine power. It is therefore an instance of confusion of thought to allege that a miracle is a violation of any law of nature. It is a law of Nature that a dead body should not come to life again, but if a new force is applied prevailing over the effect of Nature's law so that the dead comes to life, there is no more violation of law than if the man holding a stone in his hand move it upwards, and thus prevail over the tendency of gravity which is downwards towards the earth.

The possibility of a miracle is attested
1. *By the testimony of mankind.* All peoples have believed in the possibility of miracles and the universal testimony of mankind on a matter within its competence to form a judgment is a criterion of truth.
2. *By Reason.* There is no obstacle to a miracle either on the side of created beings, or on the part of God.
    (*a*) One is forced to conclude that from the standpoint of nature : (1) created beings depend on God, and are subject to the Divine Will ; (2) a miracle is not opposed to the laws of Nature ; (3) since one body can act upon another, and man can subject natural forces to his will, this power belongs in an infinite degree to God ; (4) a miracle requires merely the change of direction of a force, not the

creation of a new force. Hence the principle of Conservation of Energy is unaffected by the doctrine of miracles.

(b) If we regard a miracle from the Divine standpoint we must remember that God is all-powerful. He is not subject to the physical laws which He has made. Nor does the working of a miracle imply change in God: His Divine arrangements have been made from eternity.

C. Possibility of Proving a Miracle

To establish the genuinely miraculous character of an event three conditions should be verified:
1. The testimony of the senses.
2. The incapability of Natural causes to account for the occurrence.
3. The legitimate and necessary inference of the intervention of God.

In *certain* cases these conditions are present
1. Perception of the senses requires for present facts only the use of healthy sense organs. For past facts the testimony of History—well authenticated testimony—suffices.
2. The supernatural character of the fact is obvious in certain cases. To restore to life the dead body of Lazarus, upon which the noisome work of corruption had already begun, and to effect this restoration to life by the utterance, "Lazarus, come forth," who can deny the supernatural character of this achievement?

1st Objection. To ascertain the truth of a miracle the judgment of Scientific experts should be taken.

Answer. Certain cases of supposed miraculous intervention are doubtful. A prudent man will, in such cases, reserve his judgment. But in other cases there is not the slightest doubt as to their supernatural character, and expert testimony would be superfluous. If the torn sinews of a leg are healed instantaneously at Lourdes, the school of Anatole France would have described the fact as due to some unknown power possessed by water under circumstances as yet undetermined—a power of instantaneous healing. Needless to say that if an appeal is allowed to be made to unknown laws, and undetermined circumstances, knowledge of any kind becomes impossible.

Charcot, Renan, and others suggested that a commission of physiologists, physicists, chemists, and physicians, etc., should adjudicate upon the genuineness of alleged miraculous events. Such a suggestion is (1) impious. It means the degradation of a miracle to the level of a laboratory experiment. (2) Absurd. In regard to past miracles they cannot be reproduced for the benefit of experts. In regard to present-day miracles, e.g. those of Lourdes, medical testimony of unexceptionable character is at hand.

2nd Objection. A miracle cannot be scientifically proved.

Answer. The sciences may be grouped into three categories: (1) historical; (2) experimental; (3) philosophic.

Historical science rests on authority. Natural or Experimental science is based on experiment. Philosophic science appeals to reason.

What should be thought of a philosopher who denies that the French were defeated in the Franco-Prussian War of 1870, because there were no reasons why they should have been defeated? What should be thought of a physicist who doubts the existence of God because he has never seen or touched God? What should be thought of an historian who denies the existence of the law of gravitation because he can find no historical authority for the law? The statement, therefore, that a miracle cannot be scientifically proved is only another instance of confusion of thought.

In point of fact a miracle belongs to all three groups—Authority or sense-perception attests the fact; experiences of the limitations of natural agencies demonstrates its supernatural character; and reasoning guides us to the inference of Divine Causality.

3rd Objection. So-called miracles are the effects of suggestion, faith-healing, and the acknowledged power of mind over body.

Answer. In cases of functional trouble due to nervous derangement, treatment by suggestion, hypnotism, etc., is often successful. But in cases of organic disease such as tuberculosis, malignant tumour, fractures, caries, etc., these remedies are useless. Hence *sudden* cures of *organic* complaints afford conclusive evidence of supernatural agency. It should be remembered that tumours are sometimes non-malignant and of nervous origin.

3. The Divine causality can be proved. Though evil spirits have sometimes power accorded to them to accomplish wonderful feats, yet it is easy to distinguish between God's action and that of the devil. A superhuman fact which presents nothing false, wrong, or suspicious in the end aimed at, in the actuating motive, or in the agents employed cannot be the work of an evil spirit. It is possible, therefore, to recognise the Divine causality.

Objection. All sects claim miracles.

Answer. (*a*) Buddha's so-called miracles are metaphysically impossible.

(*b*) Erasmus said of the Reformers that they could not cure even a lame horse.

(*c*) Instances are on record of the exercise of superhuman power, but the end or motive or circumstances betray an origin which is clearly not Divine.

D. The Probative Force of a Miracle

A miracle being the work of God proves without doubt the divinity of the religion which it confirms.

1st Proof. From Reason.

God is (*a*) Truth ; (*b*) Goodness ; (*c*) Sanctity ; and therefore the suggestion is impious and absurd that He could attest a falsehood.

2nd Proof. From Testimony.

When the apostles appealed to the miracles of Christ neither Jews nor Pagans contested the authoritative force of miracles.

Moreover, all false religions are based on supposed miracles—a striking testimony to the value of miracles as a criterion of Divine approval.

Objection. God does not work miracles nowadays.

Answer. (1) The statement is false.

(2) In the early ages of the Church the need of miracles was greater. Now there is the abiding miracle of the Church which renders the need of other miracles less necessary.

III. Prophecy

A. Nature of Prophecy

Prophecy is the prevision, together with the certain and precise announcement, of a future event, knowledge of which cannot be had either in its physical or moral causes.

Three necessary elements characterise a true prophecy: (1) the certainty and precision of the announcement; (2) the futurity of the event; (3) the impossibility of knowing the event from physical or moral causes.

An occurrence of eclipse, the advent of a comet, can be predicted from a knowledge of the physical causes which determine these events, and often a clever and experienced statesman can anticipate the public will, foreseeing its development from moral causes. These instances do not constitute true prophecy.

B. Possibility of Prophecy

The possibility of prophecy depends upon two truths: (1) God knows future events, and (2) God can reveal them. It is clear that God knows the future events whose existence will be determined by necessary causes, since God is the author of these causes. But it is also true that God knows future contingent events, i.e. those dependent on the free-will of man. To deny this would be equivalent to the denial of the Omniscience, Providence, and Immutability of God. And since God knows all future things there is no conceivable reason why He should not be able to reveal certain events if He choose to do so.

It is surprising to note the flimsy and superficial character of the objections often advanced by able men. Voltaire, for instance, argued that God cannot know the future because it does not exist, forgetting that if the future does not exist for us it exists for God in His eternal present. Again, it has been said that the prescience of God is incompatible with human liberty. The true relation of God's prescience to human action is easily understood : men do not act *because* God foresees their action, but He foresees their action because they will so act.

C. True Prophecies Have Taken Place

Instances are on record where the facts predicted are numerous, minutely described and dependent upon the free-will of men. In these cases the prediction could not have been conjectural. It is worth noting how the mathematical theory of probabilities confirms the argument from prophecy. Let us suppose that the following predictions have been made

(1) That a certain nation should be made free after a definite number of years.
(2) That Christ should be of a certain family.
(3) That He should be born in a certain town, etc.

Now although the Messianic prophecies are not made in such unmistakable terms as these, still we must remember that the probability against the simultaneous verification of a number of conditions is enormously greater than the probability against the verification of any one separately. If twenty facts of the above nature were predicted, and if the probability in favour of the realisation of each of these facts were $\frac{1}{10}$, for two facts taken together the probability would be $\frac{1}{100}$, for three $\frac{1}{1000}$, and so on, so that the probability that the joint series of twenty attains realisation would be :

$$\frac{1}{100.000.000.000.000.000.000}$$

i.e. the chance of fortuitous verification is practically non-existent.

It is obvious, therefore, that the prediction when the facts are numerous, minutely described, and dependent upon the free-will of men cannot be conjectural. Nor can it be deduced from natural causes, since free-will does not depend on physical causes, and moral causes reveal human action only in a general way.

Finally, that the prediction has actually been realised is a matter of historical proof, which in certain cases cannot be questioned. The objection of Rousseau ("Emile" B. III.) that for the probative force of prophecy the witness who heard the prediction should see its realisation amounts to an elimination of Historical Certitude and merits no further consideration.

D. THE PROBATIVE FORCE OF PROPHECY

A genuine prophecy is a Divine sign and an incontestable criterion of the truth of the Religion in favour of which it is made. The veracity and sanctity of God are at stake.

1st Objection. All religions have claimed the attestation of prophecy.

Answer. Such prophecies differ from Divine prophecy in *origin*, proceeding as they usually did from the frenzy of a sibyl; in *end* which was always material, and in *content* which was ambiguous.

2nd Objection. It is claimed that in cases of Hypnotism and Somnambulism the mind of the subject foresees future events.

Answer. It is certain that the mind in a state of exaltation induced by Hypnotism has extraordinary powers. The subconscious powers—powers usually beneath the level of consciousness—have then full play, but no authenticated instance is on record of prophetic power.

3rd Objection. Prophecy may come from the devil.

Answer. The natural knowledge of the devil is greater than ours; this, coupled with his enormous experience, enables him to calculate chances with great astuteness; but the real future is beyond his ken.

CHAPTER XIII

FAITH AND REASON

I. Rationalism

RATIONALISM stands for the principle that human reason is the *adequate* measure of truth. Hence the chief aim of the Rationalistic school is war against the Supernatural, and insistence upon the claim that reason is :
1. Sole and absolute authority in the intellectual order.
2. Final judge of action in the moral order.
3. Ultimate court of appeal in the social order.
4. Guide to happiness in the material order.

To trace the origin of Rationalism fully would require much space, but all will allow that an impetus was given to the tendency by Luther and his system of Private Judgment. It will be sufficient for our purpose to state the salient principles of this school, and indicate the arguments which refute them.

The principles are three :
1. Reason is the adequate measure of truth, and therefore autonomous.
2. Revelation is superfluous.
3. Reason in its development follows an upward course.

1. Is Reason antonomous ?

Absolutely not, since man depends on God for his existence and the exercise of his faculties. It will be shown later that Revelation has " de facto " been made, and reason is bound to accept it. Hence, reason is not the only source of truth. Nor can the obligation of accepting Revealed Truth be evaded by regarding it as a benefit which may be declined.

It is indeed a benefit, but also an act of Divine will which imposes obedience upon man.

2. Is Revelation necessary?

We have already shown that for the prompt, certain, and general knowledge of natural truths Revelation is morally necessary. Much more stringent is the necessity where the truths either exceed the power of reason to attain, or where they are concerned with the free decisions of the Divine Will, which can be known only by being communicated.

3. Does reason follow an upward course?

There is need of careful distinction in answer to this question.

(a) Relatively to truths of the natural order Reason secures progress in two ways: (1) negatively by removing error; (2) positively by discovering new and strengthening the hold on old truths.

(b) Relatively to Supernatural truths there have been three dispensations, Patriarchal, Mosaic, and Christian, and the two former were perfectible objectively—not that they contained error, but in the sense that they were stages on the way.

(c) Relatively to Christian Doctrine there is no possibility of *objective* progress. The whole Revelation—the Deposit of Faith—was made once and for all. But there may be *Subjective* progress (1) extensive—the development of the explicit from the implicit, e.g. doctrine of infallibility; and (2) intensive—the acquisition of clearer and more thorough knowledge of Revealed Truth.

If the Rationalistic claim be regarded from the standpoints of History and Philosophy we shall see:

1. Reason does not tend naturally and necessarily to progress. The history of nations has been one of declension from monotheistic belief to the fetishism of savage tribes. " Je maintiens mon principe fondamental dans toute son étendue. La religion qui a précédé toutes les autres, c'est celle d'un seul Dieu, et toutes les autres, se rapportent à celle-là, comme les rayons brisés et affaiblis se rapportent à la pleine lumière du soleil" (Creuzer, Symbolique I). Moreover, wonderful achievements of art in Painting, Sculpture, Architecture, and

Poetry belong to the fourth and fifth centuries before Christ and have never been surpassed.

2. Christianity is not the product of intellectual activity. It came not from the schools of Egypt, Greece, or Rome, but from an obscure corner of Judæa.

3. It is impossible to maintain that all religions are relatively true and legitimate. To hold such an opinion would be to oppose the principle of contradiction. Truth is one and unchangeable.

II. Faith and Science

Faith and Science differ in origin and in object. As science is acquired by reason, and faith comes through Revelation, the difference in origin is manifest. Again, since the object of Science is the comprehension of natural truth, and the object of Faith the acceptance of truths, natural and supernatural, which God has revealed, the aim of one is not the same as that of the other. But whilst they differ in origin, both emanate from the same Divine source of truth as two rays from the same sun. Hence Faith and Science cannot contradict each other, and apparent contradictions are due either to misapprehension of dogma or to mistaking hypothesis for truth. Some years ago many believed that the age of man upon the earth did not extend beyond 6,000 to 8,000 years. And they had the impression that there was Scripture authority for such a view. When relics of human bodies were found in such geological situations as to require a much longer time for the antiquity of man than 8,000 years, there was no conflict between Faith and Science, inasmuch as lacunæ in the chronology given in the Bible preclude the possibility of an accurate estimate. The Church has made no pronouncement on the antiquity of man. Another misapprehension of dogma was the opinion which prevailed that the geocentric theory was supported by Scripture. The consequent condemnation of Galileo, of which so much has been made, was not an instance of conflict between Faith and Science, but an instance of erroneous theological opinion of the Congregation of the Inquisition which, needless to say, did not touch upon the domain of Faith. On the other hand, if an unproven hypothesis such as that of Materialistic Evolution be held, the supposed conflict between Faith and Science arising therefrom does not really exist, inasmuch as an unproven hypothesis does not come within the category of Science.

So far from being in conflict, Faith and Science—the product of Reason—mutually support each other.

A. Reason

1. Establishes the foundations of Faith. Natural Religion is the basis of the Supernatural, and, as we have seen, the fabric of Natural Religion is due to the exercise of human reason upon the contingent phenomena perceived by the senses. Faith therefore having its foundation in reason is not a sentiment or an instinct but a " rationabile obsequium."

2. The exercise of Reason is most valuable in the examination of Divine Truth. Such examination is necessary for its suitable comprehension.

3. By the exercise of Reason Faith is defended against error, and the history of the Church shows how continuously the need has persisted from the age of Gnosticism to that of Modernism.

4. The application of Reason gives to Theology the nature, character, and form of a true science. Scholastic Philosophy and Theology have outlived all attack, and have witnessed the advent and decay of many systems of philosophy and of belief.

B. Faith.

1. Faith illuminates reason. Both Philosophy and Science have failed utterly (Brunetière's "Banqueroute de la Science") to throw light upon man's origin and destiny.

2. Faith elevates reason. Monsabré gives an apt simile of a peasant girl lifting up a child in her strong arms so that the child may see, over the heads of those present, the contests and the games of a fête day. The beauties of Nature—sun, stars, sea, flowers, etc., are perceived by the *eye*. The world of Law is perceived by *reason*. But beyond the splendours of Nature, beyond the region of law, beyond the contemplation of the physicist, the mathematician, even of the philosopher,

there is a third world—God, His life, threefold personality, His Divine action. God has given us a power subtle and withal strong, whereby reason is raised up so that it may contemplate truths inaccessible to sense and to unaided reason.

3. Faith stimulates reason. From the standpoint of Faith, Science is a manifestation of God's wisdom, a stepping-stone to God, and an instrument of progress for man himself.

4. Faith directs reason and keeps it from error. Just as the locomotive driven by the pressure of steam tears along at the rate of sixty miles per hour, and is kept true to its direction by the iron track on which it runs, so the force of human reason exercised upon the phenomena of nature is kept true to its direction by the guidance of Faith.

C. Relation between Faith and Science.

It has been shown that Faith is superior to Science in origin and end, but the subordination of Science to Faith varies :

(*a*) On matters Scientific, Reason is autonomous.

(*b*) On matters where Faith and Science meet, Science is subject to Faith's guidance.

(*c*) On matters purely supernatural, Science is the handmaiden of Faith.

CHAPTER XIV

THE FACT OF REVELATION

1. Three Historical Phases

THE first historical phase of Divine Revelation was that known as Primitive and Patriarchal—a revelation made by God to our first parents, and lasting until the days of Moses. During this phase belief was required in certain dogmas, and in the binding force of certain precepts. The dogmas were the existence and nature of God, the creation of the world, the existence of the soul, and of angels good and bad, the fall of our first parents, and the transmission of original sin, the expectation of a Redeemer, the existence of another life with its rewards and punishments (Hebrews xi. 13-16). The precepts were those of the natural law, together with some positive precepts regarding the worship of God and the offering of sacrifice. The means given for the preservation of religion were *reason* for truths of the natural law, and *tradition* for dogmas and positive precepts. Later additional precepts were given to Abraham such as the rite of circumcision and the consecration of the first-born.

Association with pagan nations had a destructive influence upon the belief and morality of the patriarchal tribes, so that God resolved, in the words of Bossuet, " to inscribe on stone the commands which man read no longer in his heart."

The Mosaic revelation included a more explicit statement of the dogmas already revealed, the decalogue constituting a résumé of the precepts of the natural law (the determination of the Sabbath excepted), the development of government into a theocratic form, and certain liturgical and ritual observances. It was intended to prepare the chosen people for the final revelation to be given by the Messias, at whose coming the positive precepts of the Mosaic law would no longer bind.

The Christian Religion secures the full and clear development both of the dogmas and precepts of the natural law, the revelation of supernatural truths and precepts, and the giving of supernatural aids to help men to reach the Christian standard of virtuous living.

If the divinity of the Christian Faith be proved, the divinity of the two previous phases follows as a logical consequence. The three phases of the one revelation have (1) the same author, God ; (2) the same foundation, the Messias expected or actually come ; (3) the same end, the beatific vision ; (4) the same means, reason illuminated by Faith, and will strengthened by Divine grace ; (5) the same agent, man raised to the supernatural order ; (6) the same fundamental dogmas ; (7) the same moral precepts.

II. HISTORICAL AUTHORITY OF THE GOSPELS

A. THEIR INTEGRITY

Integrity of the Gospels means their substantial agreement with the original documents. The original documents do not exist, but there is in the Vatican Library, the Codex Vaticanus, which goes back to the fourth century, and the Codex Sinaiticus at Petrograd is of the same date. There are besides several versions, one of which (Syriac) belongs to the second century, and citations of Scriptural texts in the Fathers from St. Clement to St. Jerome—more than 200 testimonies.

If the text of the Gospels has been changed, it must have been before A.D. 200, because the texts of versions of this period are the same substantially as the actual existing text. Now such change was impossible for the following reasons :

1. Both Christians and heretics jealously watched over the integrity of the Gospels.

2. Before A.D. 150 a large number of copies must already have existed, all of which would have to be changed.

3. The citations in works of the Fathers must also have been changed.

B. Authenticity of the Gospels

Authenticity of the Gospels means that they were composed by the author whose name they bear.

I. Authenticity proved by tradition.

(a) 1. Papias, bishop of Hierapolis (Phrygia), wrote about A.D. 130. He mentions the gospels of St. Matthew and St. Mark; "Matthew wrote in Hebrew"—"Mark was the interpreter of Peter."
2. Tatian, about A.D. 170, wrote his "Diatessaron"—a harmony of the four gospels.
3. Clement of Alexandria wrote c. A.D. 200 his "Stromata" and "Hypotyposes." He speaks of the "four gospels transmitted to us by tradition." "The first gospels in the order of composition are those which contain the genealogies" (St. Matthew and St. Luke), "John wrote the spiritual gospel."
4. Tertullian speaks of the apostolic origin of the four gospels: "Matthew and John being apostles; Mark and Luke the disciples of Apostles" (about A.D. 200).
5. Irenæus, bishop of Lyons (disciple of St. Polycarp, bishop of Smyrna, who was a disciple of St. John), wrote his book "Adversus Hæreses" about A.D. 180, in which he says: "Matthew wrote in Hebrew; Mark, the interpreter of St. Peter, put in writing the preaching of Peter; Luke wrote Paul's gospel, John wrote his gospel at Ephesus."
6. The Muratorian Canon (published 1749 by Muratori, librarian of the Ambrosian library of Milan), composed about A.D. 170–185, refers to St. Luke's gospel as the third, and to St. John's as the fourth.

(b) The tradition is confirmed by the manner in which the adversaries of the Church—Celsus, Marcion,

Basilides, Valentine—recognised the apostolic origin of the gospels. Moreover, the following books, some authentic, some apocryphal, no one of which is later than A.D. 150, contain evident allusions to the Gospels.

Epistle of St. Barnabas, about A.D. 100.
Pastor of Hermas, A.D. 95–140.
Didache, A.D. 80–100, discovered in 1873 in the library of Constantinople by Philotheus Bryennius.
Epistle of St. Polycarp, about A.D. 110.
Epistle of Diognetus, A.D. 100–140.
Seven epistles of St. Ignatius of Antioch, A.D. c. 110.
Epistle of St. Clement, A.D. c. 96.

Thus we find at a distance from Apostolic times of only 100 years a universal, strong, precise tradition which declares that Matthew, Mark, Luke, and John were respectively the authors of the Gospels which bear their names.

II. Authenticity shown by the character of the writings.

1. The language under Greek form is Semitic.
2. The circumstances of country and people are described with an accuracy of detail which subsequent researches have abundantly verified.
3. The Gospels appeal to the reader as narratives, either of those who were themselves ocular witnesses, or of those who were associated with ocular witnesses of the events described. The apocryphal gospels presuppose the existence and authority of the canonical Gospels, as false money would not be coined and put into circulation if genuine money did not exist. In regard to the apocryphal gospels, Renan has written: "C'est faire injure à la littérature chrétienne que de mettre sur le même pied ces plates compositions et les chefs-d'œuvre de Marc, de Luc et de Matthieu" ("L'Église chrétienne").

C. The Veracity of the Gospels

1. It is clear that the Evangelists did not wish to deceive. The simple straightforward character of the narration, the holiness of the writers crowned by martyrdom, the absence of any conceivable motive which might influence them to deceive—these facts are strong testimony to their veracity.

2. The Evangelists could not have deceived. Either the Evangelists had more than transcendent ability in originating the character and doctrine of Christ, or they simply recorded the character and doctrine in accordance with their experience. Moreover, they recorded contemporary public facts and appealed to hundreds of witnesses. Again the four testimonies are in agreement and withal show characteristic differences.

3. The Evangelists were not deceived themselves. The facts which they describe were within their competence—palpable, public facts, and they were associated in the closest way with these facts. Even the enemies of Christianity did not question the facts which they relate, e.g. the miracles of Christ. Rousseau's words are well known: "The Gospel bears characteristics of truth so great, so striking, so inimitable, that its inventor would be more marvellous than its hero."

Regarding the dates of composition writers vary in their opinions. Harnack is, amongst European scholars, one of great authority in all that concerns the Christian literature of the first centuries. He writes in his "Chronologie": "In our criticism of the ancient sources of Christianity we are without any doubt in course of returning to tradition."

Catholic critics practically agree in dating the composition of the Synoptic Gospels between 50 and 70 A.D., and the composition of the fourth Gospel about 100 A.D. (cf. Vigouroux, art. "Évangile," "Diction. de la Bible," and Batiffol, "Six leçons sur l'Évangile").

III. DIVINE AUTHORITY OF THE GOSPELS

A. From the Gospels (the historical authority of which has been established) we learn that Christ founded a Church, and that He gave to this Church a doctrinal magisterium whereby she possesses the gift of infallibility in her decisions regarding Faith and Morals. It is, therefore, perfectly legitimate (from the logical point of view) that the Church should declare that the canonical books of the Old and New Testaments have Divine as well as human authority. The Vatican Council (Session III, c. II) emphasises this truth: "The books of the Old and New Testaments wholly and in each of their parts such as they are enumerated in the decree of the Council of Trent, and such as they appear in the Ancient Latin Vulgate edition, should be regarded as sacred and canonical not because being the result of human authorship they were subsequently approved by the Church, but because written under the inspiration of the Holy Ghost they have God for their author."

B. Nature of Inspiration.

Inspiration has been defined as "a charisma or special grace, by which the Holy Ghost moves, enlightens, and assists the sacred writer, so that he conceives exactly, reports faithfully, and expresses with infallible truth that which, and only that which, God intends him to write."

Certain deductions follow:

I. An inspired book is the result of a twofold causality. God is the principal cause, man is the instrumental cause, and the book is entirely the work of God, and entirely the work of man.

(a) Entirely the work of God.

1. It is the interior, immediate, antecedent, physical motion of God which decides the author to write.

2. It is the Divine light which reveals all and only the truths which God intends to be conveyed, and the suitable terms for the expression of those truths.

3. God guarantees the truth of what is written.

(b) Entirely the work of the sacred author.

The Divine motion does not interfere in any way with the liberty of the writer. He gathers materials for his book, makes researches, consults witnesses, etc. He acts precisely as a careful uninspired writer would do. His own style remains.

II. There is a distinction between Revelation and Inspiration.

1. Revelation makes known truths which, for the most part, were previously unknown. Inspiration is concerned with truths for the most part previously known.

2. In Revelation the Divine action is apparent to him to whom the truth is communicated. In Inspiration the inspired writer is not necessarily conscious of any supernatural help.

III. False definitions of Inspiration.

The Vatican Council condemns as false the opinion that Inspiration is only a negative assistance preserving the writer from error. The Council condemns also the view that Inspiration consists in a subsequent Divine approbation given to what is written.

Two other theories are false, one limiting the Divine influence to the human will, and the other making a purely passive instrument of the writer.

IV. The Bible being the word of God cannot contain formal error.

C. The aim and extent of Inspiration.

Baronius wrote " The Bible was inspired to teach one not how the heavens move but how one goes to heaven." The aim of the inspired writings is the inculcation of religious truth and the sanctification of mankind.

In regard to the extent of Inspiration we must distinguish in the Bible two kinds of writing : (1) texts which belong directly to the substance of Faith, and (2) mixed passages intimately connected with the teaching of dogmatic truths, but including also the domain of natural science or of history, e.g. allusions to nature, to chronological details, etc. The question arises can the texts which refer to truths of natural science or to some irrelevant matter be uninspired ? Cardinal

Newman in an article to the "Nineteenth Century," February, 1884, suggested the non-inspiration of what he called "obiter dicta," such as the statement of St. Paul concerning the cloak left at Troas. The encyclical "Providentissimus Deus" is considered to have condemned this opinion.

But are there not mistakes in the Bible?

Before giving a definite answer to this question it will be well to lay down certain principles.

1. There cannot be formal error in the Bible unless the writer teaches as true a statement which proves to be false.

2. Inspiration is not Revelation. The writer may have imperfect knowledge of the phenomena of nature, and if he mentions them he does so in the sense generally accepted at the time.

3. Hence, there may be an absence of scientific precision such as "the sun stood still," "he brought the shadow ten degrees backwards by the lines by which it had already gone down in the dial of Achaz" (Kings iv., xx., ii.).

But as these conventions are used nowadays, "sunrise," "sunset," etc., it would be pedantic to call them errors.

From the standpoint of Inspiration may historical statements be regarded as current views of the period not necessarily accurate?

No decision of the Biblical Commission answers the question directly, but where the decisions have touched the subject they favour a negative answer to the question. The Commission seems to say in general "whatever reads as history must be accepted as history—and true history—*unless* it can be shown on good grounds that the writer is only retailing the current view, *and* is not making that view his own." One should be careful over the wording of statements even as regards scientific matters. Leo XIII does not say that the Old Testament writers gave expression to current scientific views, but that they spoke of scientific matters in language or terms then current, and still current, and which always will be current even in the mouths of scientists when they are not writing manuals of science. The parallelism between History and Science does not hold.

CHAPTER XV

THE DIVINITY OF THE CHRISTIAN FAITH

I. Attestation of Prophecy

THE thesis, the proof of which now claims attention, may be stated in syllogistic form

If Christ is the Messias—the authoritative envoy of God—the religion which He has founded is divine.

But Christ claims to be not only the Messias but God himself, and has confirmed His claim by prophecies and miracles.

Therefore He is the Messias and the Christian Religion is divine.

The claim of Messiahship which Christ made was asserted both privately and publicly. We recall the words which He spoke to the Samaritan woman, when looking to the future coming of the Messias, she said " He will tell us all things." " I am he," replied Christ. We recall, too, the praise given to Peter when at Cæsarea-Philippi the apostle made his great profession of Faith : " Thou art Christ, the son of the living God." " Blessed art thou Simon Bar-Jona ; because flesh and blood have not revealed it to thee, but my Father who is in heaven." For an instance of the public assertion of His claim, it is recorded in the tenth chapter of St. John (vv. 23 sq.) that on a certain occasion Jesus walked in the temple in Solomon's porch, and the Jews said to Him " How long dost thou hold our souls in suspense ? If thou be the Christ, tell us plainly." And Jesus answered : " I speak to you, and you believe not ; the works that I do in the name of my Father, they give testimony of me." The Jews understood His words so well that they attempted to stone Him. Again,

THE DIVINITY OF THE CHRISTIAN FAITH 195

on even a more solemn occasion, when He was arraigned before Caiaphas the high-priest, and when the latter said
I adjure thee by the living God, that thou tell us if thou be the Christ the Son of God." Jesus replied: "Thou hast said it. I am." That Christ claimed the Messiahship in the proper sense of the word is obvious from the fact that He could not allow His hearers to form a false impression from ambiguity of phrase. To preserve His hearers from error was a duty which He owed to Himself, to His followers, and to God.

The Messiahship which Christ claimed means that He was:
1. The Liberator whom God had promised to His people.
2. The superhuman person whose attributes had been prophesied for centuries.
3. The King who would rise from the dead, judge men, restore the chosen race, and establish the Kingdom of God on earth—the Kingdom of truth and justice.

The title "Messias"—the leader of the Elect—was applicable to Our Blessed Lord during His earthly ministry, inasmuch as the new Messianic Kingdom was founded by Him. Though the Messianic Kingdom will not be fully realised till the end of time, yet it is not true to say that the rôle of Christ was exclusively, or even essentially eschatological.

"I am he." The authority of an affirmation varies in accordance with the intellectual and moral perfection of him who makes it. Needless to point out that if Christ's claim be not allowed, it follows that He was either an impostor or a madman. It is difficult to understand the frame of mind which would on the one hand disallow the truth of His doctrine, and at the same time write of Him: "If the life and death of Socrates are those of a sage, the life and death of Jesus are those of a God" (Rousseau). The claim of Messiahship was confirmed by prophecies, and it will be remembered that three conditions are necessary for the probative force of prophecy:
1. The prophecy must have been the certain and precise announcement of a future event which could not have been naturally known.

2. The prophecy must have been realised.
3. The prophecy must have been made in confirmation of doctrine or fact.

The following classification of prophecies is usually given.

A. Prophecies made in relation to Christ's passion and death.
1. Betrayal by Judas   Matthew xxvi. 21–25   Mark xiv. 20 ; Luke xxii. 21   John vi. 71, xiii. 21.
2. Abandonment by disciples   Matthew xxvi. 31   Mark xiv. 27   John xvi. 32.
3. Denial by Peter   Matthew xxvi. 34 ,   Mark xiv. 30   Luke xxii. 34 ; John xiii. 38.
4. Delivered to Priests, Scribes, and Pharisees ; delivered to Gentiles, insulted, spat upon, scourged, Crucifixion and Resurrection   Matthew xx. 18, 19 ; Mark ix. 30 ; Luke xviii. 31–33 ; John xii. 32–34.

The fulfilment of these prophecies is recorded in the xxvi. and xxvii. chapters of St. Matthew ; the xiv. and xv. chapters of St. Mark ; the xxii. and xxiii. chapters of St. Luke ; and the xviii. and xix. chapters of St. John.

B. Prophecies relative to the persecution of the Apostles and death of St. Peter

Matthew x. 17 ; Luke xxi. 12 ; John xvi. 2, xxi. 18.

The Acts of the Apostles and the Epistles of St. Paul witness to the fulfilment of these prophecies. St. Peter's martyrdom is mentioned in St. Clement's first Epistle, chapter V ; in St. Irenæus, Adv. Hæreses, III. 1 ; in Eusebius, Hist. Eccl., II. 25.

C. Prophecies relating to the coming of the Holy Ghost and the destinies of the Church

John xiv. 26 ; Acts i. 8 ; Matthew xvi. 18, xxviii. 19, 20.

The descent of the Holy Ghost is recorded in Acts ii. 4, and the triumph of the Church is a fact of history. She persists and manifests a triple immutability of being, doctrine, and love.

D. Prophecies relative to the ruin of Jerusalem and the destruction of the temple

Matthew xxiii. 37, 38, xxiv. 2, 7, 34 ; Mark xiii. 1, 2 ; Luke xiii. 34, 35, xix. 41, 44, xxi. 5, 12, 21, 24.

The destruction of city and temple by Titus in the year 70, about forty years after the prophecy of Our Lord, is well known. Eusebius tells us (Hist. Eccl., Bk. III, c. V) that before the siege of Titus the Christians had left the city and had gone to Pella, because they had believed implicitly in the truth of the prophecy. In the year 362 Julian the Apostate desired, by rebuilding the temple, to make void the prophecy of Christ. Ammianus Marcellinus—officer and pagan historian—records the miraculous occurrences which frustrated the impious design.

E. Prophecies relative to the rejection of the synagogue and the dispersion of the Jews:

Matthew xxi. 33-46, xxii. 1-10 ; Mark xii. 1-12 ; Luke xx. 9-19.

The Jews as a people are dispersed, but as a race they exist and render a perpetual testimony to the accomplishment of prophecy, whereas the Assyrians, Medes, Persians, Ancient Greeks, and Romans have either disappeared or have been profoundly changed.

The prophecies enumerated above are undoubtedly prophecies in the strictest sense. The predictions are (1) announced with certainty of their fulfilment, and the facts and circumstances are so numerous as to preclude the possibility of chance. The predictions are (2) announced with precision, and (3) concern future events. Nor (4) could the facts themselves, nor the minute details added, have been naturally inferred.

Objection. According to Strauss and Renan the prophecies were made after the events.

Answer. (a) This objection impugns the veracity of the Gospels already established.

(b) The objection is also disproved by the conformity of the Gospel narratives to the circumstances and details which existed before the destruction of Jerusalem.

(c) The prophecy in regard to the permanent dispersion of the Jews and the propagation of the Church were not realised till more than 100 years after the destruction of Jerusalem.

(*d*) The emigration of the Christians to Pella was suggested by the prophecy.

(*e*) The destruction of the City and the world are described together in prophetic vision. Had the prophecy been made after A.D. 70 the two events would not have been thus associated.

Finally, the prophecies were made in confirmation of doctrine. Christ in the 10th chapter of St. John appeals to miraculous works as the credentials of His doctrine, and He makes specific appeal in John xiii. 19 and xvi. 4 to the future realisation of prophecy as indicating the Divine origin of His doctrine.

II. Attestation of Miracles

1. The miracles classified opposite are reported by several evangelists whose good faith and honesty we know.
2. They were wrought publicly. If our Lord was anxious that the miracles should not be spoken of, this was lest there should be a political movement to put Him in power.
3. They attracted the attention of King Herod, of the Sanhedrin, of the Judges, Luke xxiii. ; John xi. 47 ; John ix. 13.
4. The miracles are appealed to by Christ Himself.
5. Their objective reality is admitted by modern critics.

Many miracles of Christ fulfil the conditions required to constitute their valid criteria :

1. They are facts cognoscible by the senses.
2. They are extraordinary.
3. They surpass the power of created nature, either substantially, or in the manner of their performance.
4. Add to the foregoing
    (1) facility wherewith they were done ;
    (2) number and variety ;
    (3) certainty of the result ;
    (4) stability of the effects, e.g. health ;
    (5) happy results on individuals and the masses.

THE DIVINITY OF THE CHRISTIAN FAITH 199

(a) Wrought on irrational beings.
1. Water changed into wine. John ii. 2–11.
2. Miraculous draughts. Luke v. 1–11; John xxi. 3–11.
3. Storm stilled. Matt. viii. 18–27.
4. Bread multiplied. Mark vi. 30–44; viii. 1–9.
5. Walking on waters. Matt. xiv. 22, 25, 29.
6. Fig tree withered. Matt. xxi. 18, 19.

(b) Wrought on human beings.

1. Maladies cured:
   (a) temporary, e.g. fever.
   (b) Chronic, e.g. paralysis.
   (c) Organic, e.g. Congenital blindness.
   1. Ruler's son. John iv. 43–54.
   2. Peter's mother-in-law. Mark i. 29 sq.
   3. Leper. Luke v. 12, 13.
   4. Paralytic of Capharnaum. Luke v. 17–26.
   5. Man with withered hand. Luke vi. 6–10.
   6. Centurion's servant. Matt. viii. 5–13.
   7. Issue of Blood. Mark v. 25–29.
   8. Daughter of Canaanite. Matt. xv. 21–28.
   9. Deaf mute. Mark vii. 32–35.
   10. Blind man of Bethsaida. Mark viii. 22–25.
   11. Man born blind. John ix. 1–11.
   12. Two blind men. Matt. ix. 27–30.
   13. Dropsical man. Luke xiv. 1–4.
   14. Lepers. Luke xvii. 11–14.
   15. Blind men at Jericho. Matt. xx. 29–34.
   16. Malchus' ear. Luke xxii. 51.

2. Demons exorcised.
   1. Man in Synagogue of Capharnaum. Mark i. 23–26.
   2. Man possessed (blind and dumb). Matt. xii. 22.
   3. Gerasenes. Matt. viii. 28–32.
   4. Dumb Demoniac. Luke xi. 14.
   5. Boy possessed. Mark ix. 16–26.
   6. Woman bent double. Luke xiii. 10–13.

3. Dead raised to life.
   1. Daughter of Jairus. Matt. ix. 18, 23–25.
   2. Widow's son. Luke vii. 12–15.
   3. Lazarus. John xi. 1 sq.

The miracles of Christ cannot be explained by magic, by physical causes, or psychical states (e.g. hypnotism), nor can they be characterised as myths or legends.

To prove that the miracles have been wrought in confirmation of doctrine note the following

1. John x. 25. "The works that I do in my Father's name give testimony of me."

2. John xi. On the occasion of the resurrection of Lazarus, Christ said expressly that He would work the miracle "so that they might believe that you (His Father) have sent me."

3. The apostles understood the motive of His miracles, John iii. 2 ; John xx. 30, 31.

4. John the Baptist (John i. 32–34), Nicodemus (John iii. 2), the Ruler (John iv. 48), the crowd (Matthew xii. 23), gave the same interpretation to the miraculous works accomplished by Christ.

III. ATTESTATION OF THE RESURRECTION OF CHRIST

The Resurrection of Christ is the keystone of all His miracles—the corner-stone of Apologetics. The transcendental importance of the miracle is attested :

1. By Our Lord Himself who appeals to it and presents it as the most striking proof of the Divinity of His Doctrine.

2. By the apostles, 1 Corinthians xv.

3. By His enemies, e.g. the Jews. The sepulchre was sealed and surrounded by soldiers.

By the Resurrection we mean that :

1. The soul of Christ, after being separated from the body, was reunited to the Body on the third day.
2. The Body was that which Christ had during His life, having still the traces of the wounds, but freed from certain material conditions, and endowed with the qualities belonging to a glorified body.

A. Christ predicted His Resurrection in confirmation of His mission.

The allusions to His Resurrection made by Christ were in me cases figurative and in other cases open and categorical.

When He had expelled the buyers and sellers from the temple and was asked for some sign in justification of His drastic action, He replied "Destroy this temple, and in three days I will raise it up." The Evangelist adds "He spoke of the temple of his body" (John ii. 18 *sqq*.). On another occasion when the Pharisees demanded a sign, Our Lord replied by reminding them that the fate of Jonas symbolised His own burial. A reference to Matthew xxvii. 63 *sqq*. will show that the meaning of the figurative language used by Our Lord was understood quite well.

The explicit allusions to His Resurrection are numerous. Compare Matthew xvi. 21, xvii. 21, 22 ; Mark ix. 30, x. 34, ix. 8 ; and Luke xviii. 33.

B. Christ arose from the Dead.
(1) He died.
    1. Witnesses worthy of belief.
        St. John xix. 30, ocular witness.
        St. Peter, Acts ii. 32, iii. 15.
        Evangelists—Matthew xxvii. 50 ; Mark xv. 37 ; Luke xxiii. 46.
        St. Paul, 1 Corinthians xv. 3–25.
        Apostles, Acts iv. 33.
    2. Attested by Jews.
        (*a*) Joseph of Arimathæa, Mark xv. 43–45.
        (*b*) Soldiers. John xix. 32, 33.
    3. Why should the Sanhedrin, Rabbis, etc., have had recourse to subterfuges, to explain the disappearance of Christ's Body, unless they were convinced of His death ?
    4. Tortures.
        (1) Agony : sweat of blood.
        (2) Scourging.
        (3) Crowning with thorns.
        (4) Crucifixion ; "crudelissimum teterrimumque supplicium" (Cicero in Verrem, Book V, Chapter 64, Section 165).
        (5) Wound by lance.
    5. The tomb for about thirty-six hours.

(2) He rose again from the dead. Attested by
   1. Evangelists and Apostles.
      (a) He appeared to them several times during the forty days.
      (b) They were upright men who cannot be suspected of fraud.
      (c) They were neither credulous nor enthusiastic.
      (d) They were willing to die in proof of their conviction.
   2. Appearances of Christ to
      (1) Magdalene, John xx.
      (2) Women returning from sepulchre, Matthew xxviii.
      (3) Two disciples on the way to Emmaus, Luke xxiv.
      (4) Peter, Luke xxiv.
      (5) Apostles without Thomas, John xx.
      (6) Apostles with Thomas, John xx.
      (7) Disciples on lake, John xxi.
      (8) Eleven apostles on Mount of Galilee, Matthew xxviii.
      (9) More than 500 disciples, 1 Corinthians xv.
      (10) St. James, 1 Corinthians xv.
      (11) Disciples at Jerusalem, Mark xvi., and on Mount of Olives, Luke xxiv.
      (12) St. Paul, 1 Corinthians xv. 8.
   3. Attested by the enemies of Christ. They bribed the guards. Why did they not convict the apostles of fraud when they preached the Resurrection?
   4. Belief of the apostles and of the world. Miracles were worked by the apostles to confirm belief in the truth of the Resurrection. Moreover, the foundation, duration, and development of Christianity must have a proportionate cause.
   5. Absurdity of the explanations given by adversaries of Christianity.
      (a) The supposed appearances of Christ were visions and hallucinations.

>> *Strauss:* A purely subjective vision or perhaps some external object gave the impression of a manifestation of Jesus."
>>
>> *Renan:* "Ce qui a ressuscité Jesus, c'est l'amour."
>>
>> *Ewald, Sabatier,* etc.

Answer. 1. A hallucination is a sensation without a palpable material cause. The risen body of Our Lord was material and palpable.

2. A hallucination does not exercise any natural influence upon surrounding objects.

3. A hallucination of the senses can be rectified by an appeal to reason unless the reason is disturbed, and the seer a lunatic.

>> (b) The appearances were pneumatic or spiritual apparitions only. The spiritualised body of Christ was revealed to the mind of the apostles.

Answer. The apostles believed in the bodily appearance of Christ. St. Paul clearly distinguishes the apparition on the way to Damascus, when Christ appeared to him, σωματικῶς, i.e. corporally (Colossians ii. 19), from the visions received in a state of ecstasy. (Acts xxii. 17-21 Acts xxiii. 11; Acts xviii. 9.)

CHAPTER XVI

"THOU ART CHRIST, THE SON OF THE LIVING GOD

1. Thou art Christ"

Realisation of Messianic Prophecy

A. It is a fact of history that the Messias was expected at the time when Christ was born. The deputation of Jews sent to the Baptist to ask him who he was (John i. 19, 20) received the answer: "I am not the Christ." And John's own disciples went later to hear Christ's reply to the momentous question (Matthew xi. 3) "Art thou he who art to come, or look we for another?" The miracle of the multiplication of the loaves evoked from those who witnessed it the exclamation (John vi. 14), "This is the prophet indeed that is come into the world." It is clear that the Gospels bear emphatic testimony to the expectation of the Messias.

The expectation was general. Gamaliel in his discourse to the Sanhedrin (Acts v. 34–39) reminds his hearers of the false claims of Theodas, and of Judas the Galilæan, each of whom posed as the Messias. Both perished, and Gamaliel points to the inference that the work of men will fall to nothing, but if the work be of God it cannot be destroyed. Even beyond the limits of the Holy Land and the chosen people, in pagan Rome and elsewhere, a vague tradition of the coming of a deliverer was cherished. (Cf. Virgil, eclogue 4.)

Moreover, the expectation of the Messias was based upon Old Testament prophecies. Witness the fact that Herod made enquiries through the official interpreter concerning the prophecy where Christ should be born. Zachary (Luke i. 68-70) alludes to the fulfilment of Divine promise: "Blessed be the Lord God of Israel because he hath raised up a horn of salvation in the house of David His servant as he spoke by the mouth of his holy prophets who are from the beginning." Philip said to Nathanael (John i. 45) "We have found him of whom Moses in the law and the prophets did write, Jesus the son of Joseph of Nazareth." St. Matthew, who wrote for the Jews, and whose object was to demonstrate that Christ was the Messias, quotes the Old Testament more than sixty times. Proofs equally strong are forthcoming from Jewish writings. The Talmud declares that "all prophecies refer to the Messias," and Maimonides acknowledges that "he who denies the coming of the Messias denies all Scripture." Edersheim in his "Life and Times of Jesus the Messias," enumerates 456 texts of the Old Testament which the Rabbis interpreted as referring to the Messias. That the prophecies are (1) genuine follows from the admission even of many Rationalists that the prophetic books were written between 800 and 500 B.C., and, as detailed in a former chapter, there is a very high probability against the realisation of a whole complexus of prophetical utterances, taken cumulatively, even if the details of some are lacking in precision and definiteness. The prophecies are (2) Messianic because they relate to a determinate individual. On the journey to Emmaus, Christ, "beginning from Moses and the prophets, expounded to them (the two disciples), in all the Scriptures, the things that were concerning him." (Luke xxiv. 27.) The prophecies give, as we shall see, many and minute details of the Messias—His birth, life, character, passion, and death. "Suppose," writes Father Pesch, "that several sculptors carve without any concerted action or agreement the different parts of a statue—the one, a hand; another, an arm; a third, a foot; a fourth, the head, and so on; is there the least probability that all these parts will suit so exactly as to form a statue as perfect as if it came from the chisel of a single artist? Equally unlikely that the different disjointed prophecies should, reunited, represent a man corresponding in every particular to Jesus (Institutiones propaedeuticae).

B. Detailed exposition of the Messianic prophecies

I. Person.

FAMILY
: Race of Abraham (Gen. xii.), of Isaac (Gen. xxvi.), of Jacob (Gen. xxviii.).
  House and Family of David (2 Kings vii. Ps. lxxxviii. Isa. xi. Jer. xxiii.).

BIRTH
: (a) Time. When Judah shall have lost the sceptre (Gen. xlix.).
  Before destruction of second temple (Aggeus ii.).
  After 69 weeks of years (Dan. ix.).
  (b) Place. Bethlehem (Micheas v.).
  (c) Manner. Born of a Virgin (Isaias vii.).

CHARACTER
: (a) Poor, laborious, despised life (Isa. liii.; Ps. lxxxvii.).
  (b) Subject to Divine will (Ps. xxxix.).
  (c) Sweetness (Is. xlii.; Ezek. xxxiv.).

LIFE
: (a) Hidden; preceded by precursor (Mal. iii.).
  (b) Public
      His preaching (Is. ix.).
      Peace and Salvation (Is. xlii.).
      Confirmed by miracles (Is. xxxv.).

PASSION AND DEATH
: Kings and Princes will conspire against Him (Ps. ii.).
  Entry into Jerusalem on an ass (Zach. ix.).
  Betrayal by His own (Ps. xl.).
  Abandoned by disciples (Zach. xiii.).
  Sold for thirty pieces of silver (Zach. xi.).
  Filling of traitor's place by another (Ps. cviii.).
  False witness (Ps. xxvi., xxxvi.).
  Silence (Is. liii.).
  Scourging and insults (Is. l.).

"THOU ART CHRIST,

PASSION AND DEATH
- Reproach of men and outcast of people (Ps. xxi.).
- Piercing of hands and feet (Ps. xxi.).
- Gall given in His thirst (Ps. lxviii.).
- Partition of garments (Ps. xxi.).
- Mockery (Ps. xxi.; Wis. ii.).
- Prayer for enemies (Is. liii.).
- Cry to His Father (Ps. xxi.).
- Earthquake and darkness (Ps. xvii.; Amos viii.).
- Cut off from living (Is. liii.).
- Pierced with lance (Zach. xii.).
- No bone broken (Exod. xii.).
- Sepulchre from a rich man, and guarded by impious (Is. liii.).

RESURRECTION AND ASCENSION
- His body will not see corruption (Ps. xv.).
- He will rise the third day (Osee vi.).
- He will be the death of death (Osee xiii.).
- Triumphant on Olivet (Zach. xiv.).
- Borne on clouds to Heaven (Dan. vii.).
- At right hand of God (Ps. cix.).
- Awaiting day of retribution (Isa. xiii.).

II. Functions.

(a) King
- Ps. ii., xliv., cix.; Dan. vii. Isa. ix.
- Spiritual Kingdom (Is. xlix., lx.; Zach. ix.).
- Pacific Kingdom (Isa. ix.; Micheas v.).
- Universal in time (Isa. ix.).
- Universal in place (Zach. ix.).
- Legislative power (Deut. xviii.).

(b) Priest (Ps. cix.; Isa. lii., liii.).
(c) Prophet, i.e. one who speaks to men in the name of God (Deut. xviii.; Isa. lxi.).

III. Work.
(a) Redemption (Gen. iii., xii., xxii.).
   Gen. xlix. (Desired of nations.)

(b) Establishment of the Church
- New alliance (Isa. xlix. ; Jer. xxxi.).
- Propagation (Isa. xliv., lx., lii.).
- Visible, Catholic, Holy, One, Indefectible, Perpetual, Magisterium, Judiciary power (Isa. xlix., ix., lxi., xlii., xix.).
- Holy Eucharist (Isa. xxv.).
- The Church would sing continued thanksgivings (Isa. xlii.).

C. Fulfilment of Prophecy.
I. Person.

RACE — Christ was of the race of Abraham, Isaac, and Jacob ; of the House and Family of David, cf. Genealogical tables, Journey of St. Joseph, cry of people " Son of David."

BIRTH — Judah had lost the sceptre.
(The edict of Artaxerxes was issued about the year 461. Christ was born 4 B.C., and His public life began about A.D. 26. Add, therefore, 461+26 which gives 487—the 69 weeks of years.)
Christ was born of a Virgin (Luke i. 34-35).
At Bethlehem (Luke ii. 1-7).

CHARACTER — Tender Father (Luke xv.).
Good Shepherd (John x. ; Luke xv. 4-6).
Good Samaritan (Luke x. 30-37).
Poor and laborious life (Matt. viii. 20; Mark vi. 3).
Submissive (John iv. 34).
Meek and Gentle (Matt. xii. 20).

LIFE — Hidden (Luke ii. 51).
Public ; preaching of the Baptist (John i. 23).
Baptism (Luke iii. 21-23).
Lived at Capharnaum, on the confines of Zabulon and Nephtali, " in order that the word of the prophet might be fulfilled " (Matt. iv. 14).
He preached peace and salvation (Matt. xxiii. 37 ; Luke xiii. 34 ; John xvii. 20-26).

PASSION AND DEATH Fulfilment evident from the Gospel narrative.

II. Functions.
(a) King (John xviii. 37).
By the merits of His work and death He " drew all to Him " (John xii. 32).
Universal power (Matt. xviii. 18).
Judiciary power (John v. 22).
Coercive power (Matt. xxv. 25 sq.; Luke xiii. 3, 5).
Legislative power (Luke ii. 22; Matt. v. 21; Matt. xix. 17).
(b) Priest. As priest He prays for Himself (John xvii. 1; Matt. xxvi. 39; Heb. v. 7; Heb. vii. 24; and for others John xvii. 9. Cf. Hebrews v. 6).
(c) Prophet. He always claimed to be the legate of God.
III. Works.
Redemption and establishment of the Church obviously fulfilled.

II. "Thou art the Son of the Living God"

The Jewish conception of the Messias did not imply a Divine Being. In their idea the Messias was the heaven-sent ambassador or envoy of God, who would lead the chosen people to a state of independence and honour.

" Son of God " may be understood as the expression of a merely moral union with God, e.g. " We are the children of God," or it may imply Divine filiation in its strict and literal sense.

Before proceeding to an examination of the exegetical grounds on which the Divinity of Christ is based, it is important to note that no such procedure is strictly necessary. Christ as the Envoy of God has established the Christian Church. God, throughout the ages, has in the most striking way attested the truth and Divine authority of the Church. It is therefore within the competence of this Church, divinely guided and infallibly preserved from error, to pronounce upon the origin and character of her founder, and needless to say the Church has, from the beginning, borne emphatic witness to the Godhead of Christ. But, though not necessary, it is interesting and instructive to set out the exegetical reasons which justify belief in this central dogma of the Christian Faith.

Two groups of Texts require separate consideration.

A. First Group of Texts

I. Passages in which Christ is proclaimed the "Son of God."
  (a) Testimony from Heaven.
    Luke i. 32. Annunciation.
    Mark i. 11. Baptism.
    Mark ix. 6. Transfiguration.
  (b) Testimony from this world.
    Matthew xiv. 33. Disciples in the boat.
    Matthew xvi. 16. Confession of Peter.
    Matthew xxvii. 40. Jews in mockery.
  (c) Testimony from Hell.
    Luke iv. 3. Temptation in the desert.
    Luke iv. 41. Various exorcisms.

II. Passages in which Christ declares Himself the "Son of God."
          Matthew xxvi. 63.
          Mark xiv. 61, 62.
          Luke xxii. 67–70.

III. Passages which describe Christ as receiving "adoration."

Matthew viii. 2 (leper); Mark v. 6 (Gerasene); Luke v. 8 (Peter); John ix. 35, 38 (blind man); Matthew xiv. 33 (disciples); Matthew xxviii. 9 (Holy Women); Luke xxiv. 52 (disciples after Resurrection).

Do the words "Son of God" quoted above imply a real filial relation?

1. *Rationalist Theory.* Christ claimed to be the Messias and nothing more. Hence, Son of God and Messias are identical in meaning (Loisy, Strauss, Renan, Harnack).

Loisy maintains that the divinity of Christ is a matter of Faith, and cannot be proved from the Synoptic Gospels. In regard to St. John's testimony he writes: " Le quatrième Évangile est un livre de théologie mystique où l'on entend la voix de la conscience chrétienne, non le Christ de l'histoire " ("Autour d'un petit livre," p. 138).

Strauss : the Gospels are mythological because they accept the supernatural.

Renan : " Qui dit au dessus ou en dehors de la nature dans l'ordre des faits dit une contradiction " ("Études d'Histoire religieuse," pp. 129, 207).

2. Catholic Critics.

(*a*) Some consider as synonymous in meaning the words " Christ " and " Son of God," because the words have sprung from Old Testament prophecies, and in these prophecies the Messias is not conceived of as divine.

(*b*) Others maintain that in the confession of Peter and the interrogation of Caiaphas, the words " Son of God " have a significance more profound. It should be remembered that when Peter made his famous " Confession," the disciples had seen Christ calm the tempest, walk upon the waters, forgive sins, etc. Christ has said " No one knows the Son but the Father " (Matthew xi. 27 ; Luke x. 22). Therefore when Christ said to Peter : " Flesh and Blood hath not revealed it to thee, but my Father who is in Heaven," etc., Christ implied that the quality of the Son of God is of an order so transcendental, so divine, so impenetrable to the mind of man that it requires for its comprehension a revelation from God.

In regard to the interrogation of Caiaphas, " *Son of God* " as claimed by Christ was understood by the Jews in its literal sense, i.e. as indicating a real filial relationship. M. Wiel, in his " Le Judaisme," has the following : " Jesus comparait devant le Sanhédrin, pour répondre à l'accusation de lèse-majesté divine." In the texts Luke xxii. 68, 70 notice :

" If thou be *Christ*, tell us."
Art thou then the Son of God ?

Compare John xix. 7. We have a law, and according to the law He ought to die, because He made Himself the Son of God," cf. John v. 18 and x. 33. The texts which record instances of adoration and prostration are significant. In Acts x. 25, 26 St. Peter deprecates the prostration of Cornelius. Does not the acceptance of this homage by Our Lord imply that He was Divine ? " The Lord thy God thou shalt adore."

The conclusion which Catholic critics maintain is that Jesus is not the Son of God, because He is the Messias ; He is the Messias because He is the Son of God.

B. Second Group of Texts

In the second group of texts it will be shown that Christ
(1) calls God His Father ;
(2) identifies Himself with God in nature and work.
(3) assumes the titles and appropriates the perfections of God.
(4) claims Divine rights and exercises Divine power.
I. Synoptic testimony.
(a) Christ is above men and angels.
 Luke xxiv. 49. Distinction between *my* Father and your Father.
 Matthew xii. 41, 42, xxii. 41–46. Christ greater than Jonas, Solomon, or David.
 Matthew xii. 5, 6, v. 33, 37. Christ greater than the Temple or the Law.
 Mark ii. 27, 28. Christ greater than the Sabbath.
 Matthew xxv. 31, iv. 11, xxvi. 53. Ministry of angels, and therefore Christ's superiority to them.
(b) Christ possesses all power.
 Matthew xxviii. 18. " All power."
 Matthew ix. 2–6. Power to forgive sin.
 Matthew xxv. 31–46. Power to judge mankind.
(c) Christ calls God His Father ; and claims to be His Son and Heir.
 Many times during His life, and twice on the cross, He called God His Father.

Mark xii. 1–9. Parable of the Vineyard.
Luke xxii. 28–30. " I give you a kingdom, etc.," i.e. the kingdom received as Son and Heir, He gives to His followers.
II. Johannine Testimony.
(a) Christ proclaims Himself of Divine origin, and Son of God.
John viii. 23. " I am not of this world."
John iii. 13, 16. " God so loved the world," etc. Cf. John xx. 17.
(b) Christ identifies Himself with God in nature and work. Nature. John x. 30. " We are one."
John xiv. 10, 11. " The Father in me, and I in him."
Work. John v. 19. " All that the Father does, the Son does."
(c) Christ assumes the titles, and claims the perfections of God.
Titles. Way, Truth, Life, John xiv. 6; Lux Mundi, John viii. 12; Panis Vivens, John vi. 51; Resurrectio et vita, John xi. 25.
Perfections. Eternity, John viii. 58; Power (1) Master of Material life, John x. 17 John v. 21 (2) Master of Spiritual life, John vi. 55; ubiquity, John iii. 13.
(d) Christ claims for Himself the worship due to God the Father.
John v. 23. Same worship to Him as to Father.
John iii. 18. Faith.
John xv. 16. Hope. Prayer in His name.
John xv. 23. Charity. Love withheld from Son is withheld from Father.

Cumulative Force of Testimony

All representative Catholic critics teach that the proclamation of Christ as Son of God, His claiming God as *His* Father in a special sense, His identification of Himself with God in nature and work, His assumption of the titles, and His claims to the perfections of God, His claim to Divine rights and power—all these constitute an argument of cumulative force which is unassailable.

Résumé

1. Divine Filiation is a " Dynamic fellowship " based upon identity of nature and operation.
2. Filiation and Messiahship are distinct.
3. Christ requires Faith in His Person as well as in His mission. Matthew x. 37, 38.
4. The DIVINITY of Christ is not a deduction from His Messiahship, but the outcome of His teaching.
5. The Divine Personality of Christ is not the result of the teaching of St. John and his school; Divine Filiation is taught also in the Synoptic Gospels, and in the Epistles of St. Paul.
6. The Divine Sonship does not date from the Incarnation, but from all eternity.
7. Thus also speak the Apostolic Fathers in regard to Christ
    St. Ignatius of Antioch   God," " Our God."
    St. Justin :   God made man."
    Tatian   " God born in the form of man."
    St. Irenæus : " God," " God made man."

CHAPTER XVII

ESCHATOLOGICAL APOLOGETICS

CATHOLICS as a rule concern themselves with eschatological teaching only so far as the subject suggests matter for meditation. The four last things to be remembered constitute the foundation of every mission and retreat. " Watch, for you know not the day nor the hour " is the practical conclusion which the exercitant endeavours to realise and to make operative in daily life. But, within the last few years, since the publication of Schweitzer's work, *Von Reimarus zu Wrede* (1906), the storm centre of theological controversy, both in Germany and in England, has shifted from other quarters and concentrated its threatening forces upon the eschatological references made by Our Blessed Lord during His public life and reported by the Synoptists and by St. John. Before consideration of the subject in detail it will be well to indicate in a general way the drift of this, the latest development of the " Higher Criticism."

It is curious to note how well the newest eschatological teaching harmonises with the trend and the chief tenet of Modernism. For Modernism—the " synthesis of all errors " —cannot disguise its antipathy to the Godhead of Christ. We may describe Modernism comprehensively as being Pantheistic in philosophy and Unitarian in divinity. And if a thoroughgoing modernist were asked to state the reasons which lead him to disbelieve in the divinity of Christ, in all probability the argument would be formulated as follows (We must ask the reader's pardon for even the bare statement of a view so shocking to the Christian mind and heart) " Christ believed in and taught the immediateness of the eschatological kingdom. In Matthew x. 13, when instructing the Apostles, who were about to begin the Galilæan mission, Christ said   Amen I say to you, you shall not finish all the cities of Israel till the Son of Man come.' The Galilæan mission was concluded, and the prophecy remained unfulfilled, with the result that Christ journeyed northwards, outside the boundary of the Holy Land, to escape the embarrassment and discredit of His mistaken anticipation. And since He was mistaken, it follows that however sublime His teaching, He was man, and man only—a teacher of marvellous insight and power, it is true, but not transcending in His instruction the limits of the human and the fallible." So argues the modernist. And thus the single word " Parousia " —the coming of Christ and of the Kingdom—suggests the fundamental principle of modernistic doctrine, as well as the central tenet of up-to-date eschatology as interpreted by Schweitzer, Loisy, and Tyrrell.

The following questions must accordingly be answered Was the immediate coming of the eschatological kingdom the chief truth emphasised by Our Blessed Lord ? What must we hold in regard to His messianic consciousness ? Has the claim of adhering closely to the Gospels—a claim made by Schweitzer and his followers—any validity in fact ? Does the eschatological interpretation of Christ's teaching support the sacramental system of the Church as Fr. Tyrrell maintained ? Can we so interpret Mark xiii. as to differentiate words relating to the destruction of Jerusalem from other words which describe the final and universal catastrophe ? Here are questions which recent writers have made of living interest. And of interest, too, are the answers given by certain divines whose controversial intentions are indeed excellent, but who incidentally reveal weaknesses in theological equipment, which are scarcely less destructive of dogmatic teaching than the thoroughgoing rationalism of Schweitzer.

Four brief notes will meet our aim in the present chapter : (1) The meaning of the words of Christ concerning the Kingdom. (2) His messianic consciousness. (3) The eschatological discourse. (4) Some concluding remarks. The review, brief though it be, will show the momentous consequences which follow upon the attempt to interpret the Written Word by unaided private judgment.

1. The Kingdom of God

It is difficult to understand how a student of the Gospels who is not under the influence of a cherished eschatological theory could interpret the " Kingdom of God " in an exclusively eschatological sense. Take, for instance, the first recorded occasion in which Our Lord used the expression. St. Mark (i. 15) describes the beginning of His work in Galilee—the preaching of the Gospel of the Kingdom of God. We are struck at once by the identity of the subject of His discourse with that of the Baptist. " The time is accomplished, and the Kingdom of God is at hand ; repent and believe the Gospel." The " kingdom of God " has been understood by the continuous interpretation and tradition of the Church to mean the New Dispensation inaugurated by the coming of the Messias and made effective for all time by His sufferings and death. But the " Kingdom " also connotes the coming of Christ as judge—a coming realised for each individual at death and collectively for the whole world at the Last Judgment. That the comprehensive intelligence of Christ did embrace all the implication of the word " kingdom " both extensively and intensively, is a commonplace of Catholic teaching, but the more obvious intention of the divine precept, " Do penance, for the kingdom is at hand," is clearly to exhort us to seize here and now the opportunity of grace offered in a manner so unique. " If I by the finger of God cast out devils, then is the Kingdom of God come upon you " (Matthew xii. 28). " The Law and the prophets were until John ; from that time the Gospel of the Kingdom of God is preached " (Luke xvi. 16). " The Kingdom of God is within you (or in your midst) " (Luke xvii. 21). " Unless a man be born again of water and the Holy Ghost, he cannot enter into the Kingdom of God " (John iii. 5). It seems incredible that a student of trained judgment could, in the face of these texts, persuade himself that the kingdom spoken of by Christ meant exclusively the final coming of the Divine Judge—a coming characterised by catastrophic accompaniments and necessitating the end of earthly life for all and the beginning of a new and perfect era.

But the above-quoted texts are not the only evidence adducible on this point. The language of the parables of the Kingdom is equally conclusive against a narrow interpretation in the eschatological and catastrophic sense. For the parables describe a gradual process of development—a process associated with Earth as well as with Heaven. In connection with the parable of the Tares there is the authoritative interpretation: "the field is the world." In the parables of the Great Supper and the Husbandman, the coming of the Kingdom is conditional upon the attitude of the Jews.

It is interesting to note how non-Catholic apologists meet the textual difficulties in reference to the Kingdom and the Parousia. One, whose exposition of the subject is in many ways most helpful, does not hesitate to state that St. Matthew and St. Luke (especially the former) have read an eschatological significance into the words of Our Blessed Lord, whereas the words in their original form and content (allowing for condensation) appear in St. Mark. It is amazing to find that the obvious consequences of such a view are either ignored or calmly accepted. For if Matthew and Luke have erroneously, in accordance with their Jewish prejudices and prepossessions, added to the teaching of Christ, how can the Written Word be inspired? Or, if Inspiration is compatible with error, what guarantee have we that the Evangelists may not have misconceived Our Lord's meaning on other more vital points—nay, in regard to His own Person and claims? And thus the foundations of the whole edifice of Faith begin to totter. We cannot wonder, then, to find the following words in "Primitive Christian Eschatology," Chapter XXIX, p. 376: "If it were essential for the maintenance of the Church's position to prove that her doctrines have continued without a change all through the centuries, or if the truth of the Christian religion depended upon the inerrancy of every passage in Holy Scripture, then the estimate of primitive Christian Eschatology, which we have formed in the preceding pages, would fail to support the claims of Christianity."

Again in Matthew x. 23 "Amen I say to you, you shall not finish all the cities of Israel till the Son of Man come." In the book alluded to the words are supposed to have been spoken with certain fixed (though unrecorded) conditions, the absence of which saved the prophecy from non-fulfilment. Contrast with this the interpretation of Fr. Knabenbauer, who understands by the "cities of Israel" the cities where Israelites dwell within and without the limits of the Holy Land. A little earlier Our Lord had said "You shall be brought before governors and before kings for my sake, for a testimony to the Jews and to the Gentiles." It seems very difficult to see how the interpretation, "you will not finish the cities of Israel (i.e. the cities visited during the Galilæan mission) till the Son of Man come," can be considered as a possible interpretation, in view of the preceding words, and especially of Matthew x. 18, where the world-wide character of the mission is plainly stated. And does not the controversy illustrate how hopeless it is to secure unity of belief unless there is some authoritative limit in essential matters to freedom of interpretation? Schweitzer and the author just quoted are poles apart in their respective conclusions, and withal each appeals to the Gospel words for confirmation of his view!

2. "The Advent of Messianic Consciousness"

The mere statement of this title is startling to a Catholic. To find commentators gravely discussing the question as to the time when Our Lord became conscious of His messianic mission reveals on their part a fundamental misconception of the doctrine of the Incarnation. Every Catholic text-book of dogmatic theology explains that Our Lord, from the first moment of His human life, enjoyed the beatific vision—a limitless source of illumination to the human nature assumed. Again it is the common teaching that Christ, as in the case of the prophets, was endowed with infused knowledge, so that if we allow that the knowledge which He acquired in a purely human and experimental way did not embrace future contingent events, nevertheless to raise the question whether He—the Divine Word—was ignorant of His messianic mission is saved from the taint of blasphemy only by the fact that the doubt reveals a deplorable want of grasp of the central doctrine of Christianity—the divinity of Christ. The words, Mark xiii. 32 "No man knoweth the day nor the hour, neither the Angels in Heaven nor the Son but the Father," cannot be interpreted as expressing the limitations of His *human* nature, for the words refer in the same sense to the Son as to the Father, namely to the Divine nature. Nor will Bishop Gore's suggestion stand ("Dissertation on Subjects Connected with the Incarnation," p. 94) "Within the sphere and period of His incarnate and mortal life, Our Lord ceased from the exercise of those divine functions and powers, including the divine omniscience which would have been incompatible with a truly human experience." For Bishop Gore's limitation is not a limitation of the human, but of the Divine, nature of Christ. The commonly accepted Catholic explanation points out that the announcement of the exact time of the Last Judgment formed no part of the divinely appointed revelation to be made by the Son in the Father's name. Fr. Knabenbauer, quoting an analogous instance, remarks that in another place Christ speaks of the Kingdom prepared by His Father—not that it was not also prepared by the Son, but to indicate that the preparation of the Kingdom (i.e. the work of predestination) was the office not of the Son but of the Father. The "kenosis" (Philippians ii. 6), therefore, admitted by Catholic theologians, does not imply limitations of ignorance nor of fallibility, but merely that God appeared amongst us in human guise, lived through a lifetime of genuine human experience, suffered in His assumed nature and died for our redemption, and was withal so great in life and death and resurrection that every tongue confesses that "Our Lord Jesus Christ is in the glory of God the Father."

3. THE ESCHATOLOGICAL THEME

The well-known discourse of Our Blessed Lord, recorded in the thirteenth chapter of St. Mark, now claims our attention. Perhaps the singular form "discourse" should not be used, for some Catholic critics of eminence hold the opinion that the Evangelist has given a blend of two discourses—one prophetic, the other eschatological—rather than one discourse on two different subjects. On this supposition a brief analysis of the chapter is necessary. From v. 5 to v. 8 a description is given of the troubles which must precede the destruction of Jerusalem. "These are the beginning of sorrows." Whereupon comes a prophecy of the persecutions, obstacles, etc., which shall always accompany the attempt to spread the Gospel when the Christian teaching of self-restraint and self-sacrifice comes in conflict with the pride and luxury of the pagan world. In vv. 14-18 the destruction of Jerusalem is again the theme. In the mind of the Evangelist the destruction of the city with its attendant horrors suggests a more momentous issue—the end of the world and the final judgment, and from v. 19 to v. 27 he depicts in graphic language the catastrophic circumstances immediately precedent (though *not* as signs or warnings), and then " shall they see the Son of Man coming in the clouds with great power and glory." From v. 28 to v. 31, a parabolic illustration is given : " now of the fig tree learn ye a parable," and these verses must accordingly be referred to the prophetical discourse. Finally, vv. 32-37 return to the eschatological theme. An arrangement of the suggested two discourses side by side will facilitate comparison and throw out into relief a series of remarkable parallelisms which constitute a strong argument in favour of the theory of a twofold discourse. I omit vv. 9-13, which describe merely the difficulties arising from hostile influences in every period of the Church's history.

A. The Destruction of Jerusalem	B. The End of the World
A Prophetical Discourse	An Eschatological Discourse
vv. 5-8, 14-18, 28-31.	vv. 19-27, 32-37.
And Jesus answering began to say to them take heed lest any man deceive you. For many shall come in my name saying; I am he; and they shall deceive many. And when you shall hear of wars and rumours of wars fear ye not; for such things must needs be; but the end is not yet. For nation shall rise against nation and kingdom against kingdom; and there shall be earthquakes in places and famines. These are the beginning of sorrows. And when you shall see the abomination of desolation standing where it ought not, let him that readeth understand; then let those who are in Judea, flee to the mountains; and let him that is on the house-top not go down into the house, nor enter therein to take anything out of his house: and let him that shall be in the field not turn back again to take up his garment. And woe to them that are with	For in those days shall be such tribulations as were not from the beginning of the creation which God created until now, neither shall be. And unless the Lord had shortened the days no flesh should be saved; but for the sake of the elect which he hath chosen, he hath shortened the days. And then if any man shall say to you Lo, here is Christ, or, Lo, he is there do not believe. For there will rise up false Christs and false prophets, and they shall show signs and wonders to seduce if it were possible, even the elect. Take you heed therefore; behold I have foretold you all things. But in those days after that tribulation the sun shall be darkened, and the moon shall not give her light. And the stars of heaven shall be falling down; and the powers shall be moved. And then shall he send his Angels and shall gather together the elect from the four winds, from the uttermost part of the earth to the

child and that give suck in those days. But pray that these things may not happen in the winter. Now of the fig tree learn a parable. When the branch thereof is now tender and the leaves are come forth, you know that the summer is very near: so you also when you shall see these things come to pass, know ye that it is very nigh, even at the doors. Amen I say to you, that this generation shall not pass until all these things be done. Heaven and earth shall pass away, but my words shall not pass away."

uttermost part of heaven. But of that day or hour no man knoweth, neither the Angels in heaven nor the Son but the Father. Take ye heed; watch and pray; for ye know not when the time is. Even as a man who, going into a far country, left his house and gave authority to his servants over every work and commanded the porter to watch. Watch ye therefore (for you know not when the lord of the house cometh; at even, or at midnight, or at the cock-crowing, or in the morning) lest, coming on a sudden, he find you sleeping. And what I say to you, I say to all; watch."

In his admirable critical analysis of these pages Père Lagrange points out that the two events—the destruction of the City and the end of the World—are differentiated in a marked way—the one is preceded by signs, not only unmistakable but clamorous in their significance, the other (though to the discerning gaze there may be indications) shall come unheralded and unexpected. The details and accompaniments of the one event had been communicated in such a manner as to make the recognition of its oncoming easy, whereas in regard to the final consummation of all things, "no man knoweth the day or hour, neither the Angels in heaven nor the Son but the Father." Christ, acting as the ambassador of the Father, has set limits to His revelation, for it is part of the divine plan to withhold certain knowledge and thereby accentuate the need of watchfulness and prayer.

Again note the curious parallelisms in the respective passages. Compare "I am he" with "Lo, here is Christ." Compare the "deceit" in v. 5 with the "seduction" of v. 22. Note the repetition of the words "take heed" in vv. 5 and 23. Note, too, that just as the signs of Jerusalem's downfall are illustrated by the fig tree, so the comparatively signless oncoming of the final cataclysm is illustrated (and the moral pointed) by the watchfulness of the porter. Note, finally, that a comparison of Mark xiii. with Luke xxi. shows that whereas St. Luke prophesies the ruin of the city, he is silent in that place in regard to the Parousia which is given by him in xvii. 22–37.

But the objection may be raised: if Catholic critics suggest that St. Mark has written down in chapter xiii. a blend of two discourses, the analysis and differentiation of which cause "un sérieux embarrass pour l'exégèse," how will these same critics harmonise this opinion with the Catholic doctrine of Inspiration? There seems to be no real difficulty here. The existence of error in the Written Word is absolutely incompatible with Divine Inspiration. But no Catholic student of the Bible regards the Written Word as a rule of Faith. To expect to find in the New Testament narrative the precise, logically developed instruction which it is the function of the Magisterium Ecclesiæ to impart is a delusion, old, indeed, but a delusion which persists. All critics recognise that the Evangelists have arranged their subject matter neither in the chronological nor in the conventional scientific order, and hence the juxtaposition of two discourses (as possibly in Mark xiii.) may give rise, in the absence of careful analysis, to "une perspective mal comprise." This much we can safely say The function of Inspiration safeguards from error the outlines of Revelation, but does not encroach upon the function of the Divine Teacher, who, for the systematic exposition of "all truth," will abide by His Church until the end of time.

4. Concluding Remarks

Concerning the answers, therefore, to be given to the questions raised by the "consistent eschatologists," the Catholic

Apologist does not hesitate. Is the chief element in Christ's teaching eschatological? Absolutely not. The chief element in all His discourses is the moral element. " *Repent*, for the kingdom of heaven is at hand." The kingdom of heaven in this life is the gift of Divine grace, whereof the consummation will be the glory of God's eternal kingdom. The wholehearted love of God is the essential feature of the New Dispensation. " This do, and thou shalt live." And in the light of this message, so often and so pointedly stressed, it is hard to understand how critics can find in all the gracious words of Christ only allusions direct or indirect, open or veiled, to the oncoming of the eschatological kingdom. No doubt Christ wished to convey that the " Kingdom " comes to each one swiftly and definitely. The kingdom of heaven begun by grace will be attained or lost by each individual soul when the portals of death are passed " Therefore, what I say unto you, I say unto all : watch."

Does the so-called " consistent eschatology " lend any support to the sacramental system of the Church? We have already seen that if the new views be carried out to their logical conclusions there can be neither Church nor Sacraments. On this hypothesis the traditional belief in the personality of the Founder of Christianity must be abandoned, and we are thrown back from Revealed to Natural Religion. One of the greatest surprises (sad surprises surely) of recent times was to find a Catholic divine of transcendent ability associated with this Arian coterie and seeking to reconcile the irreconcilable. As an instance, take the following : Christ's teaching is predestinarian in character so that the Sacraments of the Church are needed as guarantees of immunity, enabling the elect to pass through the time of tribulation and thus reach the kingdom in safety. This is the " psychologising " method indeed, not only " modern " but frankly " modernistic." And if the mighty ones of Israel can thus fall, must it not be apparent to all thoughtful men—even to those who are without the fold of the Catholic Church—that for the maintenance of Divine Faith we need, in addition to the element of Reason, an element of Will?

CHAPTER XVIII

THE DIVINITY OF THE CHRISTIAN FAITH DIRECTLY PROVED

THE direct proof of the divinity of the Christian Faith is an appeal to the moral miracle of its rapid propagation, its wonderful conservation, the transformation of the world which it has effected, and finally the number and heroism of its martyrs. A moral miracle may be defined as a fact or series of facts, flowing indeed from the exercise of human freedom, but so opposed to the ordinary conduct of men as to witness to the special intervention of God. Syllogistically the argument may be stated thus

A religion which, in spite of obstacles, humanly speaking insurmountable, in spite of the weakness of its advocates and the absence of influence and resources, has been propagated with astonishing rapidity, has preserved its doctrine and constitution for nineteen centuries, has transformed the world by its influence, and to which so many heroic martyrs have borne witness, must be divine.

But such is the Christian Religion.

Therefore the Christian Religion is divine.

The minor is proved in successive sections.

SECTION I. PROPAGATION

I. The Fact.
A. Quantitative character of the propagation.
  1st Century.
    Acts ii. 41. Pentecost: 3000 souls.
    Acts iv. 4. A few days after: 5000 souls.

DIVINITY OF THE CHRISTIAN FAITH

Acts xxi. 20. "Many thousands."
Tacitus. Annales xv. "Ingens multitudo."
St. Clement, 1 Corinthians vi. "πολὺ πλῆθος."
St. Ignatius, Epistle to Romans iii., speaks of "bishops established to the ends of the world."
Pliny, in his letter to Trajan regarding the province of Bithynia, wrote that the Christians numbered "many persons of every age and rank and sex, not only in the cities, but in the towns and country."
Harnack in his "Propagation of Christianity in the first three centuries," enumerates forty-three localities where the existence of Christian communities is historically attested in the first century; e.g. Palestine, Syria, Asia Minor, Alexandria, Greece, Macedonia, Rome, etc.

2nd Century.
St. Justin (Dialogue with Tryphon) "There is no people, barbarian, Scythian, or Greek amongst whom the name of Christ is not invoked."
Clement of Alexandria (Stromateis) bears a like testimony.
Pseudo-Clement (2 Corinthians ii.) "Christians are more numerous than Jews."
St. Irenæus (Adv. hæreses) "The churches in Germany have the same faith and tradition as those in Iberia, those amongst the Celts, in the East, in Egypt and Libya."
The pagan *Cæcilius* (in Minutius Felix) speaks of "the spread of this infamous sect."
Harnack mentions thirty-three new centres. On the other hand the persecutions lessened the numbers. Celsus (A.D. 178) writes after the persecution of Marcus Aurelius: "Scarcely does there remain anyone in hiding."

3rd Century.
Tertullian : "We fill every place except your temples."
Origen records that the pagans attributed public misfortunes to the spread of Christianity.

4th Century.
> The pagan *Porphyry*   Christians are everywhere."
> *Lucian* (martyr)   "Christians fill whole towns—fill the greater part of the world."
> The emperor *Maximinus Jovius* (Eusebius, *Hist. Ec.*, ix. 9) says that Diocletian and Maximianus persecuted because " all men abandon the worship of the gods and become Christians."
> *Renan*   " In 150 years the prophecy of Christ was accomplished ; the grain of mustard seed had become a tree which began to overspread the earth."

B. Qualitative Importance.
1. Converts of education and high rank.
   > *Sergius Paulus*, proconsul. Acts xiii. 7–12.
   > *Dionysius the Areopagite.* Acts xvii. 34.
   > *Several men and women* of rank at Thessalonica and Berea. Acts xvii. 4, 12.
   > *Pomponia Græcina* at Rome. Tacitus (*Ann.* xiii. 32). She was a matron of the highest rank, wife of Consul Plautius. In 1867 a sepulchral tablet was discovered in the crypt of Lucina with the name of Pomponius Græcinus. Thus the crypt of Lucina—one of the first Christian cemeteries—belonged to Pomponia Græcina.
   > *Titus Flavius Clemens*, consul, martyr, nephew of Vespasian and cousin of Titus and Domitian.
   > *Acilius Glabrio*, consul in 91. In 1888 in the cemetery of Priscilla was discovered a hypogeum containing the tombstone of Manius Acilius Verus and Acilia Priscilla—son and daughter of the consul.
2. Men of learning.
   > Apollo. Acts xviii. 24.
   > Tertullian.
   > Clement of Alexandria.
   > Origen.

DIVINITY OF THE CHRISTIAN FAITH

3. Army.
    12th legion under Marcus Aurelius.
    Forty martyrs of Sebaste in Lesser Armenia.

II. Supernatural character of this rapid propagation.

The supernatural character will be best appreciated if we consider:

1st, Object aimed at—the overthrow of pagan worship, the replacement of the law of Moses by the New Law, the imposition of doctrines which excited hatred and ridicule.

2nd, Obstacles to be surmounted:

(a) Internal.
　　1. Nature of the New Religion, sublimity of its dogmas, severity of its morality, transcendent character of its virtues.
　　2. Personality of its Founder—a crucified Jew.

(b) External.
　　1 Inveterate superstition of Paganism.
　　2. Corruption of morals.
　　3. Hatred of the Jews towards Christianity.
　　4. Pride of pagan philosophers and priests.
　　5. Calumnies and prejudices.
　　6. Persecutions.

3rd, Means employed.

Twelve poor fishermen. Neither eloquence nor science nor rank nor riches contributed to preach this gospel of renunciation.

4th, Effect obtained.

The Roman empire became a Christian state. Ignorance triumphed over science, weakness over strength, and the cross became the symbol of love and honour.

ST. AUGUSTINE'S FAMOUS DILEMMA

The world was converted to Christianity either by miracles or without miracles. If with them, then the doctrine was divinely attested. If without them, the conversion is the greatest miracle of all.

First Objection. Buddhism and Islamism have spread rapidly.

Answer. (1) Our argument does not rest merely upon the rapidity of the propagation, but upon the rapid propagation in view of concrete circumstances.

(2) Buddhism contains relatively pure doctrine, but is content with counsels rather than precepts. Sakya Mouni did not proscribe idolatry. Polygamy and divorce were allowed. The doctrine was propagated by a king's son. There were no persecutions. Islamism was an instance of a sensual religion propagated by force.

Second Objection. Natural causes explain the propagation of Christianity (Gibbon, Lecky, Harnack).

The natural causes are

1. Previous propagation of Judaism. There were four millions of Jews (7 per cent) in the empire. Judaism preached the unity of God and a pure morality. Its narrowness and fiercely national prejudices were the opportunity of Christianity.

2. Exterior characteristics of the time; unity of the Empire; rapid means of communication; tolerance on the part of Rome towards other forms of religion.

3. Internal characteristics.

    (*a*) decline of polytheism;
    (*b*) reawakening of religious sentiment.

Answer. If these forces were really operative they would have attracted man to Stoicism or Neo-platonism rather than to the uncompromising standard of the morality of the Gospel of Christ. Moreover, the great masses of the people were not affected by any desire for a purer morality. The arguments of Gibbon, Lecky, and Harnack do not explain how the numerous and (morally speaking) unconquerable obstacles to the spread of Christianity were so quickly and so triumphantly overcome.

SECTION 2. CONSERVATION

I. The Fact.

"Le temps, voilà le grand ennemi!" The destructive action of time is attributed to:

1. The love of Novelty — novelty has a special charm.
2. Experience: which shows the weakness or falsity of doctrines.

3. Corruption : all the empires of the past have had their youth, maturity, and decay.
4. Chance : overthrows the best conceived plans.
5. War.

Philosophic schools, religious sects, kingdoms, and empires appear, develop, and decay. But the Church, though attacked in every way, subsists. Many non-Catholic historians have borne testimony to the Church's lasting power, e.g. Hurter, Voigt, and Ranke. Macaulay's famous passage (Essay on Ranke) is well known. From within the Church Lacordaire has written powerfully on this subject in his fortieth conference, and Olivier in his thirty-fourth conference.

II. Supernatural character of the fact, attested by:
1. Aim; conservation involves power more than human.
   To conquer repeated attacks.
   To remain unchangeable in the midst of universal change and decay.
2. Obstacles to be overcome.
   (i) Number and diversity of adversaries.
       Jews, Gentiles, heretics, schismatics, Mohammedans, unbelievers, secret societies, rebellious members.
   (ii) Universality of the attack.
       Attack has been made on the life, dogmas, morality, worship, pastors, institutions of the Church. The attack has been perpetual.
   (iii) Arms of the Adversaries.
       Sword, political power, riches, sophism, science (so-called), calumny, corruption, the fatal influence of secret societies.
3. Means employed by the Church.
   Patience, Prayer, Confidence in God.
4. Result.
   The Church remains, having the same doctrine, the same constitution, the same discipline, the same worship.

Hence the Perpetuity of the Church is a witness to its divinity
1. Perpetuity in the midst of revolutions.

2. Perpetuity notwithstanding the Church's intimate association with changing institutions.
3. Perpetuity in spite of deadly attacks.
4. Perpetuity which has never stooped to compromise.
5. Perpetuity which is the result of divine prophecy.

III. Objections.
1. Other sects endure.

Answer. (1) Sects are local whereas the Church is universal.

(2) Sects have no principle of unity the seeds of decay are manifest. Whereas the Church is One in doctrine, worship, and rule.

2. The Church is in process of decay.

Answer. The same opinion was expressed fourteen centuries ago—St. Augustine replied : " Whilst they speak thus they perish themselves, and the Church remains to manifest to successive generations the power of God." (Enarr. in Psalm lxx.)

Bougaud (" Le Christianisme et les Temps présents," T. IV, 1 partie, Chapter VIII–XI) writes powerfully on the Church's triple immutability of Being, Doctrine, and Love.

SECTION 3. TRANSFORMATION OF THE WORLD

I. Fact of the transformation.
A. Before Christ.
  (*a*) The individual.

  Paganism failed to recognise the dignity of the human body. War was its ideal.

  The Gauls sold one another to pay their debts. Suicide was regarded as legitimate ; Cicero and Seneca defend it.

  In regard to the soul the intellectual faculties were cultivated in Greece and Rome, but religious belief manifested itself by a worship which was infamous and cruel. " Tout était Dieu, excepté Dieu lui-même " (Labis).

  (*b*) The Family.

  Woman. Woman was regarded as an inferior being,

a slave. The father had a legal right to kill or to sell her as a babe. Later on she was sold to the highest bidder.

Child. The Roman Law authorised the father to kill the newly-born if he chose, to expose it, even to immolate it. The child was placed at its father's feet. If the father took it into his arms it was a sign that the child was accepted; hence the phrase "liberos suscipere."

Slaves. Sparta's population was 36,000; her slaves numbered 244,000.

Athens' population of free inhabitants was 21,000; her slaves numbered 40,000.

At Rome a single individual sometimes possessed as many as 20,000 slaves.

A slave could be tortured, mutilated, crucified. Vedius Pollio threw slaves into a fishpond to fatten the eels. Augustus crucified a slave for having killed a tame quail. Domitian ordered a slave to be shut up in a furnace because the imperial bath was too hot.

Mommsen says that the sufferings of the whole Negro race compared to the suffering which resulted from Roman slavery were only as a drop in the ocean.

(c) *Society.*

Thirty thousand gladiators a year were sacrificed for the pastime of the people.

Titus sacrificed 5000 gladiators for the funeral celebration of his father.

Trajan held gladiatorial celebrations which lasted four months. For this celebration there were 10,000 gladiators and 11,000 wild beasts.

Caligula seized upon some spectators when the gladiators failed.

"Mercy is a vice" (Seneca).

"To give a poor man food and drink is folly—a loss to oneself and prolongation of misery to the man" (Plautus). "Væ victis."

B. After Christ.
  (*a*) The Individual.

  The body was regarded as an inalienable possession, sacred because intended to be the temple of God. Suicide was forbidden as a crime against nature, society, and God.

  Definite teaching was given upon man's origin and destiny, not only for the rich but for the poor.

  Heroic virtue was seen in the midst of the depravity of cities.

  (*b*) The Family.

  Marriage was raised to the dignity of a sacrament, involving unity and indissolubility. The wife became the companion, not the slave, of man; the child was regarded as a sacred responsibility. The Christian principle of the natural equality of all men had an immediate influence in mitigating the hardships of slavery.

  (*c*) Society.

  The Church reminded rulers that though seated upon a throne they were subject to God's law, and that power was given to them so that the empire of earth might serve the empire of heaven; the Church reminded subjects that all legitimate authority comes from God.

  The law of Charity was substituted for the law of egoistic cruelty. Gladiatorial combats were proscribed in A.D. 392 by Arcadius and Honorius. They were finally abolished through the heroic action of Almachius or Telemachus, who was torn to pieces by the fury of the mob because he endeavoured to separate the gladiatorial combatants, A.D. 404. Labour was now regarded as an honourable and dignified duty, consecrated by the example of the household of Nazareth. Charity extended beyond the bounds of race and country: "See how these Christians love one another."

DIVINITY OF THE CHRISTIAN FAITH

To sum up:—That this regeneration is due to Christianity the following facts are decisive evidence:
1. Christianity and the Transformation of Society are always associated.
2. Where Christianity is absent, the social conditions of paganism remain.
3. The change of manners has been proportional to the influence of Christianity.

Objection. The Latin races are a scandal to Christianity.

Answer. If Christian principles are abandoned there will be degeneracy, and the degeneracy will be more marked because of the sublimity of the principles which are contemned. "Corruptio optimi pessima." Balmes writes "These nations preserve in the midst of their degeneracy—I will venture to say, in the midst of their degradation—characteristics which bespeak their noble origin."

II. Supernatural character of the fact of transformation.

It is a law of the moral order and a law of history that a great multitude of human beings do not change convictions, conduct, and manners quickly. But Christianity has effected this change. Have we not, therefore, in this unexpected and unique event a manifest proof of Divine intervention?

SECTION 4. THE HEROISM OF THE CHRISTIAN MARTYRS

Three points claim attention
1. The number of martyrs was great.
2. They suffered for their faith.
3. Their constancy cannot be explained by invoking natural characteristics alone.

I. The number.

The number was very great.
1. Testimony of authors ancient and modern.
   > *Tacitus* writes that under Nero an "immense multitude" (ingens multitudo) suffered.
   > *Dion Cassius* relates that Domitian put to death his cousin Titus Flavius Clemens, consul, and his wife,

Flavia Domitilla (the elder), niece of the emperor, and many others.

Eusebius writes that under Marcus Aurelius the number was indefinitely large. He also states that the persecutions of the third century were more cruel still, especially under Decius. The testimony of Dionysius of Alexandria is to the same effect. Lactantius describes the sufferers under Diocletian as being executed "gregatim." Diocletian and Maximianus boasted of the thoroughness of this work—"deleto nomine Christiano."

Tillemont, Ruinart, de Rossi, Le Blant, Allard have availed themselves (the last three especially) of the light thrown on the subject by modern archæological discoveries. The most recent summary of the whole question is Allard's article "Martyre" in d'Alès' "Dictionnaire Apologétique de la Foi Catholique," Vol. III, 331–492.

The historian Dodwell (seventeenth century) denied the great number, but admitted that even his reduced estimate afforded a striking proof of the divinity of Christianity. Renan agrees cordially with the traditional estimate of the number.

2. Proof drawn from the circumstances.

(a) *Duration*, 64–313 (edict of Milan), i.e. 249 years.

	Persecutions.	Peace.
In first century	6 years.	30 years.
In second .	86	14
In third	24	76
In fourth	13	
	129	120

(b) *Universality*: Rome, Carthage, Belgium, Gaul, Britain, Spain, Asia Minor, Egypt, Syria, Persia (in the 1st Persian persecution 16,000 martyrs suffered), Armenia, Africa (under the Vandals), France (under the Saracens), Constantinople (under the Iconoclasts), Spain (under the Mussulmans), England (Henry VIII and Elizabeth), Japan, Corea, Tonquin, Mongolia, Uganda, etc.

(c) *Character of the Emperors* and sanguinary tastes of the populace.

II. The Martyrs suffered for Religion.
1. Testimony of Apologists. Justin, Athenagoras, Minutius Felix, Clement of Alexandria, Tertullian, Origen, St. Cyprian.
2. Testimony of pagan writers, e.g. letter of Pliny to Trajan, and the Emperor's response. No other charges were made against Christians except that of religion.
3. The persecutors themselves alleged Religion as the ground of their action.
4. The interrogatory dealt only with the point of religion.
5. Apostasy sufficed for acquittal.

Objection. The Christians were accused of incendiarism, hatred of the human race, superstition, infanticide, lèse-majesté, Thyestian repasts, etc.

Answer. It is now known that the burning of Rome was the work of Nero, which he attributed to the Christians. All other charges were resolved in the last analysis into that of religion.

III. The constancy of the martyrs cannot be explained by considerations in the natural order.

The early apologists emphasised the heroic *constancy* of the martyrs. The rationalists of the eighteenth century maintained that there had been religious fanaticism in all sects. The apologists replied that the martyrs were witnesses not of doctrine merely, but of facts. Pascal with his wonderful intuition wrote: " Je crois les histoires dont les témoins se font égorger." He did not write: " Je crois tout homme qui se fait égorger pour une doctrine." Hence M. Paul Allard makes the following division:

1. Witnesses of the life, death, and resurrection of Christ; 1st century.

2. Witnesses of the wonders produced by the first missionaries of the Gospel; second century.
3. Witnesses of the traditional faith of which their personal faith was the result; third and subsequent centuries.

Allard argues that if the witness element be insisted upon then we must quote the martyrs of the first centuries only. M. Laberthonnière does not see the logical force of the distinction between *fact* and *doctrine,* and believes that the strength of this argument rests upon the life, character, and death of the martyrs. But may not Mussulman and Hindoo argue in a like manner? Our contention is that the martyrdoms with all their circumstances were beyond the power of human nature. Hence the argument includes

1. The number of martyrs.
2. The martyrs were of every age, condition, and sex.
3. The terrible cruelties endured.
4. The manner in which they endured these torments—with joy and constancy.
5. The miraculous accompaniments and supernatural effects, e.g. conversions.

The true force of the argument is not that the martyrs witnessed to a fact, nor that they were beautiful in life and death, but rather that the martyrdom with all its circumstance was beyond the power of human endurance.

Objections.

1. The constancy of martyrs is explained by the hope of gain, glory, fanaticism, and expectation of rew⸺

Answer. (*a*) All gain is lost at death.

(*b*) Vain-glory was proscribed by the religion which the martyrs professed. Many died assured that their martyrdom would never be known.

(*c*) The excitement associated with fanaticism has nothing in common with the quiet, serene, charitable spirit which characterised the attitude of the Christian martyrs.

(*d*) Future invisible reward could not, humanly speaking, have influenced multitudes of Christians to suffer and die with such heroism.

2. All religions have their martyrs.

Answer. That faith and love and generous self-sacrifice have been manifested by non-Christians is a fact which is evident to the student of history. Hence the distinction between the soul and body of the Church. But our contention is that martyrdom with its attendant circumstances of (1) numbers, (2) long continuance, (3) appalling cruelty, (4) extraordinary constancy and heroism, (5) supernatural attestation, and (6) striking fruits, is the exclusive characteristic of Christianity.

3. Is not the heroism of the soldier comparable to that of the martyr ?

Answer. We are far from denying, far from depreciating the magnificent heroism of multitudes of soldiers, but there are differences between the soldier and the martyr

(*a*) A soldier's death is not always certain and he acts under the rule of military discipline. The martyr goes freely to certain torture and death.

(*b*) Soldiers have often been influenced by the hope of gaining tangible rewards, e.g. booty, honour, etc. The martyr's reward is invisible.

(*c*) The dispositions and conduct of the soldier differ frequently *toto caelo* from those of the martyr.

(*d*) Soldiers are as a rule grown-up men, whereas martyrs have included in their ranks women, children and the old of both sexes.

Résumé in the words of Lamy :

" If 12 men without influence, without knowledge, inexperienced in the ways of the world, but loving Christ profoundly, have succeeded by the aid of some poor Jews in spreading the Christian Faith throughout the Roman Empire ; if *they* have accomplished what Greece with all its eloquence, and Rome with its military power have failed to achieve ; if they have succeeded in founding an institution which has lasted for 19 centuries—an institution which has regenerated the world, emancipated the slave, rehabilitated woman, dignified family life, comforted the afflicted, uprooted vices, taught sublime truths, pure morality and heroic virtue, an institution which has resisted long-continued and dangerous destructive tendencies, undergone centuries of persecution, witnessed the passing away of kingdoms and peoples, remaining itself erect and immovable upon the ruins of time—an institution which has opposed human interests and passions—surely we have here the greatest of miracles. Unless the principle of causality be denied or the cogency of evidence called in question, it is necessary to recognise that this institution is Divine."

" Digitus Dei est hic."

BIBLIOGRAPHY

Alexander (Samuel). *The Basis of Realism.* 8°, Lond., 1914.
Allard (Paul). *Histoire des persécutions du Ier au IVe siècle.*
—— *Rome souterraine.*
Balmès (Jacques). *Philosophie fondamentale.*
Bateson (William). *Mendel's principles of Heredity.* 8°, Camb., 1909.
Batiffol (Pierre). *Six leçons sur l'Évangile.*
Billot (Ludovicus). *De Deo uno et trino; commentarius in primam partem S. Thomae.* 2 vol., 8°, Romae, 1893.
Bonniot (Joseph de). *Le miracle et ses contrefaçons.* 8°, Paris, 1887.
Bougaud (Louis Émile). *Le Christianisme et les temps présents.* 8°, Paris, Tours, 1874–1884.
Broad (Charlie Dunbar). *Perception, Physics and Reality.*
Campbell (Douglas Houghton). *Lectures on the Evolution of Plants.* 8°, N.Y., 1902.
Devivier (W.). *Cours d'apologétique chrétienne.*
Dictionnaire apologétique de la foi Catholique sous la direction d'Adhémar d'Alès.
Driesch (Hans Adolf Eduard). *The Science and Philosophy of the Organism.* (*The Gifford Lectures*, 1908.) 2 vol., 8°, Lond., 1908.
Doellinger (Johann Joseph Ignaz von). *The Gentile and the Jew in the courts of the Temple of Christ: an introduction to the history of Christianity;* trans. by N. Darnell. 2 vol., 8°, Lond., 1862.
Donat (Joseph). *The Freedom of Science.*
Farges (Albert). *Le cerveau, l'âme et la pensée.*
—— *L'idée de Dieu d'après la raison et la science.*

Frémont (Georges). *Lettres à l'Abbé Loisy.*

Garrigou-Lagrange (P. Fr. R.). *Dieu, son existence et sa nature.*

Geikie (James). *The Antiquity of Man in Europe being the Munro lecture,* 1913. 8°, Edin., Lond., 1914.

Gladstone (Reginald John). *Cephalometric Data.* (*Journ. of Anat. and Physiology,* 1903.)

Gredt (Joseph). *De cognitione sensuum externorum.*

Gründer (H.). *De qualitatibus sensibilibus.*

Hartmann (Karl Robert Eduard von). *Philosophy of the Unconscious ;* trans. by W. C. Coupland. 2nd ed. (Eng. and Foreign Philosophical Library). 3 vol., 8°, Lond., 1893.

Harnack (Adolf). *Die Mission und Ausbreitung des Christentums in den ersten drei Jahrhunderten.* (Eng. Tr., James Moffatt.)

Hettinger (Franz). *Apologie des Christenthums.* 2 vol., 8°, Freiburg-im-Breisgau, 1865–67.

———— *Théologie fondamentale.*

Johnstone (James). *The Philosophy of Biology.* 8°, Camb., 1914.

Keith (Arthur). *The Antiquity of Man.* 8°, Lond., 1915.

Lang (Andrew). *The Making of Religion.* 8°, Lond., 1898.

Lepin (M.). *Jésus, Messie et Fils de Dieu.*

Lilly (William Samuel). *The Claims of Christianity.* 8°, Lond., 1894

———— *Many Mansions being studies in ancient religion and modern thought.* 8°, Lond., 1907.

Maistre (Joseph Marie de). *Les soirées de Saint-Pétersbourg ou Entretiens sur le gouvernement temporel de la providence. suivies d'un traité sur les sacrifices.* 2 vol., 12°, Paris [1888].

Mercier, Card. *Psychologie.*

Mivart (St. George). *On the Genesis of Species.* 8°, Lond., 1871.

———— *On Truth : a systematic inquiry.* 8°, Lond., 1889.

Morgan (Thomas Hunt). *Evolution and Adaptation.* N.Y., 1903.

Rivière (M. J.). *La propagation du Christianisme dans les trois premiers siècles d'après les conclusions de M. Harnack.*

Rutten (M. H.). *L'Église et la Civilisation.*

Schanz (Paul). *A Christian Apology.* 3 vol., Dublin, 1891. (Eng. Tr.)

Sertillanges (A. D.). *Les Sources de la Croyance en Dieu.*
Sollas (William Johnson). *Ancient Hunters and their modern Representatives.* 8°, Lond., 1915.
Valvekens, M. le Chanoine. *Foi et Raison (cours d'Apologétique).*
Vigouroux (Fulcran). *La Bible et les Découvertes Modernes* (1896).
────── *Les Livres Saints et la Critique Rationaliste* (1891).
Vries (Hugo de). *Species and varieties, their origin by mutation.* 2nd ed., translated by D. T. MacDougal. 8°, Chicago, 1906.
Wallace (Alfred Russel). *Darwinism an exposition of the theory of Natural Selection, with some of its applications.* 8°, Lond., 1889.
Ward (William George). *Essays on the Philosophy of Theism;* reprinted from the "Dublin Review," ed. with intro. by Wilfrid Ward. 2 vol.; 8°, Lond., 1884.
Wasmann (Erich). *The Berlin discussion of the Problem of Evolution.* 8°, Lond., 1909.
────── *Modern Biology and the Theory of Evolution.* 1906.
Weiss (Albert Maria). *Apologie des Christenthums vom Standpunkte der Sittenlehre.* 8°, Freiburg-im-Breisgau, 1878.
Wilson (Edmund Beecher). *The Cell in Development and Inheritance.* 8°, Lond., 1907.
Windle (Sir Bertram Coghill Alan). *A Century of Scientific Thought, and Other Essays.* 8°, Oxford, Lond., 1915.

INDEX

Absolute, three windows into the, 14
Abstraction, the faculty of, 24, 117
Acilius Glabrio, 228
"Actio sequitur esse," 78, 81, 117
"Actiones sunt personæ," 114
"Actus purissimus," 35, 47, 92
Adams (astronomer), 3
Age, Primary, Secondary, Tertiary, 110, 112
Agnosticism, 51, 52
Agnosticism, Empiricist, 22
Agnosticism, Idealistic, 23
Albert the Great, 9, 14, 113
Algæ, 67
Allard, 236, 237, 238
Allelomorphs, 63
Almachius, 234
Almighty Power, 77, 78
American Tribes, Beliefs of, 163
Animism, 164
Analogical acceptation, 30
Analogical sense, 69
Analogical usage, table of, 29
Analogous things, 90
Ancestors, worship of, 19, 164, 165
Angiospermæ, 67
Anselm, St., 21
Antinomies of Kant and Spencer, 22, 23, 24, 37
Antinomies, Some supposed, 88
Anthropological Doctrine of St. Paul, 165
Antiquity of man, The, 127 sqq.
Apollo, 228
Apologetic Aim, The, 16
Apologetics, Crux of, 95
Aquinas, v. Thomas, St.
Arabia, 158
Arcadius, 234
Aristotle, 35, 47, 42, 161, 234
Assent, absolute, 26; undoubting, 26
Assyria, 157
Astronomy, 28, 109, 110, 111, 112
Atheists, 51

Athenagoras, 237
Augustine, St., 55 95, 102, 103, 109, 144, 229, 232
Augustine, St., dilemma of, 229
Augustus, 233
Australian tribes, beliefs of, 162
Australians, aboriginal, 136
Authority implies Right, 157
Azilian culture, 130, 131

Babylonia, 157
Bacon, Francis, 49
Bacon, Roger, 52
Bain, 52
Balmes, 235
Bardon, Abbé, 136
Barnabas, St., Epistle of, 189
Basilides, 189
Batiffol, 190
Being, Contingent, 38
Being, Degrees of, 40
Being, Necessary, 15, 38, 47, 108
Belief in a Supreme Being, 164
Belief of African, American, Australian tribes, 162, 163
Bergson, 19, 28
Berkeley, 3, 8
Bertrand, Eugène, 137
Bible, Inerrancy of, 193
Body and Soul, substantial union of, 127
Boëthius, 71, 96
Bonaparte, 103
Bossuet, 42, 100
Boucher de Perthes, 137
Bougaud, 232
Boule, 132
Boulenger, 66
Bourget, 49, 146
Bouyssonie, Abbé, 36
Brahmanism, 155
Brain, size of, in relation to intelligence, 118
Breuil, Abbé, 136 140

Broca, 119
Brown-Séquard, 59
Brunetière, 49, 55, 184
Brünn, 61, 133
Büchner, 53, 55
Buddhism, 154, 155, 156, 229
Budge, E. A. W., 160
Bushmen, suggested origin of, 132
Byron, brain of, 119

Cæcilius, 227
Cainozoic period, 54, 110
Cancer, prevalence of, 96
Cartailhac, 132
Catholic and Non-catholic countries, 148
Catholic Church, philosophy of the, 113
Catholic Critics and the Divinity of Christ, 211, 213
Catholicism and decadence, 149
Causality, law of, 16, 30, 32, 47
Cave men, 131
Celsus, 188
Ceratium furca, 66
Certitude, metaphysical, physical, moral, 20
Charcot, 176
Chance and theory of probability, 45
Cheddar Cave, 132
Chelidonium majus, 65
China and Japan, Religions of, 153, 154
Choice, power of (potestas eligendi), 97
Christ, Appearances of, after death, 202
Christ arose from the dead, 201
Christ's claims, 210, 212
Christ, Divinity of, 209, 214
Christ, realisation of Messianic prophecy, 204
Christian Faith, divinity of the, 194
Christian Faith, Direct proof of, 227
Christian Martyrs, heroism of the, 235
Church, Perpetuity of the, 231
Cicero, 147, 201
Clement, of Alexandria, 188, 227, 228, 237
Clement, St. (Pope), 189, 227
Cocchi, 137
Codex, Sinaiticus, Vaticanus, 187
Colour, 5, 7, 8, 10, 11, 12, 13, 14

Combe Capelle, 132
Commandments of God, 125
Comte, 23, 52
Confucius, The teaching of, 154
Conservation and Creation, 78, 80
Continuous variation, 66
Copernican system, 26
Correns, 61
Creation, 78, 79, 110
Critical Realists, 4
Cromagnon type, 132
Cromwell, 103, 119
Cuvier, 57
Cyprian, St., 237

Darmesteter, 50
Dartford skull, 136
Darwin, C., 58, 59, 60, 65
Darwin, F., 57, 58, 59
Darwin, G., 140
Darwinian Evolution, 136
Darwinism, 55
Decius, 236
Deluge, The, 130
Denis of Alexandria, 236
Dennert's chart, 49, 50
Descartes, 78
Design, overwhelming revelation of, 44
Determinism, mechanical, physiological, psychological, theological, 123, 124
De Vries, 61, 64, 65
Didache, The, 189
Diocletian, 236
Dion Cassius, 235
Dionysius of Alexandria, 236
Discontinuous variation, 66
Discourse, eschatological, prophetical, 222
Disease and preventible causes, 98
Distinctions, real, virtual, mental, 68
Distributive Justice, 74
Divine attributes, 76, 89
Divine Concursus, 81
Divine Justice, 74
Divine Knowledge, 72, 73
Divine Love, 73, 74
Divine Mercy, 76, 77
Divine Nature, difficulties, 105
Divine Nature, fundamental attribute, 69
Divine Operation: attributes related to, 72

Divine Paternity, 85
Divine Persons, 105, 106
Divine Revelations, 169
Divinity of the Christian Faith, Direct proof, 226 *sqq.*
Dodwell, 236
Dominant characters, 62
Dominic, St., 159
Domitian, 233
Driesch, Hans, 14
Duality of subject and object, 92
Du Bois-Reymond, 33, 54, 145
Duclaud, 145
Duhem, 35
Duns Scotus, 52, 88, 89
Duperron, A., 157
Dwight, 55

Earthquake at Messina, 95
Edersheim, 205
Effect, "being" and "individuality" of the, 81
Egypt, Exile in, 140
Egyptians, Early Religion of the, 160
Electrons, 27, 34
Emperor Maximianus Jovius, 228
Empiricist Agnosticism, 22
Empiricist philosophy, 21
Encyclical "Pascendi," 19; "Providentissimus Deus," 193
Energy, Conservation and Dissipation of, 39, 40
"Equivocal," meaning of the term, 90
Errors opposed to Theism, 51
Eschatological Apologetics, 215
Eskimos, Origin of, 136
Etruscans, The, 161
Eusebius, 236
Evans, Sir A. J., 127
Evil, Problem of, 95, 96, 104, 105
Evolution, 54, 56, 145
Evolution, Materialistic, failure of, 55
Evolution, Spiritualistic, 55
External and Internal Finality, 44
External World, The, 1
Eye of the Cephalopod, of the Vertebrate, 61

Faith, Divinity of the Christian Faith indirectly proved, 194; directly proved, 226

Faith and Reason, 181
Faith and Science, 183
Farges, 9
Fear, 121
Felix, Père, 149
Ferns, 67
Fichte, 3, 27, 53, 113
Fideists and Traditionalists, 17
Finality, internal and external, 44
First Being, 32, 33
First principles, ontological value of, 26
Flavia Domitilla, 236
Francis, St., 103, 159
Franck, 50
Frazer, J. G., 164
Freedom, perversion of, 122
Free-will, 97, 119–122

Galley-Hill, 137, 139
Galton, 65
Gamaliel, 204
Gambetta, The brain of, 119
Garrigou-Lagrange, Père, 29, 94
Geikie, J., 141
German Idealism, 27
Gibbon, 230
Gibraltar skull, 134
Giraffe's neck, development of, 60
Glacial periods, 129, 130
Gladstone, R., Dr., 136
God: Analogical Knowledge of, 21
  Attributes of, 70
  Commandments of, 125
  Different relations of creatures to, 93
  General view of Nature and Attributes, 68
  Immanent, 18, 71
  Immediate intuition of, 20
  Immensity and Ubiquity of, 71
  Incomprehensibility of, 72
  Intimate Life of, 84
  Invisibility of, 72
  Kingdom of, 217
  Mercy of, 76
  Sanctity of, 75
  Scientific proof of His existence, 20
  Touch of, 102, 103
  Transcendence of, 71
  Unchangeable, 71
  Uncreated, 71
  Unity of, 108

God and man, relations between, 144
God's existence, à priori proof, 21
 Proofs based on Contingent being, 38
  Degrees of being, 40
  Efficient causes, 37
  Manifestation of Order, 43
  Moving bodies, 34
 General proof, 32
 Human opinion, 47
Goethe, 14, 148
Gore, Bishop, 220
Gospels, Authenticity, 188; dates, 191; Divine Authority (Inspiration), 191; Historical Authority, 187; Veracity, 190
Gotama, 156
Grace, a participation of the Divine Nature, 86
Gredt, J., 9
Greece and Rome, Religions of, 160
Grimm, 50
Guyot, 146

Habit, psychological power of, 123
Haeckel, 53
Harnack, 190, 227, 230
Hartmann, 45, 53
Heaven, The Hound of, 109
Hegel, 3, 27, 53
Heidelberg Mandible, 134, 138, 139
Helmholz, 52, 53
Hepaticæ, 67
Hering, 12
Heroes and Hero-worship, 103
History, Religion from the standpoint of, 153
Holy Trinity, 84
Homo neanderthalensis, 134
 primigenius, 142
 sapiens, 142
Honorius, 234
Hugo, Victor, 146
Human opinion, 47
Human Relics, The oldest, 127
Hume, 2, 22, 147
Hurter, 231
Huxley, 53, 133
Huysmans, 49

Idealism and Natural Realism, 1
Idealism and physical science, 4
Idealism and scepticism, 2
Idealist, attitude of, 2
Idealistic Agnosticism, 23
Idealistic Pantheism, 34
Ignatius, St., 189; martyr, 227
Ignorance prejudicially affecting Freedom, 121
Immanence, 20
Immanence of action, 84
Immobility of inertia, of perfection, 37
Impermanence, 100
Infinite Power, 78
Inheritance, Mendel's law of, 62
Inspiration, the function of, 192, 193, 224
Instinct of animals, 46
Intensity of sound, 6
Internal and External Finality, 44
Intuitive Knowledge, 31
Ipsum Esse Subsistens, 69
Irenæus, St., 188, 227
Islamism, 229

James, W., 18, 23
Janet, Paul, 35
Japanese waltzing mice, 63
Jerusalem, destruction of, 222
Jevons, F. B., 164
Judas the Galilæan, 204
Julien, Stanislas, 154
Jurassic Period, 54
Justice, commutative, 74
Justice, identical with Divine essence, 105
Justin, St., 227, 237

Kant, 3, 8, 17, 18, 21, 23, 27, 28, 30, 37, 39
Keith, Dr., 119, 138
Kelvin, Lord, 49, 55
Kent's Cavern, 130
Knabenbauer, 219, 220
Knowledge, acquisition, 24; primary principles, 25
Kofoid, 66
Koran, the, 158
Kramberger, 134

Laberthonnière, 238
La Chapelle-aux-Saints' skull, 133
Lacordaire, 101, 231
Lactantius, 144, 236
Lagrange, 223
Lamarck, 57

INDEX

Lamy, 239
Lang, Andrew, 19, 163, 164
Langwith Cave, 132
Lansing, 132
Lao-tsze, teaching of, 154
Lartet, 132
Law of Causality, 18
Law, the Natural (sanctions of), 126
Law, Uniformity of, 109
Lazarus, resurrection of, 82
Le Blant, 236
Lecky, 230
Leibnitz, 78
Leo XIII, 193
Leverrier (astronomer), 3
Liberty, from constraint; of indifference; of contrariety; of contradiction; of specification; moral, 120
Light, change of, 8; Light and colour, 13; interference of, 11; undulatory theory of, 104
Lilly, W. S., 160
Linnæus, 65
Littré, 23, 52
Livingstone, 164
Lock, R. H., 61
Locke, John, 22
Loisy, 211
Lucian (martyr), testimony of, 228

Macaulay, 231
McEnery, Father, 130, 131, 135
Magdalene, 76
Maimonides, 88, 89, 205
Malebranche, 81
Man and God, relations between, 144
Man, destiny of, 142
Man, the nature of, 116
Man, origin and destiny of, 127
Mankind, testimony of, 48
Marcion, 188
Marcus Aurelius, 236
Mark, St., 224
Martin, Dr., 136
Martyrs, their heroism and constancy, 237, 238
    their numbers, 235, 236
    suffered for religion, 237
    various objections, 238, 239
Materialistic Evolution, 54, 55
Materialistic Monism, 53
Materialistic objections, 118
Mathematical theory of probability, 45, 179

Mauer, section of sand-pit strata, 135
Maximianus, 236
Mechanical Determinism, 123
Memory, infallibility of, 22, 52
Mendel, J. G., 61
Mendelism, 63
Mercy Divine, 76, 77
Mesozoic period, 54
Messiahship, claim of, 194; confirmed by prophecy, 195, 196, 197
Messianic consciousness, 219
Messianic Kingdom, 195
Messianic prophecy, 194 *sqq.*, 204 *sqq.*
Metaphysical movement, 36
Metchnikoff, 53
Mid-pleistocene period, 133
Mill, John Stuart, 22, 52
Minutius, Felix, 237
Miracles, 82, 83, 173-177
Miracles, Attestation of, 198
Missing Link, 138
Mivart, 9, 65
Modernism described, 215; oath against, 18
Mohammedanism, 158, 159
Molina, 81
Mommsen, 233
Monaco, Prince of, 132
Monism, 51
Monistic Idealists, 2
Monotheism (Unity of God), 108, 109
Monsabré, Père, 151, 184
Moon, birth of the, 140
Moral Law, 125, 142
Morality, Independent, 126
Mosaic Revelation, 186
Mouni, Sakya, 156, 230
Mousterian Age, 133
Müller, Max, 50, 148, 164
Muratorian Canon, 188
Musset, Alfred de, 43, 109
Mutations theory of De Vries, 64
Mysteries, 169

Natural, meaning of term, 167
Natural Law, 43, 124, 125
Natural Selection, 60
Neanderthal, 133
Nebular Hypothesis, 54, 109
Necessary Being, 15, 38, 47, 108
Negroid Aurignacians, 132
Neo-Lamarckians, 57
Neolithic Period, 128

Neo-platonism, 230
Neo-scholastics, 6, 9, 11
Neptune, discovery of, 3
Nero, 235
Newman, 30, 153, 193
Newton, 40
Newton's disc, 8, 11
Nicolas, Auguste, 122
Nietzsche, 53, 103
Nominalists, 88

Objective monistic Idealism, 3
Occasionalism, 81
Ockam, 78
Œnothera, 64
Olivier, Père, 231
Ontological value of primary principles, 28
Order, manifestation of, 43
Origen, 227, 228, 237
Overtones, 5

Palæolithic man, 131; period, 131; times, 130
Palæozoic period, 54, 110
Pangenesis, 58
Pantheism, 17, 18, 78, 113, 114
Papias, 188
Parousia, 216
Parsees, 157
Pascal, 237
Passion and Free-will, 121
Pasteur, 49
Paul, 90, 165
Payne, 164
Penck, Professor, 140, 141
Perception, Kant's categories of, 3
Perfection of immobility, 37
Perfections, Divine, 37, 91, 93
Persia, 157
Person, 105, 114
Pesch, 9, 205
Petitio principii, 4
"Philosophie zoologique," 57
Philosophy and man's origin, 145
Philosophy of the unconscious, 45
Physical science and Idealism, 4
Physiological Determinism, 124
Piette, 131
Piltdown skull, 138
Pisum sativum, 61
Pitch of sound, 7, 10
Pithecanthropus erectus, 140
Pius X, 19

Plato, 41, 146, 161
Platycephalism, 133
Pleistocene cultures, 128
Pleistocene period, 131, 136
Pliny, 227, 237
Poincaré, 35
Polycarp, St., 189
Polytheism, 50, 108, 109, 113, 165
Pomponia Græcina, 228
Porphyrius, 228
Positivism, 51, 52
Post-tertiary times, chart of, 129
Praemotio, 81
Pragmatism, 124
Prayer and God's immutability, 151
Preternatural, meaning of term, 167
Prigg, Henry, 137
Primary and Secondary qualities of bodies, 5
Primary Principles, Objective value of, 16
Primitive races, Beliefs of, 162
Pritchard, 50
Probability, theory of, 45, 179
Prophecy, 178, 179, 180, 194, 196, 197, 208
Protagoras, 160
Pseudo-Clement, 227
Psychological Determinism, 124
Pteridospermæ, 67
Ptolemaic system, 26

Quarternary Period, 128, 129
Quatrefages, 48

Ranke, 231
Rationalism, 181
Rationalists and Revelation, 171
Reade, W., 100
Realism, Natural, 4; Critical, 4
Reason, Court of appeal in Natural Religion, 16
Recessive characters, 62
Red Indians, origin of, 136
Reflex acts, soul's power of making, 117
Reincarnation, 143
Reindeer Age, 131, 133
Religion: Comparative, 163 *sqq*.
  From East to West, 153–163
  Necessity of, for individual, 144
  Necessity of, for society, 146
  Standpoint of history, 152
  Utility of, for individual, 144
  Utility of, for society, 146

Religions, approximate census of, 166
Renan, 176, 189, 197, 203, 211, 228
Resurrection of Christ, 200-203
Revelation, 167; congruity of, 168; criteria of, 172; distinct from Inspiration, 192; Fact of, 186; Necessity, moral and absolute, 19, 170, 171, 172
Réville, 165
Rolleston, 132
Rome and Greece, religions of, 160
Rossi, de, 236
Rousseau, 147, 190
Roy, M. le, 28
Ruinart, 236
Rutot, 134, 140

Sakya-Mouni, 156, 230
Savage Tribes, beliefs of, 49, 165
Scepticism, 2
Schelling, 3, 27, 53
Schmerling, 131
Schmidt, 19
Schœtensack, 134
Scholasticism, 161
Schopenhauer, 53
Schwalbe, 134
Schweitzèr, 215, 216, 219
Science and Faith, 183, 184
Scotus, 94
Sebaste, martyrs of, 229
Sense-impressions, 1, 4 *sqq.*
Sensibile commune and proprium, 5, 13
Sergius Paulus, 228
Shintoism, 155
"Si Deus, unde mala," 96
Sin, Original, 122
Sinning, power of a defect of Free-will, 122
Skull, size of in relation to intelligence, 137
Smell, faculty of, 13
Socrates, 41, 42
Solar System, 112
Soldiers v. Martyrs, 239
Sollas, Professor, 136, 140, 141
"Son of God," 209 *sqq.*
Sophocles, 161
Soul, Human, 117
　Immortality of, 142
　Materialistic conception of, 118
　Metaphysically composite, 118
　Origin of, 141

Soul, Simplicity of, 117
　Spirituality of, 116, 117
　Three faculties of, 86
Soul and Body, 127
Souls, pre-existence of, 143
Sound, 5, 6, 9
Species, origin of, 59
Species (human), unity of, 142
Spectrum, colours of, 6
Speculum Justitiæ, 75
Spencer, Herbert, 22, 29, 30, 37, 52, 57, 164
Spenger, 65
Spinosa, 53
Spiritualistic Evolution, 55
Spirituality of the Soul, 116
Sports in plant and animal life, 64
Stimulation of cold points on skin, 12
Stoicism, 230
Strauss, 197, 203, 211
Subjective Monistic Idealism, 3
Subjectivism, 1, 6
Supernatural, meaning of term, 167
Supreme Goodness, Intelligence, 33
Syria, 157

Tacitus, 227, 235
Taine, 52, 115
Taste, faculty of, 13
Tatian, 188
Tertiary Period, 54
Tertullian, 188, 227, 228, 237
Theism, errors opposed to, 51
Theists and Non-theists XV-XIX centuries, 50
Theodas, 204
Theological Determinism, 124
Thomas, St., 9, 14, 35, 42, 43, 47, 52, 55, 81, 90, 93, 99, 113, 159
Thought, direct and reflex, 25
Tilbury man, 130, 131
Tillemont, 236
Timbre of Sound, 10
Titanic, disaster of the, 96
Titus, 233
Titus Flavius Clemens, 228, 235
Traditionalists, 17, 171
Trajan, 233, 237
Transcendent value of primary principles, 28
Transcendentals, 91
Transformation of the world, 232, 233

Transformism, meaning of, 54
Transmission of acquired characters, 58
Trenton, 132
Truth, definition of, 70
Truth, Necessary, 33
Tylor, 163, 164
Tyndall, 53

Understanding, Kantian forms of, 3, 23
Undulatory theory of Light, 104
Unitarian objection against Trinity, 106
Univocal acceptation, 30, 69, 90, 94

Valentine, 189
Valvekens, Preface viii
Veda literature, 155
Vedius Pollio, 233
Verneau, 132
Vicious circle, fallacy of, 4
Vigouroux, 190
Villeneuve, Canon, 132

Virgil, 204
Virtual distinction, major, minor, 68
Voigt, 231

Wallace, A. R., 58, 100
Ward, W. G., 22, 124
Watson, 165
Weber-Fechner law, 9
Weismann, 58
Wiel, 211
Will, Freedom of, 119
Wilson, Professor, 53
Wilson, Religion of North and South Guinea, 163
Woodward, 138
World, catastrophic end of, 222
Worship, exterior, 150; interior, 150; necessity of, 150; social 151; utility of, 150
Wright, 140

Zioberg, 65
Zoroaster, 157